Lich Lord Wars Collection

The Lich Lord Wars

Marc Van Pelt

Published by Marc Van Pelt, 2024.

LICH LORD WARS COLLECTION

First edition. February 29, 2024.

ISBN: 979-8224932634

Written by Marc Van Pelt.

Also by Marc Van Pelt

Devil's Peak Chronicles
Dream Walker

Fate's Foe
Mathen's Flight

The Lich Lord Wars
Lich-El
Escape Through the Sacred Forest
The Necromancer
Paladin's Rise
Lich Lord Wars Collection

Standalone
Stories From the World of Mundial
The Doctor's Apprentice
Forest Spirit and the Dragon Queen

Watch for more at Facebook.com/catseye1979.

Timeline of the World of Mundial

Year

1MA First War of Destruction, Yucaipan Kingdom and Village of the Shadow Hunters re-established on Elvish Continent

44MA Battle North of Aguerius Forest

118MA Lich Lords

attack the Vatan Province

119MA *Forest Spirit and the Dragon Queen*

123MA *Lich-El, Escape through the Sacred Forest, The Necromancer, Paladin's Rise*

Lich Lords begin invasion of Aguerius Province

129MA *Time Mage*

983MA Necromian Kingdom established

1012MA The Forjad Consortium is formed

1024MA Formation of the Yucaipan Republic

1850MA *Mathen's Flight*

1854MA Human/Elvish War Begins, fall of the Necromian Kingdom and Yucaipan Republic. Establishment of Port Cutter

1857MA *The Merchant Ship Cree*

1862MA *The Doctor's Apprentice*

1904MA *Frost Wyrm*

MA= Mortal Age

Italics= Published Works

ACKNOWLEDGMENTS

I'D LIKE TO SAY THANKS to everyone that has supported my writing. First and foremost, my wife, Tara, for her love and support. Secondly, thanks to all of my other family and friends; for their positive support and feedback.

Forest Spirit and the Dragon Queen

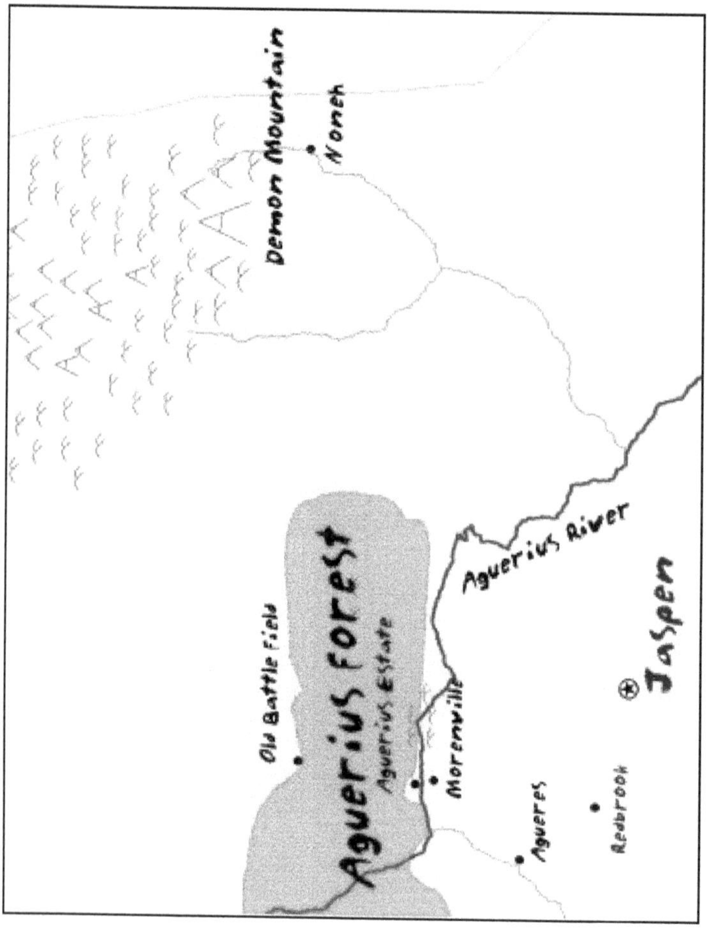
Demon Mountain
Noneh
Aguerius Forest
Aguerius Estate
Old Battle Field
Morenville
Aguerius River
Jaspen
Agueres
Redbrook

Chapter 1

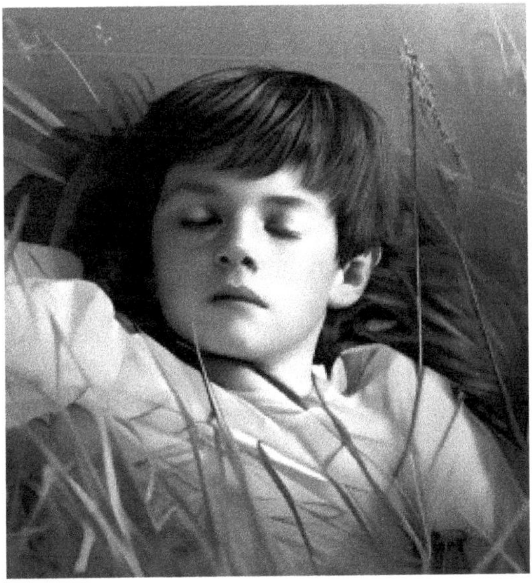

BIG BROTHERS MUST BE the dumbest, most horrible, most evil creatures in the whole world of Mundial. Even the Lich Lords of the Eastern Wastes would shudder at the pains and torments older brothers inflict on younger brothers. Of course, it would be Almas' luck to get the all-time worst.

Almas Aguerius was sure that his brother, Cree Tanis Aguerius (Almas just referred to him as Creetan), had spent his first four years of life torturing cats, learning the art of being mean and dreaming of the day he'd have a little brother to make cry. It was probably best that Almas didn't remember anything before he turned three-years-old because if they were anything like the next five years then they were most likely filled with warfare just as intense as the battles their father was involved with during his wars with the Undead.

Sure, when he was a baby Almas probably didn't cut holes in the back of all of Creetan's pants to get back at him for breaking his favorite toy horse, but they couldn't have gotten along nearly as well as their mother always claimed. There was no getting along with Creetan, you could only endure him.

Almas blamed his brother for the trouble he was in now. All he had wanted was an apple from the apple tree, but he was too short to even reach the lowest branches. Then Creetan had the nerve to sneak up on him and scare him out of his wits. Then to make things worse, rather than help him get an apple, he decides to climb up the tree, eat some apples, and call him a coward and a baby.

Now because of that, Almas was the most tired, cold, scared, and – worst of all – completely lost that he had ever been in the eight years of his life.

All he had wanted to do was spend some time in Aguerius Forest alone to prove to that 12-year-old pigheaded monster, who had somehow tricked his parents into thinking he was their first-born son, that he was not a coward.

He had gotten the idea when he had gone to the riverbank to brood. He had noticed a blue bird in a tree looking at him and had wondered if the Forest Spirit of Aguerius Forest ever had to deal with a stupid older brother. He had never been sure if there was a forest spirit – after all it was only a legend that the adults talked about, and adults had a bad habit of trying to trick children into believing absurd things. When he had asked his father, he had only said that many legends are based in truth so some of it might be real.

The legend was that the forest was cared for by a forest spirit who protected both man and beast that entered into it. Since there were no stories of anybody being attacked by wild animals in the forest, that's what gave Almas the idea to go spend the day in the woods. He had decided that it was his best chance to show Creetan how brave he really was. After all, even a safe forest could be scary when you're by yourself – couldn't it? So, after waking and eating breakfast the next day, he had told his mother that he was going to play outside. Then when no one was looking he went right into the green wood.

The day had started out great; the sun was sending bright light through the branches of the great and mighty trees. Birds were chirping happy songs while the bushes seemed to make way for him, almost inviting him into the forest. It was by far the most beautiful place he had ever seen. It was thick with green leaves and flowers on every surface. Also, there were animals everywhere from chipmunks and insects to deer and elk. After a few hours Almas decided that he had been out long enough to show Creetan who was brave. Not to mention he needed to get home before it got dark – for his mother's peace of mind, of course.

It was then he realized that he had no idea which way home was. Picking the direction, he was sure would at least take him to the river that he could follow home, he had set off at what he meant to be a nice easy trot, but ended up more like one that resembled a deer being followed closely by a pack of wolves.

It was shortly after this that things began to go wrong for him. The friendly forest seemed to change with every step. First the friendly songs of the birds stopped, followed by the trees reaching out and blocking the light of the sun with their branches, while the bushes and shrubs began to grab and claw at him as he tried to find his way home. From time to time the forest seemed to play a game where it would start to brighten and give Almas hope, only to destroy it by suddenly becoming darker and more menacing.

It was just as the sun was beginning to set that Almas learned where he was. He stepped out into a clearing to find the site of an old battlefield. The clearing was mostly dead earth with clumps of tall, brown grass scattered about; much the same as the instruments of war that littered the field. Everywhere he looked he could see armor and weapons of all sorts. He realized as he looked among broken swords and shields that he was on the completely wrong side of the forest. His father had told him how 75 years ago his great grandfather had led the king's army against the Lich Lords and drove them to the eastern wastes, and that the battle had taken place on the other side of the forest.

First, he hesitated. The place was spooky, and Almas was scared enough as it was. But curiosity in the objects littering the ground overcame his fear and he entered the field. He began to wander around and study the relics of a battle long past. Why had no one claimed these treasures? As eerie as the place was, he had to take a look at some of these artifacts. Was that a real ruby in the hilt of that sword? The metal it was embedded in looked like gold! If he brought something expensive home maybe his mother wouldn't kill him for being late. At least he'd be able to make Creetan jealous.

For a moment he was so lost in his curiosity that he forgot about being scared. But then as he was looking at a helmet in the tall grass that looked like it might have a diamond embedded in the front, he felt something odd under his foot. Searching the ground where he had stood, he saw a small, gold chain partially hidden in the ground. He pulled the chain from the ground and found a small pendant attached to it. The pendant was round and somewhat flat, and like the chain, was made of gold. There was also a green gem embedded in the center of it.

As Almas looked over the pendant, he wondered how much something like this would be worth. The last thing he expected was an answer to his unspoken question.

"I am what you would call priceless."

"Who said that?" Almas yelped as he searched in all directions for the source of the voice.

"I did you fool. You're holding me," came the reply.

Almas looked down at the pendant. Was the pendant speaking to him?

"Idiot child, of course I'm speaking to you. Do you see anyone else around?"

At that moment Almas realized that the voice he heard was only in his own head. Almas stared at the pendant and asked, "What are you?"

"I am Lightbringer, a powerful fielis. Figures that I would be found by an ignorant, runny-nosed human child... An Aguerius at that, by the looks of the symbol on your crest."

Almas looked at his crest hanging on his neck that bore his family's symbols. How could this thing see it and what was a fielis? Almas thought he had heard that word before but couldn't remember where he heard it or what he had heard about it. He was about to ask more but the thing called Lightbringer spoke first.

"You don't have to speak out loud; I can hear your thoughts just fine. But explaining these things to you probably doesn't matter since I don't expect you to escape this place alive. Do me a favor and put me down. I really hate getting eaten along with fools – even if the slime behind you doesn't get you then the forest dragon that claims this land will surely track you down. He hates intruders. Few grave robbers that have come here have escaped. If you do survive, send someone back worthy to hold my greatness."

Almas turned around and, sure enough, not far behind him was a big, slug-like blob about the size of a large cat. He had never seen a slime before but had heard that they were boneless creatures that could spray a stream of acid five feet away. The acid was used to dissolve its food before eating it and to defend itself from predators. They certainly didn't live in his family's forest; it was yet another reminder that he was far from where he was supposed to be.

This gray colored slime seemed to be eating an old shield, and Almas decided there was no point in sticking around and handing it an easier-to-eat dessert. If the pendant wanted to stay that was fine with him. He dropped Lightbringer, cutting off the pendant's maniacal laugh and ran back into the forest.

Almas wasn't sure how long he had been running. Ten minutes? Thirty? He just knew he needed to put as much space between himself and that field as he could, yet when he tripped as he passed through a dense grove of trees, he knew he couldn't get up. His legs felt dead, and his chest felt like it was on fire. By now it was completely dark, and all Almas could do was focus on breathing.

Rolling on his back he cried and cried till he heard a strange sound. Looking up he saw in the tree a songbird singing to him. At least he was pretty sure it was to him. It seemed to look right at him. The song reminded him of a song his Uncle Marpel used to play on a harp to help him and his brothers and sister go to sleep. He had always accused his uncle of casting a musical spell on him, as bards like his uncle were known to do, but tonight he would've welcomed the peace his uncle's music would have brought. Slowly the fire in his chest went away and he felt that he could breathe again. He knew he should get up and get moving again, but he just didn't have the strength. He quickly faded off to sleep.

As he slept, he dreamt of home. He dreamt of his mother tucking him in for the night and singing gently to him. It was a nice dream and Almas slept peaceably and warm well into the morning.

Almas awoke with a start to the sound of the songbird chirping and fluttering its wings in obvious panic. He found himself under a blanket of tall grass which he didn't remember being there the night before. Searching for the cause of the bird's agitation he sat himself up to find the same gray slime from the evening before right next to his feet. At least he was fairly certain it was the same slime; part of the slime's body had expanded and shaped itself into a small tendril that was holding the magic pendant that had called itself Lightbringer.

Almas quickly began crawling backwards but only went a couple of feet before hitting his head hard on a tree. Before Almas could make any movements, a stream of acid shot right past him and the tree that his back was against. Almost instantly a large roar filled the air behind him, and Almas felt something big crash into the tree he was against. Rolling away from both the slime and whatever the slime had just attacked, Almas decided that if anyone wanted to question his courage, they were welcome to do it. He just prayed to whatever gods might be listening that he could get home alive; he didn't care what names his brother called him. Looking to the tree he had rolled away from; he saw a forest dragon that was franticly dragging its head on the ground as it tried to scrape off the burning acid from its face.

Forest dragons were small for dragons and had no wings, but still twice the size of a large bear. They were colored green and brown to blend in better with the forest. Almas had seen many forest dragons before – many warriors used them as war mounts, his own father included – but this one was nothing like the tamed ones he knew. First, this was the biggest one he'd ever seen; second, this one was now looking at Almas with what seemed a mixture of hunger and anger.

Almas knew he should be running but his legs betrayed him and refused to move. The forest dragon took a step towards him, but another stream of acid shot right in front of the beast. Almas glanced at the slime. Was it actually moving between him and the dragon?

The dragon eyed the slime, then Almas, then back to the slime. It seemed the dragon was deciding if Almas would make a meal worth the sting of the slime's acid. After a short eternity the dragon suddenly looked off to the left and emitted a low growl. Almas turned to discover, to his great shock, an older boy, perhaps just a little younger than his brother Creetan, standing between two trees. He had light brown hair and stood only a couple inches taller than Almas himself. He wore brown and green clothes and had nothing on his feet. While it was clear the boy was a child, it was also clear the boy wasn't human – his ears were more pointed on top.

The blue-eyed boy stared at the dragon and the dragon stared back. Then suddenly the dragon charged at him. The boy just continued to stare the charging beast right in the eyes and at the last minute jumped, planting his bare feet on the trunk of the tree next to him. He then took two quick steps up the tree trunk and grabbed onto a branch. The dragon, unable to slow down, passed right under the boy who dropped onto the dragon's back, then did a front-flip off of it and landed right next to the slime. As the dragon turned and once again charged, the boy quickly took Lightbringer from the slime and held it up to the charging dragon.

"Don't look directly at the pendant!" he yelled.

Almas wasn't sure why he needed to look away but decided to trust the boy. He turned his face away just as the pendant exploded with bright light. Even looking away from the light everything was so bright that Almas threw his arm over his eyes to protect them.

The light dimmed and, as Almas blinked the afterimage from his eyes, he heard the sound of the dragon crashing through the forest away from them. Soon the sound of roaring and trees being knocked over faded. The boy continued to stare in the direction the dragon went for a few moments longer, then walked over to Almas and collapsed against the tree next to him. Only now did Almas realize how out of breath the boy was.

"Do you...(gasp)...have any idea...(gasp)...how much trouble you've caused me...(gasp)...these last couple days? That dragon is a lunatic about protecting his territory, which includes the old battlefield. It picked up your scent and tracked you down. I had to sprint for the last 20 minutes and still almost didn't make it in time."

Almas just stared at the boy. "Are you a forest spirit?"

"No, I'm an elf."

"Why do they say there is a forest spirit here then?"

"There is what people believe and then there is the truth."

The boy stood up and walked over to the slime; he removed his shoulder bag and scooped the slime into it. Putting the shoulder bag back on he added, "We should get going before Grumpy gets his eyesight back and returns for breakfast. I don't think he believed me when I said my father was nearby."

"I didn't hear you tell it anything."

"I don't need to talk out loud to speak to the animals and plants of the forest," the boy answered as he wrapped Lightbringer in a cloth and placed it in his pocket. "Now come on; I'll take you home."

Almas eyed the pocket the boy had put Lightbringer in. "That thing is bad."

"Lightbringer is bitter, selfish, and annoying but like all of his kind, harmless to those who hold him. Now let's get going."

Almas stood up and followed the boy who started walking away. "My name is Almas Aguerius."

"I know."

"How?"

"Little happens in or near this forest that I don't know about, not to mention your family has been protecting my family since they settled this area. It was my father who gave this forest to your family."

"But my family has owned this forest for a hundred years! How old are you?"

"One hundred and nineteen."

"That's older than my father!"

The boy laughed, "Much older."

"What's your name?" Almas asked as they started walking.

"Just call me Ulec."

Chapter 2

ULEC WASN'T SURE WHAT to make of this small human creature. Maybe if he would close his mouth for longer than two seconds, then Ulec could decide.

"So how big is your family?" Almas asked.

"What's that?"

"Your family. You said my family has been protecting your family; how big is your family?"

"Just my parents, my little sister, and me," Ulec answered.

"I have an older brother, a younger brother and a younger sister along with my parents. Do you have a house here in the forest?"

"The forest is our house."

"Oh," Almas said thoughtfully, "don't you get wet when it rains?"

"The trees can keep us dry if I ask them to."

Realization came to Almas' eyes. "Was it you that made the forest scary yesterday?"

Ulec was glad the boy was following behind him and couldn't see his face turn red. "Well, I was trying to help you get back home. I... I thought if the forest was only scary when you were going the wrong way, you'd find the right way. It didn't work very well."

"Oh... sorry."

Ulec felt bad. He had tried to lead Almas back home, but all he had managed to do was scare the kid out of his wits and almost get him killed. If he had just been more open and gone personally to help, he could've led Almas back home without him ending up in danger.

They walked for a minute in silence, and then Ulec turned and asked, "Would you like to see the best view of the forest, see it as I think of it?"

"Yes, please!"

"Follow me."

Ulec could normally move quickly through the forest, but the boy moved slowly, even with his help. Eventually they came to a huge tree. Ulec didn't even slow down as he got to the tree; he took three steps up the trunk of the tree and effortlessly swung himself onto one of the lower branches. Almas stopped and stared.

"Hey! How did you do that?"

"Do what?"

"Run up the tree like that. I can't do that."

"I ask the tree to help me. It holds onto my feet, so I don't slip as easily. Here let me help you up."

Ulec reached down and took Almas' hand. He helped pull him up and the two boys began climbing up to the top of the tree.

"Only citizens of your kingdom wear them. I'm not part of your kingdom. I've seen them from a distance but never up close. How come your crest has two pictures on it?"

"They are pictures of my parents' crests; the one with the owl is my father's and the one with the anvil is my mother's. Children's crests always show both their parents' crests to show who they belong to. Then when we grow up, we get our own."

"And the foxes around the edges of your crest?"

"Every kid has his own border around the crests. That way every child in the family has a crest that is a little different. My dad said that once only nobles had them but since everyone in the kingdom now are descended from those that fought in the War of Destruction, an old king declared everyone to be of noble blood."

"Oh," Ulec responded as he handed the crest back. "My parents also fought in that war."

"Really? My dad told me that very few who fought in that war survived. And it was about one hundred and twenty years ago. Are your parents old?"

"Elves live 10 times longer than humans. So, for elves I guess they would be about middle aged," Ulec answered with a shrug.

After another moment of silence Almas spoke up, "I was wondering. That pendant, Lightbringer, said it was a fielis. Do you know what a fielis is?"

"It's a magic item made by a group of elves that died off long ago. They made the items by taking part of someone's soul and binding it to an item. That item gains the personality and abilities of that soul."

Almas asked something else, but Ulec didn't hear. His attention was suddenly elsewhere in the forest. That forest dragon was heading their way again – fast. The creature's eyes still hadn't recovered from the flash from Lightbringer, but the dragon was probably following their smell.

"What's wrong?"

Ulec turned back to Almas, "I should get you back home. Your family is worried about you."

"Uh, sure," Almas responded with a quizzical look.

The two boys began climbing down. It was slow at first as Ulec showed Almas how to grab hold of a branch and step off the limb which they were standing on. The branch they were holding on to would then slowly bend, lowering them to a lower branch. They then could repeat the process. Almas was scared at first but soon began enjoying it. When they got to the bottom Ulec reminded Almas not to try doing that without him, since the branch could break, and he'd probably fall to his death. Almas nodded and the two boys started on their way.

Ulec tried to hurry Almas along as quickly as possible, but the young human just wasn't fast enough.

"What's wrong? Why can't we rest a while? It's after noon and I haven't eaten in over a day."

"I'm sorry, Almas, but we have to move fast. The forest dragon is following us again. I thought I could get you some place safe before he caught up but he's moving too fast. I'll have to try something else."

"What?"

"No time to explain. Come on!"

Ulec led Almas to another large tree. "Up the tree, quickly. He's almost here."

He helped Almas get up to a large, high branch. Almas looked around, then called down to Ulec, "I see him! Hurry and get up here!"

"No matter what, stay up there."

"Are you crazy?! What are you doing?"

"Trust me!"

Ulec ran over to another tree. As the dragon came into view, he grabbed hold of a long, thick branch. He asked the tree for the branch, and it immediately separated from the tree. Ulec decided he must have lost his mind as he held up his makeshift staff and watched the dragon sniff the air.

The dragon still couldn't see very well but it smelled Ulec and charged. At the last second Ulec sidestepped and hit the dragon's leg with the branch with all his strength. The dragon didn't even seem to notice. It simply turned towards Ulec and lunged at him. Ulec tried to move but he knew he wouldn't be able to move out of the way fast enough. He mentally sent a plea for help to the slime that was still sitting inside his shoulder bag hanging at his side. He lifted the flap of the bag and a stream of acid shot out and again hit the dragon in the face. With the dragon's lunge disrupted, Ulec took the opportunity to get out of the way and quickly climbed up a nearby tree.

As the dragon once again used the dirt to scrape the burning acid from his face, Ulec took a moment to open his mind completely to the forest. Ulec had lived in the forest a long time. The plants and animals there knew him, and he asked them all for help.

The dragon charged the tree Ulec was standing in. As it charged, branches from the surrounding trees began to fall like spears on it and the shrubbery grabbed and clawed at the dragon's legs. Most hit harmlessly on the dragon's hard scales. The dragon threw itself against the trunk of the tree Ulec was on and the tree fell over.

Ulec managed to jump and grab onto the branch of another tree as the one he'd just been on came crashing to the ground. The dragon only took a moment to sniff the air and find Ulec's new position and charged once again. As it came, a pack of wolves leapt from some surrounding bushes and onto the dragon. The dragon stopped its charge and tried to shake the wolves from its back, but they just sank their fangs deeper till the dragon finally rolled onto its back. The wolves scattered to avoid being crushed but Ulec felt his mental connection to one of them suddenly disappear. The wolves grouped up again, but the dragon went after them, and they were forced to scatter in order to avoid the dragon's attack.

Ulec looked around in desperation. The wolves didn't stand a chance and he was out of ideas. The dragon stopped chasing the scattered wolves and once again came right at Ulec. He pulled Lightbringer from his pocket, held it towards the dragon and channeled as much magic as he could into it and once again the pendant exploded into light. At the same time a dark voice entered into his mind.

"That won't work. That beast is no longer using his eyes to hunt you."

"Help me!" Ulec thought back to the pendant.

"Why should I do that?"

"If I get eaten, you go with me."

"Hmm, as entertaining as you're getting eaten would be, I really would prefer not to pass through the insides of that beast again. You don't want to be eaten? Then the answer is easy...run. With your power over the forest, you can move much quicker than that blind beast."

"If I did that, Almas would be killed. I'm not leaving him."

"Why would the son of Lady Alixia risk his life for a mere human? Have you no pride as an elf?"

"The Aguerius family protects this forest, protects my family. I have to try."

The tree Ulec was in began to fall over as the dragon crashed into it. This time there were no nearby branches to jump to, so all Ulec could do was jump clear of the falling tree. As he tried to get up Lightbringer's voice returned. "*Run, boy. Human lives are short anyway. Just run.*"

As he tried to stand, Ulec's ankle felt like it was on fire, and he collapsed back onto the ground. There was no way he'd be able to avoid the dragon with it.

"*No, it's too late for that now,*" he thought to the pendant.

The dragon came at Ulec, mouth open to consume him. Suddenly a rock struck the dragon's head and both the dragon and Ulec turned their heads to see the source.

"Leave him alone," Almas yelled. He had dropped down from the tree and was picking up another rock to throw while the dragon took a step in his direction.

"*Well, at least I'll be able to enjoy watching both you and that annoying human get eaten. With any luck the dragon will choke on your dead body and cough me up.*"

"Choke!" Ulec exclaimed aloud attracting the dragon's attention once more to him.

"*What? No! I can see your thoughts, you ca–*"

Ulec pushed himself onto one hand, the dragon over him, mouth open once again. With his other hand Ulec aimed quickly and threw the pendant down the air hole of the dragon's throat and rolled away as quickly as he could.

ALMAS HAD WATCHED MOST of the fight from his tree, too terrified to even speak. For a moment he was sure he was about to watch his new friend get eaten right before him. He then realized he couldn't let Ulec die because of him. So, he had jumped down, picked up a rock and threw it as hard as his 8-year-old arm could throw it. Then suddenly it was over.

Now the dragon lay motionless on the ground and Ulec limped over to where the wolves had gathered around their pack member that had been crushed by the dragon. Ulec looked over to Almas and motioned him to come over. So, he walked over to Ulec, keeping an eye on the motionless dragon.

"Are...are you alright?" Almas asked as he came near.

"My ankle hurts but I don't think it's bad. I just twisted it wrong when I fell from the tree. Thanks, by the way. *That* is what being brave is all about. You saved my life there," Ulec responded, and then looking at the wolf said, "They came and saved us too. Even knowing that they were no match for a forest dragon, they came to protect me."

Almas turned to the lifeless wolf.

"I'm sorry. If I hadn't gotten lost..."

"I need you to do me a favor."

"What?"

Ulec picked up a branch from a fallen tree and began to bend it as if it was clay, and in a couple of moments he had fashioned a walking staff to help him with his hurt ankle.

"Follow me," Ulec said and limped away with the help of his new staff.

Almas followed him and the wolves to a small cave in the side of a hill. Ulec reached in and pulled out a wolf cub.

"He's still too young to survive without his mother. He needs a place to live and someone to take care of him. I can't take both the slime and the cub."

Ulec handed the small cub to Almas. The wolf cub was shivering, so he wrapped his shirt around it and answered, "I don't think my mother would let me."

"Just ask. Explain what his mother did for us. I think you might be surprised."

"Sure, I'll try."

ALMAS WAS SILENT THE rest of the trip home. Ulec found him some berries to eat but he was still tired and drained from everything that had happened. Never again would he do something just to show his stupid brother he wasn't a coward.

As evening approached Ulec turned again to Almas and asked, "Can I ask you another favor?"

"What?"

"My parents don't want other people to know about our being here in this forest. Your parents are the only ones who know about us, so will you promise that you won't talk about us with anyone except for them?"

"Not even with any of my brothers or sister?"

"Not for now. Your younger brother and sister would have a hard time keeping the secret. I'm not sure if I trust your older brother. If any of them accidentally told other people about us, we might have to leave. But maybe later; I'll have to discuss it with my parents."

"Why does your family need to hide?" Almas asked.

"After the War of Destruction there were only a few humans and elves left. Humans can increase their population faster than elves. So, there are still very few of us compared to humans. We need time."

"Ok, I sort of understand – I promise."

"Thank you. I'm going to have to say goodbye now. I've brought you as far as I can."

"But...but I still don't know the way from here."

"Just follow the voices in the air."

"What voices?"

Then suddenly he heard it, his name being called out in the distance.

"That sounded like my Uncle Jerad," Almas said looking in the direction of the voice. "OVER HERE!" he yelled. "They are looking for me...Ulec?"

When Almas turned back towards Ulec, the young elf had completely vanished. He only had a moment to contemplate how someone with a hurt ankle could disappear so quickly and quietly when he heard his name called again. The voice was very close now and soon a large man with a hand axe strapped to his side appeared. It was his father's best friend, who also served as commander of his father's men when he was away.

"Uncle Jerad!" Almas ran to the man and gave him a sideways hug, being careful not to crush the wolf cub.

The man laughed, "Well, well. I was beginning to think the spirits of this forest had kidnapped you." Turning his head, he spoke to someone behind him. "Would you take a look at what I found wandering the forest alone?"

"Now why'd you have to go and find him for? You have any idea what it costs to feed that kid?" said another familiar voice.

Almas peeked around Jerad to see his father standing there with a huge teasing grin.

"FATHER!"

This time Almas leapt into his father's arms. "You're home! You're home!"

Almas' father scooped him up and, laughing, swung him around and put him back on the ground. "Yes, I arrived home last night to find I was short one child. Now seeing I still had three out of four of my kids, I was all set to call it good enough and just write you off, go to bed and get some rest. But you know how your mother is. She started to fuss and fuss, so I figured I might as well come out and find you."

"You were worried about me," Almas said, giving him a knowing smile.

"Me? Never. Now let's get you home and get you a bath. Then you can tell me why you smell like slime acid and have a wolf cub wrapped in your shirt. I've a feeling it's an interesting tale," Almas' father said with a grin and a wink as he put a hand on his son's shoulder and led him home.

ULEC SAT IN A TREE long after Almas and his father were out of sight. He had opened his shoulder bag and let the slime out, which was munching on pinecones at the moment. Ulec decided to call the slime Metal, since, while it appeared to be willing to eat just about anything, it seemed to have a special liking for metal, as Ulec had found out upon finding the remains of his small knife in the bag.

After watching Metal eating for a few minutes, Ulec spoke, "Are you mad?"

A voice answered from below him. "Mad about what? That you missed a lesson in order to save and help a boy lost in the forest, or that you seem to once again have adopted yet another pet?"

"I thought I could do it myself, without any help. I almost got us both killed."

"Yes. If you had left me a trail to follow, I might have been in a place to help you when you finally called for it. There is no shame in asking for help when lives are at stake. On the other hand, all your life I've been trying to teach you the importance of serving others. You have demonstrated that you have learned and understood the most important lesson I could ever teach you – service. So no, I'm not angry. I'm very proud."

"Thank you, Father," Ulec looked down to where his father was leaning against the tree. "So...can I keep Metal?"

Ulec's father sighed and smiled. "Like I really have a choice with you and your pets."

Chapter 3

A WEEK HAD PASSED SINCE Almas and Ulec's last adventure in Aguerius Forest. Almas couldn't contain his excitement as he stood at the forest's edge, waiting for Ulec to arrive. His father, High Lord Gidon Aguerius, observed his son's restless anticipation with a chuckle.

Almas fidgeted with a leaf that had fallen on his shoulder. He glanced at his father and said, "Father, do you think Ulec will remember me? It feels like forever since we last saw each other!"

Gidon smiled warmly as Almas brushed off another leaf that had fallen on his shoulder. "Oh, my dear Almas, a week may feel like an eternity to an eight-year-old like you, but I'm sure Ulec remembers you. After all, he's been eagerly awaiting this reunion too. Not to mention you never forget friends who risk their lives for you."

Almas' father smiled as yet another leaf landed on his son's shoulder. Just as Almas finished brushing the leaf off, a mischievous giggle filled the air. Almas looked up to see Ulec perched on a branch above him, a wide grin spread across his face. Almas burst into laughter, realizing that Ulec had been hiding in the tree, playfully dropping leaves on him.

Almas climbed onto the lowest branch to join Ulec, his laughter still echoing through the forest. Ulec's eyes sparkled with mirth as he greeted Almas, "Hey there, buddy! Missed me, didn't you?"

Almas chuckled, trying to catch his breath. "You bet, Ulec! You've got quite the talent for surprising entrances."

Ulec hopped down from the branch, landing gracefully on the forest floor. He glanced at Almas and said, "Well, I couldn't resist a little prank. But now, let's have some real fun!"

Almas looked to his father who nodded and said, "Go have fun, just be back home by supper time."

Almas and Ulec wasted no time and took off. They ventured deeper into the forest and soon Ulec's ability to communicate with animals and plants became evident. They encountered a family of deer grazing peacefully, and Ulec projected his thoughts towards them, sharing a silent conversation. The deer responded with gentle nods and playful leaps, conveying their joy to Almas through their graceful movements.

As they made their way through a shimmering meadow, Ulec's gaze shifted to a group of singing birds perched on a branch. He switched to speaking aloud, addressing them directly for Almas' sake, "Lovely tunes, my feathered friends! Mind teaching us a few notes?"

The birds chirped in delight and began a melodious chorus. Ulec and Almas joined in, their laughter and voices intertwining with the bird's song, filling the forest with a joyous symphony.

As evening approached, Ulec turned to Almas with a mischievous glint in his eyes and asked, "Can I make a request, Almas?"

Curiosity sparked in Almas' eyes. "What is it, Ulec?"

Ulec's voice dropped to a conspiratorial whisper, "I've heard that your father is quite the skilled warrior, just like me. How about a friendly sparring match? I've been told I'm a formidable opponent."

Almas' eyes widened in excitement. "You want to spar with my father? He's a master swordsman!"

Ulec grinned. "Well, I've been around for quite some time, and I've honed my skills. What do you say? Shall we put our swordsmanship to the test?"

As they arrived to the place that he had arranged to meet his father, Almas quickly asked his father if he would spar with Ulec. Lord Aguerius agreed and so Almas led Ulec and his father to a clearing on the edge of Aguerius Forest. They armed themselves with short swords and prepared for the friendly duel.

Ulec's movements were lightning-fast, his elven agility allowing him to maneuver with grace. Almas' father met his strikes with skill and precision, their swords clashing in a flurry of metal.

The forest echoed with the sound of their blades, the clash and clang of their intense bout. Almas watched in awe as Ulec matched his father's every move, his elven reflexes giving him an edge.

As the duel continued, Ulec's skill and finesse shone through. His movements became fluid and mesmerizing, as if he were dancing with the sword.

With a series of swift strikes, Ulec disarmed Almas' father, sending his sword flying through the air. The duel had reached its climax, and Ulec stood before Almas' father, victorious.

Almas' father laughed heartily, a mix of surprise and admiration in his eyes. "Well, Ulec, it seems you truly are a weapons master. That was an impressive display!"

Ulec bowed respectfully. "Thank you, High Lord Aguerius. It was an honor to spar with you."

Almas' father extended a hand to Ulec, a warm smile on his face. "The honor was mine, Ulec. Your skill with a sword is unmatched, and I can see why Almas holds you in such high regard."

Ulec accepted the handshake with a grin. "Thank you, High Lord Aguerius. It was a pleasure to test my abilities against such a formidable opponent."

They shared a moment of camaraderie, the forest filled with laughter and respect. Almas felt a surge of pride witnessing the bond between his father and his elvish friend.

As the sun started its descent, painting the sky in hues of gold and orange, Almas knew their time together was drawing to a close. He approached Ulec, a mixture of excitement and sadness in his voice.

"Ulec, this has been an incredible day. I don't want it to end."

Ulec placed a hand on Almas' shoulder, his gaze filled with warmth. "Fear not, my friend. Our paths will cross again. Aguerius Forest will always be here, waiting for us to create new memories."

Almas nodded, a smile tugging at his lips. "I can't wait for our next adventure, Ulec. Until then, take care."

Ulec nodded in return. "You too, Almas. Stay curious, brave, and kind."

With a final embrace, Almas bid farewell to Ulec. As he walked back home with his father, the echoes of their laughter and the memory of their sparring match filled his heart, fueling his anticipation for their next meeting.

"OUCH! CRUSTY, NOT THE fingers!" Almas exclaimed, trying to suppress a laugh.

It had been a few months since Almas had received the wolf cub, Crusty, in the depths of Aguerius Forest. Almas had taken on the responsibility of raising him, and the joys and trials of wolf cub parenting were becoming apparent.

One sunny morning, Almas was sitting at the breakfast table with his family. Crusty, now a lively ball of fur, had playfully nipped at Almas' fingers under the table.

His mother chuckled and shook her head. "Almas, dear, maybe it's time to teach Crusty some table manners."

Almas' older brother, Creetan, smirked. "He's already got the manners of a wild animal. What's next, howling at the moon during dinner?"

Almas shot Creetan a playful glare. "Hey, watch it! Crusty's still learning. We all have to start somewhere."

Almas' parents had decided to keep Ulec's existence a secret from his siblings, as it could be dangerous if the wrong people found out about an elvish family living in the forest. Instead, they told them that Almas had found Crusty while he was lost in the forest.

During a family gathering in the evening, Almas' younger sister, Cady, poked Almas with curiosity sparkling in her eyes. "Almas, how did you find Crusty in the forest? Tell us the story!"

Almas' father chimed in; his voice full of mischief. "Well, you see, Cady, your brother has a knack for attracting all sorts of woodland creatures. He's got a secret language with the animals. They just can't resist following him."

Cady's eyes widened, and she gasped in amazement. "Wow, Almas! You're like a real-life animal whisperer!"

Almas winked at his father, playing along with the tale. "That's right, Cady. They call me Almas the Animal Whisperer. I have a special bond with the creatures of the forest."

As Crusty grew, so did his mischievous nature. He would often disappear into Aguerius Forest, only to return covered in mud and leaves, a mischievous twinkle in his eyes.

One day, Almas and Crusty ventured out to the nearby meadow. Almas watched as Crusty rolled around in the grass, kicking up clouds of pollen.

Almas sneezed; his voice muffled. "Crusty, you're turning me into a walking sneeze factory!"

Crusty tilted his head, as if to say, "Oops, sorry!" before darting off into the meadow, chasing butterflies.

Almas chuckled and shook his head. "That cub sure knows how to keep us on our toes!"

ONE EVENING, AS ALMAS sat under a tree with Crusty by his side, he contemplated the wisdom of his furry companion.

"Crusty, sometimes I wonder how you know things without being told. It's like you understand the world in a way we humans can't."

Crusty perked up his ears, his gaze meeting Almas'.

Almas continued; his voice filled with wonder. "You remind me of Ulec. He had a similar way of seeing things, of understanding nature and its secrets."

Crusty let out a soft howl, as if in agreement. Almas smiled and scratched the wolf cub's ears. "I bet you and Ulec talk, Crusty. I bet Ulec uses you to see what we are doing here. Tell Ulec I can't wait till we get a chance to play in the forest again. But for now, let's enjoy our own little adventures."

As the sun set, Almas and Crusty walked back home, their bond growing stronger with each passing day.

As the days went by Almas' siblings had become accustomed to the wolf's presence, unaware of his true origins.

One evening, as the family sat around the hearth, Almas' youngest brother, Giddy, turned to their father with a mischievous grin. "Father, can we go on an adventure in the forest? I want to find a wolf friend like Almas did!"

Almas' father chuckled and exchanged a glance with Almas' mother. "Well, Giddy, wolves are wild creatures. They're not easy to find or befriend. Besides, Almas was lucky to have found Crusty. It's not something that happens every day."

Creetan smirked and nudged Almas. "Yeah, Giddy, you'd better leave the wolf whispering to Almas. I hear he's got a secret language with animals and can call them with just a whistle!"

Almas grinned, playing along. "That's right, Creetan. Just a simple whistle, and they come running. Maybe someday, you'll learn the whistle too."

Giddy's eyes widened, filled with wonder. "Wow, Almas, you're so lucky!"

Almas glanced at Crusty, their silent understanding growing stronger by the day. Yes, he was lucky indeed to have a wolf friend and a secret only shared by a few.

WITH A SKIP IN HIS step and Crusty bounding alongside him, Almas made his way into Aguerius Forest. It had been some time since their last encounter with Ulec, and Almas was eager to reunite with his elvish friend.

As they ventured deeper into the forest, Almas looked all around before calling out as loud as he could, "Ulec! We're here!"

"Over here," Ulec called back. Almas turned and saw Ulec sitting on a moss-covered rock that he could've sworn had been empty just a second before. Ulec's eyes sparkled with delight as he waved to Almas and Crusty. "Almas! It's wonderful to see you again, my friend. And I see you've brought Crusty with you!"

Crusty wagged his tail, his excitement evident. Ulec reached into his shoulder bag and carefully released Metal, the slimy creature plopping onto the ground and assuming its blob-like form. Crusty approached with curiosity, sniffing the peculiar creature.

Almas grinned. "Metal, this is Crusty, my loyal wolf companion. Crusty, meet Metal, Ulec's slime friend."

Metal jiggled in response, emitting a soft, gurgling sound. Ulec chuckled. "They're going to be fast friends; I can already tell."

As the trio ventured deeper into the forest, Almas noticed a glimmering light dancing through the foliage. "Ulec, do you see that? It looks like a hidden treasure!"

Ulec smiled with mischievous excitement. "A treasure? Let's go investigate!"

Crusty barked eagerly, his tail wagging in agreement. They followed the trail of sparkling lights, their laughter echoing through the forest.

They soon stumbled upon a clearing, where an enchanting waterfall cascaded into a crystal-clear pool. And there, around the pool was a sea of bright flowers their colors mixing giving the appearance of a bed of sparkling gems.

Almas gasped, his eyes widening with wonder. "Ulec, it's even more beautiful than I imagined!"

Ulec grinned mischievously. "Indeed, it's a treasure worth discovering. But remember, true treasures lie not in gold and jewels, but in the simple moments with friends in nature."

Crusty, with his tail brushing against the flowers, seemed to understand, his gaze fixed on Almas and Ulec. They basked in the magic of the moment, cherishing their friendship and the hidden treasure they had uncovered within themselves.

As the afternoon wore on, the sun cast a warm glow upon the forest. Almas, Ulec, Crusty, and Metal reached a tranquil stream, its gentle current inviting them to play.

Ulec's eyes twinkled mischievously. "Almas, Crusty, how about a game that uses my ability to communicate with the animals of the forest? Let's call it the Mind-Link Game!"

Almas gave Ulec an intrigued glance. "How does it work?" Almas asked, his curiosity piqued.

Ulec explained with a grin, "I will close my eyes and connect my mind with a forest creature. Without speaking or making any physical gestures, I'll try to guide the animal to find you. It's your job to stay hidden and see if you can outwit our furry friends!"

Crusty wagged his tail, eager to participate. Almas nodded, excitement bubbling within him. "That sounds amazing! Let's do it!"

Ulec closed his eyes, his brows furrowing in concentration. Slowly, he reached out with his mind, seeking a connection with a forest dweller.

After a moment, Ulec's eyes fluttered open. "I've established a link with a mischievous squirrel named Nutmeg. Prepare yourselves, my friends!"

Almas and Crusty hid behind a cluster of bushes, their hearts racing with anticipation. Ulec focused his thoughts, mentally guiding Nutmeg towards their hiding spot.

Minutes ticked by, filled with suspense. Suddenly, a rustling sound echoed through the forest, drawing closer. Almas and Crusty exchanged glances, trying to suppress their excitement.

Then, with a triumphant chirp, Nutmeg leaped onto the bush, landing right in front of Almas. He burst into laughter, delighted by the squirrel's clever sleuthing.

Ulec clapped his hands in glee. "Well done, Nutmeg! You've found Almas!"

Crusty wagged his tail, barking his approval. Almas stepped forward, patting Nutmeg gently on the head. "You're a brilliant detective, Nutmeg. Thank you for playing with us!"

Ulec beamed with pride. "The forest creatures are incredible allies and friends. We can share adventures and games like this, any game you can think of."

And so, they continued their game, connecting with different forest creatures through Ulec's mind-link. From playful squirrels to wise old owls, the animals of Aguerius Forest joined in the joyous pursuit, making memories that would last a lifetime.

As the day drew to a close, Almas and Ulec sat atop a mossy log, their faithful companions by their side. The sun cast a warm, golden hue upon the forest, bathing everything in a tranquil glow.

Almas sighed, a mix of happiness and longing in his voice. "Ulec, this has been the best day ever. I wish it would never end."

Ulec placed a hand on Almas' shoulder, his voice filled with warmth. "I feel the same, my friend. But remember, the forest will always be here, waiting for our return. And who knows what new adventures await us?"

Crusty nuzzled against Almas, as if in agreement. Metal gurgled softly, its slime quivering with contentment.

Almas smiled, his heart brimming with gratitude. "You're right, Ulec. We'll come back to this magical place, with Crusty and Metal by our side. Until then, we'll carry the memories of today in our hearts."

And with a promise to return, Almas, Ulec, Crusty, and Metal made their way back through the forest, their laughter and whispers blending with the rustle of leaves, creating a harmonious melody that would linger in Aguerius Forest, a testament to the enduring bond of friendship.

Chapter 4

AS THE SUN CAST ITS warm glow over the Aguerius Estate, Almas and Creetan eagerly mounted their horses, accompanied by their father, High Lord Gidon Aguerius. The air buzzed with anticipation as they prepared to embark on their journey to Jaspen, the capital of the Aguerius Province, where the King of the Yucaipan Kingdom awaited their arrival.

As they trotted away from the estate, Crusty trotting along with them, Almas couldn't help but feel a mischievous spark within him. This journey presented the perfect opportunity to engage in some brotherly rivalry. Not to mention get back at Creetan for all the mean things he did to him, most of which he couldn't remember, but that wasn't important.

On the first day of their journey, as they made their way through lush meadows and winding forest trails, Almas seized every opportunity to pull something off against Creetan. He surreptitiously tied knots in Creetan's saddle straps, causing him to struggle with disentangling them. Almas would stifle his laughter, pretending innocence as Creetan shot him suspicious glances.

But Creetan was not one to be outdone. When they stopped to rest by a babbling brook, Creetan seized the chance to strike back. As Almas took a refreshing drink from his water flask, he spluttered in surprise, realizing Creetan had swapped his flask with one filled with tadpoles in it.

As they continued their journey towards Jaspen, the mischievous rivalry between Almas and Creetan escalated, leaving a trail of laughter and bewildered reactions in their wake.

One sunny afternoon, the travelers found themselves passing through a small village nestled amongst rolling hills. The village buzzed with excitement as news of the High Lord and his sons' arrival spread like wildfire. Villagers lined the streets, waving and cheering as they trotted by, adding to the festive atmosphere.

Almas glanced around, spotting a bucket perched precariously on a rickety wooden beam above the road. A mischievous grin spread across his face as he nudged his horse closer to the beam, positioning himself directly underneath it.

With a swift tug on the reins, Almas feigned a stumble, causing his horse to rear up. Startled, the horse kicked its hooves, jolting the beam and sending the bucket flying through the air. The bucket arced gracefully before landing squarely on Creetan's head, dousing him in a cascade of water.

The onlookers erupted into fits of laughter, their cheers echoing through the village square. Almas struggled to contain his own laughter, his shoulders shaking as he watched Creetan's stunned expression.

Their father, High Lord Gidon Aguerius, raised an eyebrow, his eyes twinkling with amusement. "Boys, I hope you know the villagers will remember this day for a long time."

Almas and Creetan exchanged sheepish glances, their faces turning scarlet as they tried to stifle their laughter. Their father chuckled softly, unable to suppress his own amusement.

The escorts, stoic and composed throughout the journey, finally cracked a smile, their stern expressions giving way to hearty laughter. They had witnessed the mischievous escapades of the two brothers and had become secretly entertained by their antics.

As the laughter subsided, Creetan removed the drenched bucket from his head, his wet hair plastered to his forehead. He looked at Almas, a mischievous glint in his eyes. "Well played, brother," he said with a smile. "But remember, the day is not over yet."

Their pranks continued into the evening when they arrived at the welcoming village of Redbrook. The inn, a cozy retreat adorned with wooden beams and flickering candlelight, provided a warm respite for the travelers.

As they settled into their rooms, Almas' mind buzzed with ideas for the night's prank. With a mischievous glint in his eye, he realized he had the perfect plan.

Under the cover of darkness, Almas tiptoed into Creetan's room. With careful precision, he rearranged Creetan's belongings, leaving them in amusingly disarrayed positions. Shoes were placed atop the bed, while his clothes were arranged in a comical fashion.

Almas stifled his laughter, his heart racing with anticipation for Creetan's reaction. With his mission complete, he stealthily retreated to his own room.

The following morning, Almas awoke with a mix of excitement and curiosity. He couldn't wait to see Creetan's face when he discovered the prank. As they gathered for breakfast, he cast a furtive glance at Creetan, noticing the bewildered expression on his brother's face.

As they mounted their horses, ready to continue their journey, Almas couldn't help but chuckle to himself. He was already plotting the pranks for the day, determined to outwit Creetan once again.

With a mischievous glint in his eye, Almas spurred his horse forward, eager for the day's adventures and the inevitable retaliation from his brother. The prank wars had only just begun, and the journey to Jaspen promised to be filled with laughter and surprises.

The journey to Jaspen continued, and the prank wars between Almas and Creetan showed no signs of slowing down. Their mischievous spirits seemed to infect even their father, High Lord Gidon Aguerius, who found great amusement in their antics.

As they rode through quaint villages and picturesque countryside, the brothers seized every opportunity to outdo each other. Almas carefully placed a frog in Creetan's saddlebag, causing a comical commotion when Creetan discovered the unexpected visitor. In retaliation, Creetan managed to discreetly tie a fake spider to the back of Almas' saddle, resulting in a wild dance as Almas swatted at the imaginary arachnid.

Crusty, the loyal wolf cub, observed the ongoing pranks with curiosity and amusement, occasionally joining in the fun in his own unique way. He playfully nipped at Creetan's boots or hid Almas' belongings, adding a touch of furry mischief to the mix.

As they neared Jaspen, the anticipation grew. The brothers realized that their time for pranks was coming to an end as they approached the solemnity of the capital city. They reluctantly agreed to one final prank as a grand finale before their meeting with the King.

Late in the evening, they arrived at Jaspen, weary but exhilarated from their journey. They sought refuge in a cozy inn, their laughter echoing through the corridors as they settled into their rooms. Almas and Creetan exchanged mischievous glances, knowing this would be their last chance for a prank before the morning.

The inn had a large bath, a luxury they gladly indulged in, but little did they know the misadventure that awaited them.

As the two brothers entered the bath, their playful spirits took hold once again. The large space offered plenty of opportunities for splashing and mischief. Almas couldn't resist dunking Creetan under the water, and in retaliation, Creetan unleashed a cascade of water on Almas. Laughter filled the air as they playfully wrestled and made quite the mess of the bath area.

By the time they were finished, the bath resembled a wild sea, with water splashed across every surface and bubbles floating in the air. The innkeeper's eyes widened in shock as he surveyed the aftermath of their aquatic escapades. Almas and Creetan sheepishly gathered their belongings, apologizing profusely as they left the now-drenched bath area.

As he returned to his room and under the cover of darkness, Almas thought up a plan that involved Creetan's boots and a jar of harmless but smelly ink. With silent precision, he executed the prank, leaving Creetan's boots stained a vibrant shade of blue.

As he retired for the night, Almas couldn't help but chuckle at all the mischievous escapades. He knew that the following day would bring a different atmosphere, one of formality and respect in the presence of the King.

Almas could hardly sleep that night, as he was too excited about meeting the King the next day. He had always dreamed of seeing the Provicial palace, where his father often went for important meetings. He wondered what the King would look like, and what he would say to him. He hoped he would make a good impression and not embarrass his father.

He also hoped that his final prank on Creetan would work out as planned. He had spent all day planning for it, and he was confident that it would be the best one yet. He had secretly replaced Creetan's boots with identical ones, except that they were dyed blue with an ink that smelled of blueberries. He had hidden the original boots in his own room, and had waited for the right moment to switch them.

He smiled to himself as he imagined Creetan's reaction when he saw his blue boots. He expected him to be furious, but also amused. After all, they had agreed to end their prank war with a bang, and Almas had delivered.

He finally fell asleep, dreaming of blue boots and golden crowns.

He woke up early the next morning, feeling a rush of adrenaline as he remembered what awaited him. He jumped out of bed and got dressed, eager to start the day. He wore his finest clothes, a dark green tunic with black trousers, with a silver belt and a matching cloak. He also wore his own boots, which were black and polished.

He left his room and waited in the hallway, pretending to be casual. He heard Creetan's door open and saw him walk out, carrying his saddlebag and wearing his blue boots.

Almas felt a surge of satisfaction as he saw Creetan's expression. He looked shocked, angry, and embarrassed all at once. His blue boots contrasted sharply with his otherwise elegant outfit, making him look ridiculous.

Almas greeted him cheerfully, trying to act innocent.

"Good morning, brother," he said. "You look...blue."

Creetan glared at him, knowing that Almas was behind this prank.

"This is not funny, Almas. This is the worst prank you've ever pulled. How could you do this to me on such an important day?"

Almas shrugged, enjoying Creetan's discomfort.

"It's just a harmless joke, Creetan. Don't be so uptight. Besides, blue suits you. It brings out your eyes."

Creetan snorted, not falling for Almas' flattery.

"You know what else brings out my eyes? Rage. And you're about to see it if you don't apologize right now."

Almas shook his head, still smiling.

"I'm sorry, Creetan, but I can't do that. This is our last prank, remember? We agreed to go out with a bang. And I think I've achieved that."

Creetan opened his mouth to argue, but was interrupted by their father's voice.

"Boys, are you ready? We have to leave soon."

They turned to see High Lord Gidon Aguerius walking towards them, dressed in his finest clothes and looking dignified and regal.

He wore a dark blue coat over a white shirt, with gold buttons and embroidery. He also wore black trousers and boots, and a gold chain around his neck. On his head he wore a black hat with a white feather.

He stopped in front of them and scanned them with a critical eye.

"You both look very handsome," he said approvingly. "But Creetan...what's with the blue boots?"

Almas felt a surge of amusement as he saw his father's expression change from pride to confusion.

He quickly came up with a lie to cover for Creetan.

"He likes them, father," he said innocently. "He thinks they make him stand out."

High Lord Gidon raised an eyebrow, not buying Almas' explanation.

"Is that so?" he asked Creetan.

Creetan hesitated, not wanting to admit that he had been pranked by his brother. He looked at Almas, hoping for some mercy or sympathy. But all he saw was a wicked gleam in his brother's eyes. Creetan sighed and nodded reluctantly.

"Yes, father," he lied. "I like them."

High Lord Gidon shrugged and smiled.

"Well, then, I suppose they do make you stand out," he said kindly. "But I hope you don't mind if I stand a little further away from you when we meet the King."

He chuckled and patted Creetan on the shoulder.

"Come on, boys," he said warmly. "Let's go."

Their father led them towards the palace, leaving Almas feeling triumphant and proud. He had pulled off the best prank ever, and had made Creetan wear blue boots in front of the King. Almas sure hoped that the King would have a sense of humor.

Or at least poor taste.

Chapter 5

AFTER A FINAL CHECK that their clothes were clean and fresh, the brothers joined their father, High Lord Gidon Aguerius, on their way to the palace. The anticipation in their hearts grew with each step as they entered the grand halls of the Provincial Palace, their footsteps echoing through the opulent corridors.

Upon reaching the King's chambers, they were greeted by King Yucaipa, a kind and elderly man who exuded wisdom and warmth. His eyes sparkled with recognition as he saw the boys standing before him. "Ah, Almas and Creetan! How you have grown since I last saw you. It warms my heart to witness your journey into young adulthood."

Almas and Creetan bowed respectfully. "Thank you, Your Majesty," they replied in unison.

The King smiled, his voice gentle and filled with grandfatherly affection. "Your father has informed me of your adventures in the forest and the mischievous pranks you played on your journey here. It is good to see young spirits full of life and laughter. It brings light to the sometimes-weighty duties of the crown. By the way Young Cree, I must say I love your boots, perhaps I could get your parents to tell me where I could get a pair like that for myself. Now you will need to excuse me and your father."

Before they could respond, King Yucaipa turned his attention to their father, signaling that he had matters to discuss. "High Lord Gidon, I require your guidance on a matter of great importance. Would you be so kind as to accompany me to my study?"

Their father nodded respectfully. "Of course, Your Majesty. Almas, Creetan, I trust you will behave yourselves while I am away. You may explore the Provincial Palace, but remember to show respect to all those you encounter."

As their father departed with the King, Almas and Creetan found themselves alone in the vast palace, filled with curiosity and a sense of adventure. They embarked on their exploration, marveling at the grandeur of the architecture and the exquisite artwork adorning the walls.

However, their wanderings soon led them to an encounter that dampened their spirits. Turning a corner, they stumbled upon the prince, a stark contrast to his father. Unlike the benevolent King, the Prince possessed an air of arrogance and disdain.

"Well, well, what do we have here?" the prince sneered, eyeing the brothers with disdain. "Lost little nobles wandering through my palace. Shouldn't you be following your nursemaids?"

Almas clenched his fists, his face reddening with anger, while Creetan shot the prince a defiant glare. "We are not lost, Your

Highness. We have been given permission to explore the palace while our father attends to matters of state."

The prince scoffed, his voice dripping with contempt. "You have been given permission to explore the palace? How generous of my father. He must have taken pity on you, living out in the farmlands like peasants instead of the Provincial Palace like real nobles."

Creetan stepped forward, his voice calm but firm. "Remember your Highness, by decree of the first king of the New Yucaipan Kingdom there are no peasants. We are proud to live in the farmlands, where we can see the fruits of our labor and the beauty of nature. Our father wants us to be close to the people he serves, and he wants us to know and understand the people of the province. He says that is what makes a true noble, not the walls of a palace or the jewels on a crown."

The prince's eyes widened, his face turning red with rage. He was not used to being challenged by anyone, let alone two young boys. He opened his mouth to retort, but before he could utter a word, Almas and Creetan had already walked away, leaving him speechless and fuming.

The prince's lip curled into a sneer as he called after them. "Permission or not, while my father and I are here, this is my palace, and I do not take kindly to your presence here. Know your place, little boys."

Almas and Creetan exchanged glances as they continued to walk away, their determination unyielding. They knew their father had taught them to respect others, but they also understood the importance of standing up for themselves.

They continued their exploration, leaving the prince behind. The encounter had left a bitter taste in their mouths, but they refused to let it overshadow their excitement for the grandeur that surrounded them.

As they roamed the palace, they stumbled upon stunning gardens, magnificent tapestries, and halls filled with history. The intricate details and stories embedded within the Provincial Palace captivated their imaginations, allowing them to momentarily forget the unpleasant encounter with the prince.

As the sun began its descent, casting long shadows throughout the palace, Almas and Creetan found themselves outside the King's chambers once again, eagerly awaiting their father's return. Their hearts brimmed with stories of their exploration, ready to share their adventures and misadventures.

AS THE SUN BEGAN TO set, casting a warm glow over the city of Jaspen, High Lord Gidon Aguerius emerged from his meeting with the King, his expression a mix of concern and determination. Almas and Creetan eagerly awaited their father's return, sensing that something important had transpired within the walls of the Provincial Palace.

Walking briskly alongside his sons, their father's voice held a weight of urgency. "Boys, the King has entrusted me with a crucial mission. He wishes for me to journey to the remnants of the Elvish Kingdom, beyond the Dividing Mountains. It seems we are on the precipice of another conflict with the Lich Lords, and the King seeks to secure an alliance with the Elves."

Almas exchanged a worried glance with his father, understanding the delicate nature of this mission. The Elves had become reclusive over the years, isolating themselves from the affairs of men after their near annihilation during the war of destruction. Almas knew from Ulec's tales that their welcome would be anything but warm.

"We have just lost the Vatan Province, and the King is determined not to let another one slip away," their father continued, his voice tinged with both responsibility and concern. "I will leave in the morning with my guards, while the two of you will return to the Aguerius Estate later tomorrow morning, escorted by a contingent assigned by the King himself."

Almas listened intently, his mind racing with conflicting thoughts. He was proud of his father's important role, but he couldn't shake his worries about the reception they would receive from the Elves. Ulec had made it clear that their kind regarded humans with suspicion and caution.

Yet, Almas knew he couldn't voice his concerns in front of Creetan. The promise he made to Ulec, to keep the secret of his forest friend hidden, weighed heavily on him. He had to protect Ulec and his kin. Luckily, he knew his father was aware of the same information that Almas was.

Returning to the inn, the weight of their impending separation settled upon them. Almas and Creetan began their preparations for their respective journeys. The room was filled with a mix of excitement and melancholy, knowing that the next day would bring significant changes to their lives.

Almas observed his father, watching as he meticulously packed his belongings, his mind focused on the task at hand. The High Lord's determination to secure the alliance and protect their land was unwavering, and Almas admired his father's strength.

As they gathered their belongings and made final preparations, Almas stole a moment alone with his father. "Father, please be careful on your mission," he said, his voice laced with genuine concern. "The Elves... they may not be as receptive as the King hopes. Their fear toward others runs deep."

High Lord Gidon's gaze softened, a mixture of appreciation and understanding. "Thank you, Almas. I am aware of the challenges that lie ahead. But I will do everything in my power to find a common ground and convince the Elves of our shared purpose. I trust you and Creetan to make your way home safely."

Almas nodded; his heart heavy with unspoken worries. They had to trust in their father's skills and the bond of family that united them. As they joined Creetan back in the room, their eyes met, understanding passing between them. Tomorrow would mark the beginning of a new chapter in their lives, and they would face it with courage and resilience.

With the evening sky fading into twilight, they settled into their beds, their minds swirling with thoughts of the future. As they drifted off to sleep, dreams of alliances, adventures, and the unknown danced in their heads, each determined to fulfill their respective roles in the days to come.

Chapter 6

THE SUN HAD BARELY begun to peek over the horizon when Lord Aguerius roused his sons from their slumber. Almas and Creetan rubbed their sleepy eyes, trying to grasp the reality of their father's departure. He stood before them, dressed for the journey, his countenance a mix of pride and concern.

"Remember, boys, behave yourselves and show respect to your escort," their father reminded them, his voice firm but filled with fatherly affection. "You'll be returning to the Aguerius Estate under their protection. I have faith in you both."

Almas and Creetan nodded, their expressions a mixture of determination and reluctance. They understood the gravity of the situation and the need to maintain composure. With a final embrace, their father bid them farewell and headed towards his own destiny.

As the morning sun rose higher, Almas and Creetan, accompanied by their escort, made their way back to the Provincial Palace. The King and the Prince awaited them at the entrance, offering their good wishes and ensuring their safety.

"Safe travels, my young friends," King Yucaipa said, his voice warm and reassuring. "I have personally selected this escort to accompany you. They are among the finest soldiers in the kingdom."

Almas couldn't help but feel a shiver crawl up his spine as he caught a glimpse of the prince's smirk. There was something unsettling about the way the prince regarded him, an undercurrent of mischief that he couldn't quite decipher. He wondered if the prince might have had more of a hand in picking their escort than the King. If that was true it could be a problem, particularly since they would be walking this time and were only bringing a pack horse and no mounts.

With a courteous bow, Almas and Creetan accepted the King's wishes, their expressions masking their growing apprehension. As they set off on their journey, Almas couldn't shake the eerie feeling that this escort might not be what it seemed.

As the day wore on, Almas noticed a shift in the demeanor of their escorts. They became increasingly short-tempered, their patience wearing thin at the slightest provocation. Even Crusty, usually a playful and friendly companion, growled and snarled at the guards, sensing their malevolence. He stayed close to Almas and seemed to be extra protective.

Creetan's unease became palpable, his normally confident demeanor giving way to nervous fidgeting. Almas observed his older brother's discomfort, his own worries mirrored in Creetan's eyes. Something was amiss, and they couldn't ignore the signs any longer.

"It feels like we're taking a different route," Creetan whispered to Almas, his voice laced with worry.

Almas glanced around, noticing the unfamiliar surroundings. His brow furrowed as he realized that their escort had indeed veered off the usual path. His suspicions deepened, but he knew they couldn't confront their guards directly without risking further danger.

"Our leader said it's a shortcut," Almas responded, his voice hushed after making a subtle observation to the escort leader. "But I don't trust them. We need to stay alert and watch our backs."

The afternoon sun beat down upon them as they continued their journey, their path twisting through unfamiliar terrain. The tension hung heavy in the air; the atmosphere charged with uncertainty. As dusk settled, the escort finally announced that they would make camp for the night.

Setting up their modest camp, Almas and Creetan exchanged worried glances. They couldn't shake the feeling that they were at the mercy of their treacherous escorts, and their hearts sank with the weight of the unknown.

As darkness enveloped the camp, they huddled together, seeking solace in each other's presence. Almas couldn't help but wonder what the next day would bring. Their fate rested in the hands of those who were meant to protect them, and the uncertainty gnawed at his core.

With a silent prayer for their safety, Almas closed his eyes, hoping that their journey would soon lead them back to the familiar embrace of the Aguerius Estate. Little did they know that the trials they would face were only just beginning.

And so, under the watchful gaze of the moon, they slept, their dreams haunted by shadows of the unknown, their minds racing with unanswered questions.

ALMAS STIRRED FROM his sleep as Creetan's arm flopped onto him, jolting him awake. He grumbled and pushed his brother's arm aside, about to settle back into slumber when he heard Creetan's hushed voice, barely audible.

"Almas, pretend to wake me up," Creetan whispered, feigning sleep. "Tell me you need to go take care of business, but you're scared to go alone. We need to talk."

Curiosity piqued, Almas followed his brother's lead, shaking him gently and pretending concern. "Creetan, wake up! I really need to go take care of something, but I'm scared to go alone."

Creetan stirred, his eyes fluttering open as he groggily sat up. "What's the matter, Almas?"

"I need to go... you know, do my business," Almas said, gesturing towards the trees. "But it's dark out there, and I don't want to go alone. Will you come with me?"

Creetan nodded, playing along. They both rose from their bedrolls, making their way towards the outskirts of the camp where they could speak without being overheard.

Once they were out of earshot, Creetan leaned in closer to Almas, his voice barely a whisper. "Listen, Almas. Something's not right with this escort. They're heading straight towards the Vatan Province, controlled by the Lich Lords. We need to find a chance to escape."

Almas's eyes widened with a mix of fear and determination. The Lich Lords were a formidable force, and being caught in their clutches meant certain doom. Almas knew they had to seize any opportunity that presented itself.

"When the moment comes and I tell you to run, don't hesitate," Creetan continued, his voice filled with urgency. "We can't afford to be caught. Stick close to me, and we'll find a way to escape."

Almas nodded, his heart pounding in his chest. He understood the gravity of the situation and the need to trust his brother's instincts. They couldn't let themselves be led into the clutches of the Lich Lords.

But time was of the essence. Almas glanced back towards the camp, knowing that their prolonged absence would raise suspicions. With a silent agreement, they returned to their bedrolls, their minds swirling with plans and uncertainties.

As they settled back into sleep, Almas couldn't help but feel a mix of anticipation and trepidation. The next day would bring challenges they couldn't yet fathom, but they were resolved to face them together, brothers bound by an unbreakable bond.

In the darkness of the night, their dreams were filled with flickers of escape, their imaginations conjuring pathways to freedom.

THE MORNING SUN CAST dappled shadows on the forest path as the group resumed their journey. Almas couldn't shake the feeling that something was amiss. The guards seemed to be sticking closer to him and Creetan, their eyes watchful, suspicion evident in their expressions. It was as if they anticipated the boys' next move.

Lost in his thoughts, Almas suddenly heard a faint melody carried by the wind. It was enchanting, drawing him closer with each passing note. The music grew louder, resonating through his being, its hypnotic pulls impossible to resist. Deep within, a voice cautioned him of the magic entwined within the melody.

A sense of urgency gripped Almas as he realized the others were succumbing to the allure of the music. Their faces softened, tension giving way to a tranquil acceptance. Almas fought against the enchantment, his mind racing for a way to break free.

But before he could devise a plan, the source of the music came into view—a man standing tall, playing an instrument that resembled a blend of a battle staff and wind instrument. His attire, adorned with symbols of mourning and a skull mask, marked him as an avenger—a figure of vengeance and solemn purpose.

The avenger ceased playing, and the magical hold on the group dissipated. Almas stood rooted to the spot, trying to shake off the lingering effects, his heart pounding in his chest. He exchanged a knowing glance with Creetan, their unspoken recognition of the avenger's identity hanging in the air.

The avenger lowered his instrument, his eyes piercing through the skull mask. He spoke in a low, raspy voice, "Where are you taking the sons of Lord Aguerius?"

The leader of the escort, a burly man with a scarred face, sneered at the avenger. "That's none of your business, stranger. Move aside or face the consequences."

Sensing an opportunity, Creetan took a step back, as if seeking shelter behind their escorts. With three quick taps on Almas's shoulder, then two, and finally one, Creetan initiated their daring escape plan. The brothers darted to the side, disappearing into the dense forest, their nimble movements aided by Crusty, who bravely fended off one of the guards.

The sounds of struggle echoed behind them as they fled deeper into the woods, including the clanging of weapons and notes played by the instrument of the avenger. Almas's heart pounded with each step, adrenaline fueling their flight. They wove through the underbrush, guided by the instinct to survive and the flicker of hope that burned within.

In the midst of their escape, Almas spared a moment to reflect on the avenger's voice—it was hauntingly familiar. But now was not the time for introspection. They had broken free from their captors, and their priority was to put as much distance as possible between themselves and their pursuers.

With the forest as their refuge, Almas and Creetan pressed onward, determined to navigate the unknown and seek sanctuary from the dangers that loomed ahead.

Chapter 7

ALMAS'S BREATH CAME in ragged gasps as he ran alongside Creetan, their feet pounding against the forest floor. Thoughts raced through his mind, the revelation of who the avenger could be sending shockwaves through his being.

Amidst the chaos of their escape, Almas voiced his suspicion, his voice strained with disbelief. "Do you think that avenger was Uncle Marpel?"

Creetan's breaths were heavy, but he managed a nod. "It's possible, Almas. I never thought I'd see him again, not after what happened to Vatan Province."

Uncle Marpel, their mother's brother and the High Lord of the now-devastated Vatan Province, had vanished during the province's fall. The brothers had mourned his loss, fearing the worst. The sudden appearance of their enigmatic uncle raised questions about his fate and the hardships he must have endured.

Almas hesitated, his heart torn between their own safety and the potential danger faced by their uncle. "Shouldn't we go back and help him, Creetan? If that was Uncle Marpel, he might need us."

Creetan's voice held a mix of caution and determination. "As much as I want to believe he's alive, Almas, we must prioritize our own escape. Uncle Marpel is a skilled bard; he can defend himself. Never underestimate the power of a High Lord. But we need to focus on getting away and not burdening him with our protection."

Agreeing with his brother's reasoning, Almas suppressed his concerns and concentrated on their immediate survival. After what felt like an eternity of running, they reached a river—a respite amidst the wilderness. They knelt by the water's edge, gulping down cool, refreshing sips to quench their parched throats.

Creetan glanced up, his eyes scanning their surroundings. "We should walk along the river for a while, Almas. It might help throw off anyone who might be following us."

Almas nodded, the icy water numbing their feet as they trudged alongside the riverbank. Time seemed to blur as they forged ahead, their bodies growing weary with each passing step. But they knew they had to press on, relying on their resilience and the hope of evading their pursuers.

Just when their strength waned and despair threatened to take hold, a small bird alighted upon Almas's shoulder. Its presence startled him, but the bird's purpose soon became clear as it took flight, perching on a nearby branch and peering back at Almas.

A spark of intuition ignited within Almas. "Creetan, I think we should follow this bird. Perhaps it can lead us somewhere safe."

Creetan's weary eyes met Almas's, exhaustion mingled with curiosity. "We don't have many options, brother. Let's trust the bird's guidance."

With renewed determination, they followed the bird's lead, their steps guided by a creature in tune with the forest's secrets. As the sun dipped below the horizon, casting long shadows, the bird guided them to a concealed cave—nature's sanctuary hidden from prying eyes.

Realizing the gift they had been granted, they entered the shelter of the cave, grateful for its protection. As darkness enveloped the world outside, the brothers huddled together, seeking solace and security within the hidden refuge, their thoughts consumed by the events that had unfolded and the mysteries that awaited them.

AS THE MORNING LIGHT seeped into the hidden cave, Almas and Creetan stirred from their restless slumber. The events of the previous day and the encounter with their mysterious uncle still lingered in their thoughts. The bird that had guided them to safety now flapped its wings anxiously, as if urging them to follow.

Almas and Creetan exchanged glances, their unspoken agreement evident. They would trust the bird's instincts once more. Following its lead, they ventured towards a nearby cluster of berry bushes, their empty stomachs grumbling in anticipation of a much-needed meal.

The boys savored the sweet taste of the berries, their nourishment providing a small measure of comfort in their dire situation. But their respite was abruptly shattered as the bird suddenly erupted into panicked flapping, its distress reverberating through the air.

Confusion etched across their faces, Almas and Creetan turned their attention to the source of the commotion. To their shock, three members of their escort had emerged from the forest, encircling the boys with malicious intent.

"So, you thought you could get away from us, said one if the men insincerely, "Sorry boys but we are being paid good money to deliver you to the Lich Lords."

Fear and defiance mingled in Almas's voice as he demanded answers. "What are you doing? We trusted you!"

The men sneered, relishing in their deceit. But just as they closed in, a young voice echoed through the clearing, commanding them to stop. All eyes turned to the unexpected presence nearby—Ulec, standing with an air of confidence, Crusty at his side.

With his elvish features hidden beneath a bandana, Ulec appeared as nothing more than an eleven-year-old boy to the men. They laughed, underestimating the danger that stood before them. Ignorance would prove to be their downfall.

One of the men drew his sword, his intentions clear. Ulec, however, effortlessly dodged the swing, his movements graceful and agile. With a swift series of strikes from his staff, the man crumpled to the ground, unconscious.

The remaining two men approached Ulec more cautiously, their wariness apparent. They attacked simultaneously, swords flashing through the air. Ulec's skill and agility were put to the test as he deftly evaded and parried their strikes.

The fight waged on, each clash of metal resounding through the forest. Almas and Creetan watched in awe as Ulec demonstrated his prowess. Eventually, the other two men joined their comrade on the ground, defeated.

Almas wasted no time in asking Ulec about who he thought was his uncle. "Ulec, do you know if that was Uncle Marpel that helped us yesterday?"

Ulec responded, "Yes. He is okay, just a small wound to his leg. When I noticed you were in trouble, I had a bird write a message on the ground during the night telling him how to find you guys. But we can't worry about him right now, it's your dad that I'm worried about, we need to catch up to him."

Creetan's eyes widened, his voice filled with astonishment. "Who is this boy, Almas?"

Almas spared a brief moment to exchange a knowing glance with Ulec before responding. "He's a friend, Creetan. I'll explain everything on the way, but for now, we must catch up with Father. If Ulec believes that Father is in trouble than we need to believe him."

Ulec nodded, his expression serious. "We need to warn High Lord Gidon and ensure his safety. Time is of the essence."

With renewed urgency, the group set off, their steps propelled by a shared purpose. Almas, Creetan, Ulec, and Crusty moved swiftly through the forest, their determination unwavering. As they navigated the treacherous path.

Chapter 8

THEY CONTINUED THEIR trek through the forest, aware of the gravity of their mission and the perils that awaited them. After a while, they came across a river, its soothing sound offering a brief relief.

Almas took the chance to slip away, heading towards the bushes to take care of some urgent personal business. But as he was just finishing up, he heard a loud roar that made his blood run cold. Suddenly right in front of him he saw a huge bear, its mouth open and its eyes fixed on him.

Almas froze, his eyes wide and his mouth dry. He was about to scream when Ulec showed up seemingly out of no where, standing between him and the beast, unfazed. "Seacra, cut it out. That's not funny," Ulec said in a slightly annoyed tone.

The bear changed shape in an instant, becoming a young elvish girl with long blonde hair and a mischievous smile. The elvish girl giggled at her own joke, enjoying the scare she had given Almas.

"Who are you!" Almas gasped, clutching his chest. "You nearly gave me a heart attack!"

"Sorry, sorry," the girl said, not sounding sorry at all. "I couldn't resist. You looked so funny with your pants down and your face all pale. I'm Seacra, Ulec's sister."

Almas felt his cheeks burn with embarrassment. He quickly pulled up his pants and tried to act casual. "Ha ha, very funny. You're quite the comedian. How were you a bear a moment ago?"

Ulec rolled his eyes at his sister's antics. "Almas, Creetan, meet my sister Seacra, she is a shape-shifter. That's how she was a bear."

"A shape-shifter?" Creetan asked, fascinated. "That's amazing! How do you do that?"

Seacra shrugged. "It's a gift. I can change into any animal I want, as long as I've touched it before. It's fun and useful."

"Useful for what?" Almas asked, still feeling a bit annoyed.

"For pranks, of course," Seacra said, grinning. "And for spying, escaping, hunting, traveling... you name it."

"Wow," Creetan said, impressed. "You must have had a lot of adventures."

Seacra nodded. "Oh yes, I have. I just turned 100 years old after all. I've seen many places and met many creatures. Some friendly, some not so much. But I always manage to get out of trouble."

"Sounds like you're quite the troublemaker along with being a spy," Almas said.

Seacra winked at him. "Maybe I am. But I'm also loyal to my family and friends. And you two are my brother's friends, so you're my friends too." She hugged them both, making them feel welcome.

"Thank you," Almas said, smiling.

"Thank you," Creetan echoed.

ULEC SMILED AT HIS sister's warmth. He was glad she was here. He knew they would need her help in their quest. He hoped she would take it seriously.

He decided to tell her where they were going and why. He hoped she would understand the urgency and the danger of their mission.

He hoped she would laugh less and listen more.

He hoped he wasn't hoping too much.

Seacra's grin didn't fade as she asked them where they were going. Ulec told her that they were heading to stop Lord Aguerius before he reached elvish lands, and Seacra burst into laughter again. "The Dragon Queen is going to roast him alive before he can cross the Dividing Mountains!" she exclaimed.

Ulec's serious expression showed his worry. "Seacra, this is no laughing matter. Their father is in trouble, and we need your help."

Seacra sighed, but agreed to help, though she still had a playful glint in her eyes. She winked at them and said, "Hop on, boys. Let's see how fast you can hold on," right before she transformed into a magnificent horse.

Almas, Creetan, and Ulec climbed on the horse, eager to catch up with Lord Aguerius and their destiny. Seacra took off with a gallop, making the wind blow their hair and their fears away, for a moment. They rode as one, a strange alliance formed by common goals and new friendship. The forest flew by, the once-frightening journey now filled with the warmth of old and new friends.

THE JOURNEY HAD TAKEN its toll on Almas and Creetan. As Seacra came to a stop and transformed back into her elvish form, the boys stumbled off the horse, their legs barely able to support them.

"I think... I might have left my legs behind," Creetan mumbled, trying to steady himself.

Ulec looked concerned. "You both need rest. We can't afford to push ourselves too hard."

Crusty whimpered softly, exhausted from chasing the horse for hours on end. He curled up next to Almas, seeking comfort and warmth.

Ulec put down his shoulder bag, and as he opened it, Seacra let out a startled shriek. "What is that... thing?"

Almas chuckled sleepily. "Don't worry, Seacra. That's just Ulec's pet. It's called Metal."

Creetan's eyes widened as he saw the slime oozing out of the bag. "A pet? That... that thing is a pet?"

Almas nodded. "Yeah, it's a slime. Ulec found it in the forest."

Seacra still seemed uneasy. "It's so... slimy."

"Hey, Metal might not be the prettiest creature, but it's harmless if you're a friend," Almas reassured her, stifling a yawn. "It's actually kind of helpful."

Seacra raised an eyebrow, unconvinced. "Helpful in what way?"

Ulec chimed in, defending his peculiar companion. "Metal can eat pretty much anything and has a knack for finding useful things in the forest. It's like having a walking scavenger with us. Not to mention the time it saved Almas from a forest dragon."

Forest Dragon, when did you encounter a forest dragon?" Creetan asked Almas right before realizing the answer, "Wait was that when you were lost in the forest?"

"Yep," Almas answered, that is where I met Ulec for the first time also.

Creetan still gave the slime a skeptical look but was too tired to argue. "I suppose it is okay to have around then, as long as it doesn't eat us in our sleep."

Almas chuckled again, feeling a wave of exhaustion wash over him. "Trust me, Metal won't do that, unless you were made of metal since that is what it likes best to eat. It's loyal to Ulec."

Seacra found a spot as far away from Metal as possible and settled down to sleep. "Fine, but it's still gross."

With that, the three boys and Crusty quickly fell asleep, their bodies finally getting the rest they needed. Hours later, Seacra gently woke them up.

"Time to go," she said softly, looking at them with a mixture of concern and determination. "Ulec went on ahead. We need to catch up."

Almas and Creetan rubbed their eyes, still feeling the fatigue but knowing they couldn't delay any longer. They thanked Seacra for the rest and for being their guide.

Seacra smirked playfully. "Just don't expect me to carry you all the way."

Almas grinned, his humor returning despite his weariness. "Wouldn't dream of it."

With newfound energy, they set off once more, Seacra leading the way with her characteristic confidence.

Chapter 9

THE TRIO PRESSED ON, following Seacra's lead as they reached a cave at the foot of the imposing Dividing Mountains. Seacra explained that these mountains split the continent into two halves, with the humans inhabiting the southern side and the elves the northern.

"The only way through is these caves," Seacra explained. "The passes are too high, and the air is thin and unbreathable."

Curiosity sparked in Creetan's eyes. "So how do we get across then?"

Seacra smiled mischievously. "Just follow me, and you'll see."

The cave they entered was illuminated by glowing stones, casting a soft, eerie light. Creetan couldn't help but marvel. "What makes these stones glow like this?"

Seacra laughed. "It's slime acid! Ulec had Metal spray the stones as he passed through. Clever, isn't it?"

As they ascended, the air grew colder, and soon the chill was biting into their skin. Seacra seemed unaffected as she transformed into a magnificent salamander, radiating warmth to keep Almas and Creetan from freezing.

"Thanks, Seacra," Almas said, feeling the soothing heat surround him.

Seacra grunted an acknowledgement and continued walking.

Finally, they reached the mouth of the cave, stepping out into a vast snowy valley. The silence was interrupted by angry roars that echoed through the mountains.

Almas tensed. "That doesn't sound good. What do you think it is?"

Seacra's eyes narrowed, her senses heightened. "I don't know, but we should be cautious."

The chilling wind whipped around them as they ventured further into the snowy valley, the imposing mountains casting shadows over them. As they moved forward, the roars grew louder, and the ground trembled beneath their feet.

Creetan said, "Whatever it is, I hope it's not hungry."

As they approached the center of the valley, they saw a large crater, surrounded by jagged rocks. Smoke billowed from the crater, and the roars became deafening.

As the temperature was much warmer near the crater, Seacra shifted into her natural elf form and said, "That's odd. There shouldn't be any volcanoes here. This must be a recent eruption."

She shifted into a hawk and flew over the crater, scouting for danger. She returned quickly, looking alarmed.

She shifted back into her elf form and said, "Guys, we have a problem. There's a young mountain dragon in there!"

Almas and Creetan gasped. "A young mountain dragon? How is that possible?"

Seacra said, "I don't know, but it looks like it's trapped. It must have been sleeping under the mountain and woke up when the volcano erupted. It's trying to break free, but the rocks are blocking its way."

Almas said, "That's terrible. We have to help it!"

Creetan said, "Are you crazy? It's a mountain dragon! It could eat us in one bite!"

Seacra said, "Not all mountain dragons are dangerous, Creetan. Some are friendly and wise. Besides, if we don't help it, it could cause more damage to the valley and the mountains."

She looked at Almas and Creetan with determination. "We have to free the dragon."

Creetan gulped. "How do we do that?"

Seacra said, "We need to clear the rocks that are blocking its way. I can use my fire to melt some of them, but I'll need your help to move them."

She transformed into a salamander again and headed towards the crater.

Almas followed her, feeling a surge of courage. He said, "Come on, Creetan. Let's do this."

Creetan hesitated, but then nodded. He said, "Okay, okay. But if we get eaten, I'm blaming you."

He joined Almas and Seacra as they approached the crater. The young elder dragon saw them and roared angrily, snapping its teeth at them. Seacra used her fire to melt some of the rocks that were blocking the young elder dragon's exit. Almas and Creetan used their strength to push and pull the rocks away from the crater.

They worked together as a team, dodging the dragon's snapping jaws and clearing its path. After a while, they managed to create a large enough opening for the young mountain dragon to escape.

The mountain dragon crawled out of the crater, shaking off the ash and dust from its scales. It looked at Almas, Creetan and Seacra with gratitude in its eyes. It bowed its head and made a low rumbling sound that seemed to convey thanks.

Almas smiled and said, "You're welcome. We're glad you're fine now."

Creetan said, "Yeah, yeah. No problem. Just don't eat us, okay?"

The dragon chuckled and made another sound that seemed to convey amusement. It spread its wings and gestured for Almas, Creetan and Seacra to climb on its back.

Seacra shifted into her elf form and said, "What is it doing?"

She realized that the young elder dragon wanted to repay them for their kindness.

She said, "I think it wants to take us across the valley."

Almas said, "Really? That would be awesome!"

Creetan said, "But what about our father? We have to catch up with him before he meets the Dragon Queen!"

Seacra said, "Don't worry. The mountain dragon will fly faster than we can walk. We'll get there in no time."

She climbed on the dragon's back and helped Almas and Creetan join her.

They found the dragon to be very warm so at least they wouldn't need Seacra to be in salamander form for the ride.

The young mountain dragon took off into the sky with a powerful flap of its wings.

Almas, Creetan and Seacra held on tight as they soared over the snowy valley. Almas just hoped it would be in time for his father.

Chapter 10

AFTER BEING DROPPED off by the mountain dragon, Almas, Creetan, and Seacra, back in her salamander form, soon reached the overlook, where they were met with a sight that took their breath away. An enormous Elder Dragon stood before the cave leading to Elvish lands, chasing a group of men. Almas recognized his father and the escorts among them, and his heart pounded in his chest.

Creetan's voice quivered with awe, "Is that the Dragon Queen?"

Seacra, still in her salamander form, grunted nodded solemnly.

Almas felt a surge of urgency to go help his father, but Seacra growled and blocked his path. Creetan seemed to understand, saying, "It's too dangerous, Almas."

Almas turned to Seacra, desperation in his eyes. "But we have to do something!"

Seacra lowered her heat, and then raised it again. It dawned on Almas that she couldn't go help because without her warmth, they would quickly succumb to the freezing temperatures.

"Right... we wouldn't last long without you," Almas muttered.

Almas saw some arrows from his father's escort and some bolts of holy energy strike the dragon but seemed to have little to no effect on the monstrous dragon. Where was Ulec? Had they flown past him? Was he still on his way?

They watched as the dragon breathed fire at the men, but Lord Aguerius summoned a golden shield to protect them. For a moment their view of the group of humans disappeared as flames engulfed them but the golden magic shield held and they were visible once the flames stopped. Now the dragon charged forward snarling ready to tear the men apart with her claws and teeth. Worst of all, Almas could see that his father was weakening. Desperation grew inside him. He had to act.

He couldn't just stand there and watch his father be swallowed by the dragon. "STOP!" Almas yelled at the top of his lungs, his voice carrying across the ridge.

The dragon paused, searching for the source of the voice. The Dragon Queen seemed to stare right at Almas for a moment before it returned its attention to the men, but this time, standing between them and the dragon was Ulec. The young elf looked small and insignificant compared to the massive creature yet the elvish boy looked at the beast calmly.

“Leave these men alone!” Ulec ordered as he looked the dragon in the eye, but the dragon snarled in response. It seemed like the confrontation would escalate until Ulec firmly commanded, "Mother, stop. That's enough!"

In a mesmerizing transformation, the dragon turned into a tall elvish woman with long golden hair. She glared at Ulec, "Humans had no right to trespass there. Move aside boy and let me deal with them!"

Ulec stood his ground, his voice strong, "You should give them a warning before you try to cook them. They didn't know any better."

At that moment, Seacra nudged Almas and Creetan, leading them down the ridge to where Ulec, his mother, and the men were. They continued to hear heated arguing as they climbed down and arrived just as Ulec was introducing his mother to Lord Aguerius and his men.

Almas couldn't believe it – Ulec's mother was the Dragon Queen herself! The tension in the air was palpable, but for now Ulec's bravery had saved his father and the others from disaster.

AS SEACRA, ALMAS, AND Creetan approached with Ulec, Lady Alixia's eyes narrowed with disapproval. "Why have you brought more humans here, Seacra? Have you forgotten the danger they pose?"

Seacra shifted uncomfortably and grunted but stood her ground.

Ulec stepped forward, his voice determined. "They are our friends Mother. Not to mention the Aguerius family has always been faithful in protecting us. They came seeking help against the Lich Lords. The King asked Lord Aguerius to seek assistance from the elves."

"Their reasons don't matter; humans are not allowed here! You know that!" Lady Alixia nearly roared.

..nas was afraid she was about to go Dragon Queen again when a soft voice spoke, "That is enough Alixia. You know the Aguerius family means no harm."

It was an elvish man who had silently joined the group.

"Father," Ulec said not nearly as surprised as the rest of the group was at the elf's sudden appearance, "Thank you for coming."

The tall elf nodded to his son while motioning for Ulec to approach him and his mother. "Maybe we should listen to what our son has to say."

The elves began to speak among themselves while Lord Aguerius, his expression a mix of relief and confusion, embraced his sons. "I'm glad you're safe, but why aren't you back at home?"

Creetan quickly explained their journey and the danger they faced to their father as Ulec tried to explain to his mother the human peoples need.

"Are those really Ulec's parents?" Almas asked.

His father answered, "Yes, I have met Ulec's father a few times. His name is Teanas and is the brother to the elvish king. I have never met Ulec's mother but she fits the descriptions I have heard."

The elves finished their conversation and Lady Alixia's tone was curt as she addressed the humans, " I understand your need for help but I am afraid we have our own battles to fight. I am too occupied with other tasks right now to deal with destroying the Lich Lords at the moment."

Lord Aguerius, undeterred, tried to persuade her. "But your lands are also threatened, once we fall, they will turn their eyes on you. We need to unite against this common enemy."

Lady Alixia scoffed, "Your affairs are not my concern. I will deal with the Lich Lords in my own time."

Before Lord Aguerius could respond, Ulec stepped in, his voice respectful but firm. "Lord Aguerius, the Elvish Kingdom really isn't in a position to help at the moment. It would be best to return

Almas and Creetan to a safe place before Seacra's magic wanes. We didn't have time to get warm clothing for them."

"I'm sorry my friend but my people are not strong enough right now. Plus, there are dangers you don't understand in putting elves and undead against each other, dangers that could be the doom of humans." Ulec's Father added.

Reluctantly, Lord Aguerius agreed. He knew he couldn't force an alliance, and his sons' safety was his priority. He bid Lady Alixia farewell and thanked Ulec for his help.

As they made their way back to the cave leading to human lands, Almas couldn't help but feel a sense of disappointment. He had hoped for an alliance between the humans and elves, but it seemed it was not to be.

However, he was grateful for Ulec's presence and the friendship they had formed. As they crossed the valley back to human lands, Almas knew that their journey was far from over, but he also knew that he had gained a true friend in the elf boy named Ulec.

AS THEY DESCENDED THE cavern back to human lands and the warmth returned, Seacra transformed back into her elvish form. She immediately turned to Lord Aguerius with a mischievous glint in her eyes. "You must be very strong, Lord Aguerius, to withstand my mother's first attack."

Lord Aguerius chuckled, his tension easing. "Well, I must admit, it was quite a surprise. But I'm grateful we're all safe now."

Lord Aguerius sent his men ahead to find and help his brother-in-law, High Lord Marpel Vatan, who had aided Almas and Creetan in escaping their treacherous escort. He also sent men to ask the king to investigate and organize a search for those treacherous men. Turning to Ulec and Seacra, Lord Aguerius thanked them sincerely. "I can't thank you enough for looking after my sons and helping them get back to safety."

Ulec smiled warmly. "It was our pleasure, Lord Aguerius. Almas and Creetan are our friends now, and we'll always be there to lend a hand when needed."

Seacra nodded enthusiastically. "Yes, and you can always count on me to keep them warm!"

Almas and Creetan grinned at each other, remembering Seacra's transformation into a salamander during their journey. Her playful attitude had added a spark of humor and warmth to their otherwise perilous adventure.

Lord Aguerius was touched by the genuine bond that had formed between the four children. "I'm grateful for your friendship, Ulec, Seacra. You've shown great courage and loyalty."

Ulec looked at Almas and Creetan. "Your sons are brave and resourceful. They handled themselves well in a challenging situation."

As they continued on their way, Lord Aguerius explained how he would protect the identity of Ulec and Seacra, not wanting any association with Aguerius Forest to be revealed. "I'll tell my men that you met Almas and Creetan on the way to the Vatan Province. That way, they won't connect you to our home."

Ulec nodded in appreciation. "Thank you, Lord Aguerius. It's best if our presence in Aguerius Forest remains a secret."

As they reached the cave's exit and stepped back into the human lands, Lord Aguerius felt a mixture of relief and gratitude. He knew that the friendship forged between his sons and the elvish siblings was something special and would endure.

Almas looked at Ulec and Seacra, grateful for their help and friendship. "Thank you, Ulec, Seacra. You're welcome in our home anytime."

Seacra grinned mischievously. "Oh, don't worry, we'll be back, and I'm sure I'll find a way to cook up some more fun!"

They all laughed as they parted ways, each carrying with them memories of an adventure that had changed their lives forever. As they returned to the Aguerius Estate, Lord Aguerius knew that the bond between humans and elves might still be elusive, but the friendship between their families would remain unshakable.

Lich-El

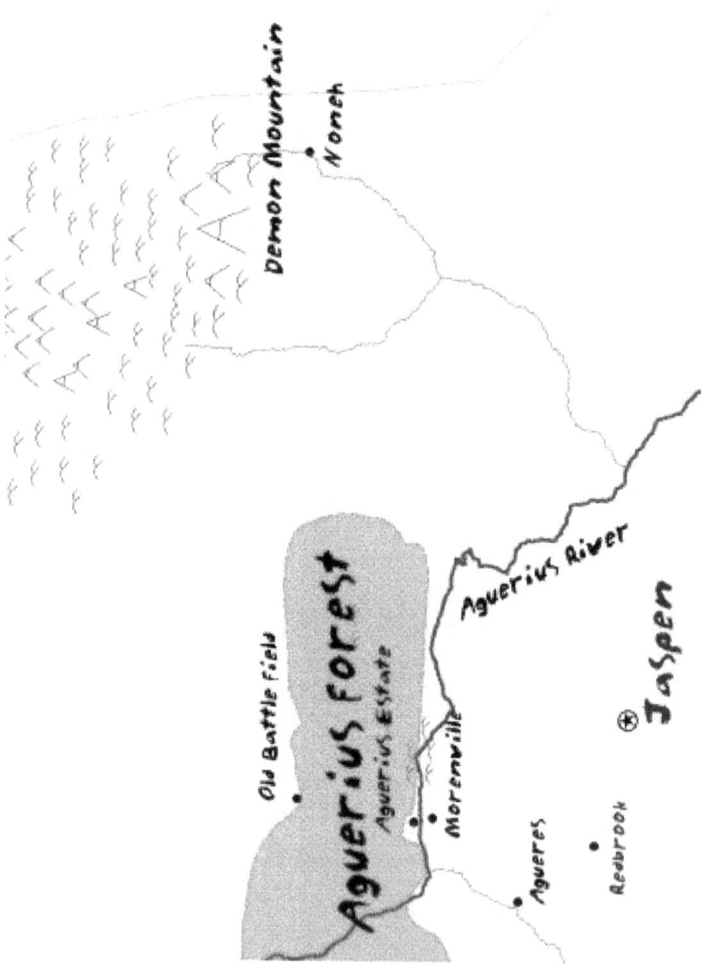
Demon Mountain
Aguerius Forest
Aguerius Estate
Old Battle Field
Aguerius River
Morenville
Jaspen
Agueres
Redbrook

Chapter 1

"I THOUGHT I WOULD FIND you here today, my lady."

"Why have you come here, creature?"

"The same reason as you, to remember the dead, and to pay respect to friends long past turned to dust. Do not think this field and monument is your own private grieving ground. I also once stood on this field, shoulder to shoulder with gods, elves, and men. I also lost many friends that day so long ago."

"What can a monster like you remember of friendship? I should destroy you now and let the world be rid of you."

"My dear Lady Alixia; first of all, you're no longer sure you could defeat me alone. Second, you remember what friendship is, even if I don't."

"How dare–"

"But while I may be a bit... hazy...on friendship, I still remember honor. And that honor compels me to pay old debts."

"I forgive you of all debts. Now leave and corrupt this sacred ground no longer with your presence!"

"Just as soon as I say this: Tornal has begun his experiments again."

"And just what is he working on now?"

"He seeks to make more of us."

"Odd. I was just thinking this world needed fewer of you."

"He also seeks to give himself, and the others he makes, power not unlike your own, only with his own dark twist. He seeks to steal what you merely mimic. In fact, he says that he has one last experiment to make, and he would like an elvish subject."

"Then he has far to travel to find one."

"He has heard rumors there might be one to be had in human lands. It seems poachers have been spreading tales about strange happenings in Aguerius Forest."

"Tornal shouldn't listen to rumors."

"That's what I told him. He never would listen to me. If there are any elves there, I hope they watch themselves."

"Hunting elves is very dangerous. Finding the wrong one would be the end of him."

"Yes, but finding the right one, such as one young and inexperienced, would be easy prey for a Lich Lord of Tornal's power."

"Are you insinuating–"

"Nothing. I insinuate nothing. Just giving information I thought you might find interesting. Now I must bid you farewell. Give my regards to your husband and children, wherever they may be."

"Farewell? A creature like you comes here to this field of sacrifice to mock and threaten me, and you bid me farewell? You think I would let an abomination such as yourself simply leave after such disrespect?"

"Here I am. Stop me!"

"Gladly."

CADY WASN'T JUST DIZZY. She was very dizzy. Yet she kept moving around and around, watching the trees. She was determined to make sure no pesky elves snuck up on her this time. Her brother, on the other hand, didn't even try anymore.

"I've told you, Cady, you're not going to see him arrive."

Cady's 12-year-old brother, Almas, just sat there, sitting with his back resting against the tree, playing his lap harp. She would never admit it to him, but he was starting to get good at it. But practicing music wasn't going to help her catch Ulec when he arrived.

The rest of her family was just as useless. Creetan was 16 now and more interested in shooting arrows at a target; her father, Lord Gidon Aguerius, was wrestling with her 8-year-old brother, Giddy, and Mother was in her shop making who knows what. So, it was up to her, a little girl of only 10 years, to keep the vigil and guard the family against young trespassing elves.

"I'm going to catch him this time. I will not let Ulec sneak up on us again," Cady informed her brother as she stumbled a little but caught herself before falling down.

"Good luck with that. In four years, I've never spotted Ulec before he wanted to be seen," Almas responded with a sigh and continued playing a quick jumpy sounding tune on his harp.

Ulec was a young elf that Almas had met while he was lost in the forest four years before. He had saved Almas from becoming lunch for a forest dragon and they had been best friends ever since. Now every once in a while, Almas would announce that Ulec was coming over to visit. She wasn't sure exactly how Almas always knew, but she was sure it had something to do with Ulec's ability to talk to animals and plants. Cady was always amazed at how plants and animals seemed to do whatever he wanted.

Cady continued spinning, determined to catch the elf trying to sneak up on her like he always did. She was scanning the trees when she heard the tune Almas was playing abruptly change and a force, like a very strong wind, pushed her and she toppled to the ground.

"Hey! You pushed me!" she yelled at Almas.

Almas gave the most disgustingly false-innocent look she had ever seen and responded, "What? Me? I never touched you. I was just practicing. You know me better than that."

Cady knew that Almas didn't need to touch her. The last few years their mother and Uncle Marpel had been teaching Almas both music and how to use magic through it. As Almas got better at music, he also got better at casting spells with it. It was called bard magic and she was about to retort that he used it to push her but a voice above her spoke first, "Yes, she knows you well. That's how she knows it was you."

He'd done it to her again. In just the moment that it took for her to fall, Ulec had just appeared out of nowhere. Looking above her, she saw Ulec sitting on a branch in the tree with his back to the trunk and one leg hanging lazily, as if he'd been sitting there waiting all day! It wasn't fair! She had been looking right at that spot when Almas pushed her.

"How do you do that?" she asked.

Ulec slid off the branch and landed noiselessly on his bare feet and asked with a sly grin, "Do what?"

"Appear out of nowhere like that!"

"I didn't come from No Where. I came from over there. I've never been to No Where," Ulec answered, pointing behind him.

"But we never see or hear you come," Cady protested.

"I apologize for not moving through the forest making noise like a huge lumbering bear."

"Cady isn't that loud," Almas cut in as he stood up and stepped over to his friend.

"Actually, I was referring to you."

"Hey!"

Ulec laughed as Almas tried to push him but missed as he easily stepped aside. "You need to move faster than that! Or maybe you should stick to the harp," Ulec said right before they all heard a soft snap above them. They all looked up to the tree for the source of the sound and Ulec started to step to the side when a large, furry animal landed on him, knocking him to the ground. Cady gave a surprised shout as she recognized a panther standing on Ulec with its large paws on his chest.

Rather than being frightened, Ulec looked annoyed and spoke calmly to the large cat, "Seacra get off! That hurt."

He pushed the panther off him and in an instant, it transformed into a young elvish girl who laughed and said triumphantly, "That time you weren't fast enough."

It was Ulec's younger sister, Seacra. She was almost 20 years younger than her brother, but even though she was a little over 100 years old, she didn't seem any older – or act any older for that matter – than Cady. Ulec got up glaring at her and brushed the dirt off of himself. It was in that moment they heard Giddy yell as he ran over, "Ulec, Seacra!" Behind him their father approached at a much more leisurely pace.

"Seacra, you're back!" Giddy exclaimed.

Cady was also happy to see Seacra. She was away most of the time up north in elvish lands and when she was gone, Cady missed having another girl around to play with and couldn't help asking, "How long are you here for?"

"A couple of weeks," Seacra replied.

"Seacra! So good to see you," Cady's father said as he arrived. "Is Lady Alixia staying also?"

"No, Mother is up north, on the other side of the Dividing Mountains. It's been 125 years since the War of Destruction. She wanted some time alone to visit the monument."

The Dividing Mountains was a mountain range that ran northeast the whole length of the continent. It divided the elvish lands and the human lands and were so tall no one could cross them. At least that's what Cady had heard.

"I see," Gidon said in response to Seacra.

Cady noticed a quick look of relief cross her father's face, and apparently Seacra noticed it, too. "Are you scared of my mother?" she giggled.

Ulec answered for Lord Gidon and grumbled, "Everyone is scared of Mother, at least anyone who knows her. Even the gods feared her."

"Can she really turn herself into a dragon?" Giddy asked excitedly.

"Yes," Gidon answered his son. "But before you ask, no, you can't see."

"You don't want to see her as a dragon, Giddy," Seacra added. "She only turns into a dragon when going into battle and that would be very dangerous."

"That's enough of such talk. So, what is the plan today?" Gidon said, ending the topic. Cady's father always seemed to dodge any conversations about Lady Alixia and any war stories about her. Almas had once told Cady that he and father had met Lady Alixia four years earlier right, after Almas had first met Ulec. He had told her she was a shape shifter like Seacra but could turn into more powerful creatures than Seacra could. He said she had attacked her father. Then Ulec and Ulec's father had to stop her from hurting him but that's all anyone would tell her.

It was Ulec who answered Gidon's question. "I wanted to show Almas some plants I'm growing from seeds that my mother brought from the north."

"I want to go!" Cady chimed in. Cady liked plants, and plants from Elvish lands sounded interesting.

"Sounds like fun," Gidon said. "I need to see to some business and get Creetan's armor. See if he's able to brag about his archery skills shooting with some thick leather weighing him down and impairing his movements. Just don't stay out too late or your mother will have both our hides."

"What about me?" Giddy asked excitedly.

"Sorry, short stuff," Gidon answered. "Maybe in a year or so. You stay here with Creetan."

With that, Gidon walked away. As soon as he was out of earshot, Seacra remarked to Ulec, "All the stuff you can do in the forest and you're going to go look at some blue flowers. I thought you were boys."

Cady giggled at the comment but didn't dare say anything that might keep her from seeing the flowers. Ulec, on the other hand, rolled his eyes and turning to Almas asked, "Want to trade sisters?"

"Don't tempt me; I've had enough of silly, giggling sisters," Almas responded.

Silly? Could she help it if Seacra made a good joke at the boys' expense? "Why are brothers so mean?" she asked Seacra.

"They think it's their job."

"See what you did, Ulec," Almas said. "Now they're mad at us and we'll have to listen to them whine all day."

"If that's the way you feel, we will just go play by ourselves. We don't need you. Come on, Cady. We can go see those plants on our own if you want. And better ones along with them," Seacra said as she got up and started leaving.

"And good riddance," Cady added as she left to follow Seacra. It would be a lot better without any annoying brothers around acting like jerks.

WHAT CADY AND SEACRA failed to notice as they walked away was Almas smiling and whispering to Ulec, "Works every time." Then both the boys were off.

In the four years that Almas had known Ulec he had learned to move through the forest pretty quickly. Yet he still often had a hard time keeping up with his friend. Ulec moved through the forest like they were one entity, as if the forest sped him on his travels.

"So how many are there?" Almas asked as he tried to keep up.

"Only three of them," Ulec responded.

Every so often poachers would enter Aguerius Forest. Mostly these were inexperienced hunters testing to see if the rumors about poaching being impossible in the forest were true or not. Ulec always made sure they went home empty handed. In cases where the poachers were near enough, Ulec would let Almas watch the show from a safe place.

"This is the spot here. You should be able to watch everything from that branch," Ulec said, pointing to a tree near the edge of a small clearing.

Almas climbed up to the spot Ulec indicated; the branches concealed him from view although he could see the entire field. Ulec meanwhile went out into the clearing and disappeared into some tall grass. After a short time, three men appeared at the far side of the field.

As they drew near Almas could hear them speak.

"This grass sticks like nothing else. It's almost like it's grabbing at us."

"I told you to keep silent. You'll scare our prey away."

"What prey?" asked the third man. "We haven't seen a single living creature in this forest. I'm beginning to think there is something to the rumors here."

"I said keep quiet. Look at those trees up ahead. The branches are moving," the man who appeared to be the leader said.

"That's just the wind," replied the first man.

"What wind? There is no wind."

All around the clearing branches on trees swayed as if there was a heavy wind, except the lower branches where Almas was perched swayed a lot less. The three poachers only had a moment to watch when all around the clearing multiple wolf howls rose up from the trees.

Almas almost felt sorry for the poachers, watching the fear and confusion on their faces. Yet that was the price of trying to poach game in Aguerius Forest. Ulec had the power to speak to both plant and animal and ask them favors. Mostly he just did little tricks here and there, but at times like these Almas got to see just how much influence Ulec could have over the forest.

The three poachers loaded arrows into their bows at the sound of wolves moving through the tall grass. As one caught a glimpse of a wolf, he aimed his bow to shoot, but a small rock flew from the grass hitting his hand that held his bow, knocking off his aim and making him drop his bow. Two more rocks flew from the grass and two more bows hit the ground.

Holding his hurt hand, the leader said to the others as he glanced around, "I've seen enough, let's get out of here."

Pulling out their swords and keeping their backs together, they cautiously made their way back through the meadow. As they left, they didn't even notice the grass had stopped clinging to their legs and had even made a little path for them to leave by.

CADY WAS USING SOME of the flowers she had picked to show Giddy how to decorate hats. He was a good student, and she wondered how long it would be before he decided such things were too girlie for him like her other two brothers.

Glancing at the forest Cady wondered what was keeping Almas and Ulec. She hadn't seen them anywhere near the flowers, which didn't say much for Ulec as he was only seen when he wanted to be.

She had asked Seacra if she knew where they had gone off to, and the elvish girl had told her to wait at home and she'd go find them. Cady didn't think it would take this long.

"Hey, Uncle Jerad is here," Giddy stated, pulling Cady from her thoughts.

Looking in the direction Giddy was pointing, she saw her father's best friend walking purposely toward her father at a brisk pace. He had a concerned look on his face. He walked up to her father, who greeted him, but his face turned somber almost instantly as Jerad started to converse with him. Cady couldn't hear what they were saying, but she saw him turn to Creetan and say something then started walking over toward her and Giddy.

"Cady, do you know exactly where the boys went?" her father asked as he approached.

"We didn't see them near the flowers Seacra showed me. She said she was going to go look for them. Is something wrong?"

"Nothing to worry about, I think. A couple of my scouts failed to report in. Probably just running late. But to be on the safe side, Jerad is taking you and Giddy back to the house, and Cree and I are going to go retrieve Almas."

"What about Ulec and Seacra?" Giddy asked.

"I'll make sure they are also fine, but I think Ulec and Seacra can take care of themselves. Right now, you two get going. I'll be home shortly," her father said with a grin.

Cady watched a moment as her father and brother walked into the forest, then said to Giddy, "Guess we'll have to finish the hat in the house." Giddy helped her gather some of the flowers then walked over to where Jerad was waiting for them.

"You two having fun today?" Jerad asked as they came within speaking distance of him.

"We were making a flower hat," Giddy told him excitedly.

"Do you know why the scouts didn't report in?" Cady asked.

"That's what we are looking into, and that's a nice-looking hat. Let's get it to the house so you can show your mother."

"THAT WAS PRICELESS," Almas exclaimed as he dropped down from the low branch to the ground.

Ulec sat down and rested with his back to the tree. "Yeah, the look on their faces were great."

One of the wolves happily came over to Almas, who rubbed the side of his head. "Hi Crusty!"

Crusty was the pet wolf that Ulec had given him four years previous when they had first met. He had raised him from a cub and now the wolf was grown and spent as much time in the forest with the other wolves as it did at the Aguerius Estate.

Almas glanced at Ulec and noticed he was half asleep and looked paler than normal. With some concern he asked, "Are you okay? You don't look so well."

"I'm fine, just a little tired," Ulec responded.

Almas was about to respond when a voice above them spoke first. "You'll be more than tired if Mother or Father find out you were using Vithal magic."

Looking above them, they found Seacra sitting on the branch that Almas had just dropped down from.

"Dang it, Seacra! It's bad enough when Ulec scares me doing that. Don't you start now," Almas complained.

"I thought you were showing the flowers to Cady," Ulec said in an annoyed tone.

"I showed her all the flowers and realized you weren't anywhere near the place you said you would be. So afterward I took her back home and came looking for you to see what you were really up to. You mean you didn't notice?"

Ulec turned red. He normally kept good tabs on everything happening in the forest. Almas had never seen anyone sneak up on him before.

"I was distracted," he responded.

"I know. It's rare I ever get the drop on you, let alone twice in one day."

Ulec sighed, "There just seems to be a lot more poachers in the forest than normal lately. I just thought I'd give this group a good show and maybe discourage others from coming."

Seacra slid off the branch and dropped lightly to the ground next to Almas. Meanwhile Ulec opened up his shoulder bag and let Metal out, which began rolling and oozing towards Seacra.

"Ulec! Keep that thing away from me. That thing is gross."

Ulec smiled lightly and responded, "Mention any of this to Mother or Father and you just might find him sleeping next to you one morning. He likes you."

"Okay, just get it away from me."

"Good," Ulec said as he closed his eyes and leaned his head against the tree. "Now just let me rest a moment here."

As Ulec closed his eyes and relaxed, Metal oozed over to some rocks, settled over the top of them, and soon the smell of acid on rock filled the air. Almas shook his head and laughed, "Those rocks must have a little iron ore in them. Some day that thing is going to be metal plated."

"That thing is just plain creepy," Seacra muttered.

"That thing saved my life once," Almas responded back. "It attacked a forest dragon to protect Ulec and me."

Seacra shrugged and after a few moments of silence, Almas spoke again, "What did you mean earlier when you said something about Ulec using Vithal magic?"

Seacra answered with a question, "You know the difference between elvish magic and human magic, right?"

Almas thought back to conversations he had had with his parents and with Ulec. "Humans have to make their magic by some sort of action, like when I play my harp, and Ulec once told me elves use energy given off by living things, which is why you live in the forest. Lots of life means lots of magic for you."

"That's right; there were three races of elves during the War of Destruction: Elder elves, Shadow elves, and Desert elves. Elder and Shadow elves use Natela magic, Desert elves use Vithal magic, and humans use Trabar magic. Elder and Shadow elves have a large source of magic, but we all use the same source and can feel when someone is using it and how much they are using."

"So, you and Ulec can't use magic without your parents knowing it?" Almas asked.

Seacra answered, "Normally no, but our mother is only half Elder Elf. Her mother was an Elder Elf, and her father was a Desert elf."

"And that makes her different?"

"It makes her, Ulec and myself a little different. Desert elves were a race of elves that lived in the great northern desert that were wiped out during the War of Destruction. Since there is very little Natela magic in the desert, they learned to tap their own life force as a source of magic. So, when one of us uses Vithal magic we draw the magic from ourselves so no one else can sense it," Seacra explained.

"That sounds like it would hurt."

"More like exhaust you," Seacra corrected, nodding toward Ulec who was now sleeping. "But you need to be careful not to use too much. If you do, then it can shorten your life. That is why our mother would be very angry if she caught Ulec doing it."

Almas took a moment to digest everything Seacra said. He wasn't sure what to say after that. After a while Almas spoke up, "Well, it's starting to get late; I should be heading home. Tell Ulec I said goodbye when he wakes up."

"Okay."

Chapter 2

"OUR SCOUTS REPORT CONTACT."

"Very good, Keshen. Did they see any more traces of Aguerian scouts in the forest?"

"No, it seems our sources are true; Lord Aguerius keeps scouts on the border of the forest but not in it — not that we can see."

"Excellent. Let's go see if we can draw out this forest spirit and have a visit with him. Just be sure to remember Lich-El's orders concerning the boy."

"I'll remember alright, Tornal, but you know accidents happen sometimes."

"Take care none do, or you'll be the one to explain it to Lich-el."

TEANEAS HEARD HIS VISITORS before he saw them. Not that they were loud. Compared to most humans they were quite stealthy.

Born an elf prince, Teaneas lived much of his life as a warrior and as a champion for the gods that had created Mundial, their world. He was also one of the great heroes of the War of Destruction. Now he spent his days here in this forest, with but one common title given by his children, living with but three people –when two of them weren't away up north–and he couldn't imagine being happier.

The last hundred years of living in this forest had been the happiest years of his life. He had often wished that things could always remain the same, yet in his heart he knew it was an impossible wish.

He wasn't sure why, but these were the thoughts that came to him as his guests came into view, these thoughts along with a feeling of foreboding.

The first of his guests was Gidon Aguerius. While humans were creatures of chaos, of all the humans Teaneas knew, Gidon was one not unlike himself. He was a man of many titles, and a man who fought for and loved his people with all his heart. Most of all he was a man who valued the title given to him by his family the most: The title of father.

His companion was his eldest son, Cree Tanis Aguerius, nicknamed Creetan by his younger brother Almas, which had caught on with the rest of the family. At age 16 the boy seemed to have reached his man's height. Both had visited before, so it wasn't their arrival that brought the feeling of foreboding but the quickness and the tension in their walk. They also had their weapons and armor, although they often did while they were training. Gidon had on his leather armor along with his bow, broadsword, shield, and although he couldn't see them, Teaneas was sure he had at least a half dozen other weapons hidden on his person. His son, on the other hand, only had on his leather armor, bow and a dagger.

"Behold the mightiest warrior the human race has to offer. If I had a body, I'd die laughing," a voice came to Teaneas' mind.

Teaneas didn't even glance at the ring on his right index finger as he thought back, "*It was thinking like that, that led to the death of your previous owner.*"

The response came, *"He died at your hands. At least you're of elvish blood, which is a step up from human blood, although still a far cry from the blood of the desert kin."*

"Just remember that the desert kin are gone now thanks to inferior elves and humans, using an inferior human's battle plan."

"And a traitor," the voice grumbled as Teaneas felt the voice withdraw into the ring.

By this time Teaneas and his two visitors had closed the distance between them and Teaneas asked, "Is something wrong?"

Gidon smiled and responded, "I hope not; two of my scouts watching the southeastern border of the forest are missing. I wondered if you knew where the kids are. Cady said Seacra went looking for them since the boys weren't where they said they were going to be. I'd like to know where they are until we sort this out."

"Hmm," Teaneas took a moment to think before answering. "I think Seacra went off to the east. She and my wife are the only ones who can track Ulec provided he isn't hiding. It's possible she followed the boys."

"East...Right in the direction of the missing scouts..." Gidon said with concern growing on his face. "We need to get going. I'll feel much better when I know where he is."

"I'll join you," Teaneas said. "I'm sure if something was going on Ulec would give me a sign, but something still feels wrong about this situation."

THE RIVER WAS HIGH with spring runoff. Almas was following the river west towards his home. The river bordered Aguerius Forest along its south borders.

Almas hurried along, his pet wolf Crusty following. The sun was getting low, but he was sure he'd get home before it got too late. It was his night to spend with his father doing what he wanted, and Almas' favorite thing to do with his father was to play a game called Chintal, a strategy game.

Almas loved to play the game and was good at it. Sadly, he couldn't find many people that enjoyed it, at least not many that enjoyed playing it with him. Maybe if he learned to let his opponents win once in a while like his father often did with him, he'd be able to get some more enthusiasm from others.

At least he was pretty sure his father let him win. He was the royal strategist, so it wasn't surprising that his father was a master at the game. Ulec was a pretty good challenge at the game also. As bright as Ulec was, he just didn't care much for the game. Ulec was more of a hands-on person. Almas had watched him practice with various weapons and even watched him spar with Almas' father before. He could respond to situations brilliantly and instantly, and Almas thought it was a shame that Ulec couldn't bring that brilliance to games that he enjoyed.

Almas started working on the opening moves he'd make and how he might counter some of the moves his father might make when a commotion in the forest erupted nearby. It seemed like every bird in the area had taken flight at the same time. The sky was full of birds of every kind. His first instinct was that Ulec was playing a trick on him. But this was big even for his elvish friend. Then he heard Crusty growl, and he looked behind him at his pet wolf.

Crusty was facing the forest, the hair on his back bristling, growling at the forest with the scariest look that Almas had ever seen. Something was upsetting the animals and Almas decided he didn't want to find out what it was. Turning his face towards home, he commanded Crusty to follow him and took off in a run.

"ULEC... ULEC WAKE UP!"

Ulec had continued to sleep after Almas had left and was still sleeping with his back to the tree and Metal right next to his leg, doing its normal imitation of a gross puddle of slime.

Now Seacra was going to have to get physical to wake her brother up. Moving to the slime-free side of her brother, she grabbed his arm and started to shake him.

"Ulec, get up now! Something weird is going on. Every bird in the forest has freaked out."

Finally, Ulec began to stir, "Mmmm... What's going on?"

"I told you. It's like every bird in the forest just took off at the same time."

"Birds?" Ulec asked, still in the mental fog of just waking up. Confused, he looked up at the flocks of birds fleeing some unknown danger for a few moments, then his eyes opened wide, color drained from his face, and all trace of sleep was gone instantly.

"Almas!" he yelled in alarm as he leapt to his feet, scooping up Metal and dropping him into his shoulder bag as he did so.

"Wait! What's wrong?" Seacra cried as Ulec took off running.

"Just go find father," Ulec yelled as he vanished into the forest.

GIDON KNEW SOMETHING was horribly wrong even before the entire forest erupted into chaos. He had become nervous when two of his scouts failed to report on time, but it was as they were heading east, searching for his son and his playmates, that an eagle dropped out of the sky, landed in front of him and his companions, and transformed into an elvish woman, that he knew that this good day was turning into a nightmare.

He knew the woman. Lady Alixia was the wife of Lord Teaneas. She also had the same talent as her daughter, Seacra, of assuming the forms of animals. In fact, the first time he met her she had been in the form of a dragon that had tried to toast him to a crisp. Suffice it to say he preferred to avoid her.

But right now, it was her current form that shocked Gidon. She had a large cut on her face and a hastily bandaged arm in a sling. He'd seen her in action and couldn't imagine anything with the power to injure her so.

"Lady Alixia," Gidon started to ask, "What hap–"

"Where are the children?" she interrupted, speaking directly to Teaneas and ignoring Gidon and his son.

Teaneas answered immediately, "East."

Alixia turned to face east and took one step when the sky in that direction filled with squawking birds. Alixia hesitated a moment and glanced at Teaneas who at once ordered, "Go now!"

Instantly she was an eagle again rising to meet hundreds of other birds.

Gidon wasn't sure what was going on, but he knew things were beyond anything he had expected. Turning to his son Creetan he quickly ordered, "Go home now and tell Jerad to outfit and bring me my mount. Full battle gear."

"But Father!"

"Go now!"

Creetan looked like he was ready to argue more, but suddenly the forest grew dark. Looking up, Gidon could see the trees had spread their branches to block out the sun except for a few beams of sunlight touching the ground and marking a path through the forest.

"I said GO!" Gidon ordered his son again before joining Teaneas as he ran down the lighted path. Both the human and the elf knew Ulec was now calling for assistance and giving them a path to follow.

ALMAS FIRST FELT RELIEF when the forest came alive. Ulec controlled it so that meant the plants and animals were on his side. Then he heard the sound of trees crashing to the ground. Ulec had never made trees fall, even years back when the two of them had been attacked by a forest dragon. That meant either Ulec was really desperate or something else was knocking the trees down. Either way Almas decided to keep running but only got a few more feet when an arrow suddenly embedded itself in a tree directly in front of his face. Going too fast to stop, the shaft of the arrow hit him in the face as if it was a low branch. The arrow broke off the tree and while it didn't hurt, the impact still caused Almas to lose his balance and fall.

Almas sat up and looked in the direction from which the arrow had come. Coming out of the woods was a man armed with a bow and the Aguerius crest on his tunic. It was one of his father's scouts, but something was wrong. Even from this distance he could tell his skin was pale and dry. He could also see running up both arms what looked like spikes. The most eerie thing was his face. It was completely emotionless, blank, like there weren't any thoughts or feelings behind eyes that appeared devoid of life.

All those years of his father telling stories of battles against the Undead could never have prepared Almas for meeting his first revenant.

Revenants were completely lifeless, which meant there was a Lich Lord in the forest controlling it, and most likely more of them. This one was reloading his bow and Almas was just sitting there, completely unable to will his body to move from fear. The revenant pulled back the arrow and Almas was hit hard with the realization that he was about to die. Suddenly, before the revenant could release the arrow, Crusty leapt on it. In a moment the revenant had fallen to a flurry of fangs.

As the remains of the revenant began to crumble to dust, the sound of Crusty's growls and snarls turned to yelps as an arrow from a location to Almas' left hit the wolf above his hind leg.

"Crusty!" Almas yelled as he started to get up.

Without thinking he took a step toward his injured pet but stopped cold when he spotted the second revenant, another one of his father's scouts, then spotted a third and a fourth coming out of the forest. The other two weren't any of his father's men. Their clothes and armor looked much older and worn. In a short time, Almas found himself being closed in by eight undead creatures. They were forming a half circle around him, and with the river 50 feet behind him at the bottom of a 40-foot drop, they had effectively trapped him.

The revenant that had shot Crusty loaded another arrow into his bow and took aim directly at him. As the revenant released the arrow, everything went into slow motion. He knew he needed to move but like in nightmares he couldn't move quickly enough. Then a running form entered the side of his view. Ulec ran into the path of the arrow, snatched it out of the air with his right hand, and with a twist of his body and a flick of the wrist, he sent the arrow back to the revenant. After the arrow struck the undead creature in the throat, it instantly crumbled to dust. Ulec wasted no time in backing up to Almas and saying, "Move back."

Almas started moving but said as he went, "We're backing up into a dead end!"

"I know," Ulec quickly responded. "We just need to buy a little time. Help is on the way."

Ulec was breathing hard. To Almas it looked like he was about to pass out. Another crash back in the forest behind the revenants made Almas realize that Ulec must be dealing with more undead creatures than just the ones present. Out of the corner of his eye he saw one of the visible revenants step to avoid a falling branch that had dropped like a spear towards the creature. Almas couldn't believe his friend could divide his attention to multiple fights in different locations. As wolf howls began to sound nearby, Almas looked at his friend again; he had turned pale and was sweating. He remembered what Seacra had said about the danger of overusing his own magic, Vithal she had called it. Why wasn't he using the other one, the Natela one?

He didn't get much time to think because suddenly all the revenants he could see charged at them. He thought he heard Ulec swear under his breath before saying, "Wait here, and stay alert."

Almas heard a cracking sound above him and watched a branch fall from the tree next to them and drop right into Ulec's hand. It was a straight branch that was thick and pointed on one side, making it look like a sort of mace.

As soon as Ulec caught the branch, he charged the oncoming revenants, which all began converging on him.

Upon reaching the first revenant, he ducked and sidestepped to avoid its short sword, spun around the side of the revenant and planted the knot at the end of his stick into the back of its head.

As the revenant began to crumble to dust, Ulec let go of his stick and grabbed its short sword as it fell to the ground. By now two more revenants were coming up behind Ulec with swords raised. Grabbing the bottom of his shoulder bag, he spun around and in one motion, he flung Metal out of the bag and into the face of the first revenant and flung the short sword into the throat of the second.

As the latest two revenants crumbled to dust, Almas could see only four left. Almas couldn't tell if the one Metal killed crumbled or melted from the slime's acid, but either way he could only see four more. Three of them started to surround Ulec as the fourth held back.

Ulec picked up the stick he had used on the first revenant and backed towards a tree. He was too small and lacked the strength to block or parry the attacks from the Undead, but he was quick, and Almas could barely follow him as he dodged and used his stick to redirect blows as much as his strength would let him. The revenants seemed to be taking him more seriously, fighting much more defensively. That wasn't good for Ulec. Almas could see Ulec starting to slow down and felt absolutely helpless.

Almas was racking his brain trying to think of a way to help Ulec when the revenants backed Ulec up to a tree. Almas saw Ulec's plan a moment before Ulec sprang his trap. As he backed up to the tree, the one revenant wielding a spear charged Ulec as the other two revenants moved to the left and right side the elvish boy to block him from escaping. Ulec, having nowhere else to go, planted his bare feet on the side of the tree trunk and took four backward steps up the tree as the tip of the weapon embedded itself into the tree just below him.

Ulec let himself drop onto the shaft and brought the end of his stick down hard on the head of the revenant. At the same time about 10 branches dropped onto the other two revenants like falling stalactites. The revenant on Ulec's left disintegrated from a hit by one of the falling branches. The one on his right managed to avoid all the falling spears only to fall to Ulec's follow-up strike.

The final revenant continued to stand back and size Ulec up. Then it smiled and Almas realized for the first time that this one wasn't a revenant. There was intelligence behind this creature's eyes. He was a Lich Lord.

"It seems our little outing here has been successful," the creature said, drawing his sword with his right hand.

"What do you want?" huffed Ulec.

"Just you," said the Lich Lord as he pulled a dagger out of a sheath with his left hand and charged.

Ulec was suddenly on pure defense. As fast as Ulec was, the Lich Lord was surely using magic to enhance his speed. Almas couldn't even follow the Lich Lord and from the look on Ulec's face, it seemed he was having trouble tracking him, too.

The Lich Lord seemed to be herding Ulec closer to Almas, despite Ulec's best efforts to move in a different direction. Ulec was slowing down noticeably when the Lich Lord's sword caught Ulec's stick in the middle cutting it in half.

Ulec was in trouble and Almas felt he needed to do something. Suddenly an idea came to him, and he cursed himself for not thinking of it sooner. He quickly unstrapped his small harp from his back and started playing a quick, energetic tune and tried to send those feelings towards his friend.

It seemed to work as Ulec looked like he was moving faster as he stepped and ducked under his opponent's sword. With a jab upward and a twist with his now shortened stick, he sent his opponent's sword flying. The Lich Lord tried to counter with his dagger, but Ulec stepped out of range. Using his free hand, the Lich Lord pulled a bone spike from his left arm and threw it like a dagger – not at Ulec but at Almas.

"Almas, look out!" Ulec yelled.

The bone spike missed, just grazing his shirt, but he fell to the side out of shock. The Lich Lord, taking advantage of Ulec's distraction, attacked again with his dagger and caught a piece of his arm, giving him a nasty gash a little below his shoulder.

Ulec staggered a bit but managed to avoid a second slash from the dagger. The attack, however, was a faint, as the Lich Lord took the opportunity to side-step behind Ulec and caught him with his fist on the back of his head. The Lich Lord positioned his dagger for a final blow as Ulec crumbled to the ground.

"Ulec! Look out!" Almas yelled standing up again.

The Lich Lord ignored Almas' yell but didn't ignore the screech of a hawk above him. Ulec rolled away as the Lich Lord looked up to see the bird diving at him. He raised his dagger to defend himself but somehow Ulec managed to push himself to his knees and hit the Lich Lord in the hand with a well-aimed rock, making him lose his grip on the dagger. The Lich Lord glanced at Ulec, then back up at the bird, only instead of finding a hawk he found a full-size grizzly bear falling on him. The lich attempted to step out of the way but instead tripped and fell. He had failed to notice grass had grown around his feet and ankles and wrapped around his legs to prevent him from escaping.

The Lich Lord had no time to react before the large bear landed on him with a loud thud. The bear wasted no time finishing off the undead creature. Once the Lich Lord had turned to dust, the bear took a step towards Ulec and transformed into Seacra, who ran to her brother. Almas also hurried over to join the siblings.

"Ulec!" both Seacra and Almas cried and once arriving to where he was, Almas added, "Are you okay?!"

Ulec started to get up and said, "I'm fine," right before collapsing once again.

"Your body seems to disagree with you," Almas pointed out.

Ulec started to get up again, still clearly dazed. "Have... to go... more coming."

Almas felt a chill go down his spine. If he were to write a list of things he didn't want to hear, that would've been the top of it.

"Take his other arm and let's get out of here," Almas said to Seacra as he helped his friend up and put his arm around his own shoulder.

ONLY A FEW MOMENTS after Seacra and Almas began helping Ulec move, they found themselves surrounded by more revenants. The three were quickly boxed in at the top of a 40-foot cliff above the river.

Looking down Seacra could see lots of rocks and fairly shallow water. Jumping or falling would not be a good idea.

The revenants made up a semi-circle around the children before a Lich Lord appeared from the forest wearing a large robe and a wicked grin.

"Well now," the Lich Lord said. "I was hoping to find an elf here, and I flush out two elflings. Sadly, I only need one of you."

"What...do you want?" Ulec managed to ask. "Why..."

Ulec didn't seem to have even the energy to finish his question, which the Lich Lord ignored anyway and continued, "As impressed as I am with the fighting skills of the boy, I'm afraid I couldn't possibly pass up a shapeshifter."

Seacra's heart sank with that last statement. At the same time, she felt Ulec tense up and stand up straight without any help. His eyes were blazing with anger, and she could feel magic around him. She still hadn't felt him once using any Natela magic. He must have been saving it for her and their father, who must be close by now, but to use this much of his own life force was crazy.

"You will not touch my sister!" Ulec growled at the lich. Then moving faster than Seacra had ever seen her brother move, he charged at the revenant between him and the Lich Lord. Easily dodging an attack from the revenant, he stepped around the undead creature pulling a dagger from the revenant's sheath. Although Seacra didn't see it Ulec must have then made a lighting fast attack on the revenant, because it began to crumble to dust as Ulec rushed the Lich Lord.

The Lich Lord pointed his staff at Ulec, who was enveloped in a sudden whirlwind. As the strong wind lifted Ulec off his feet, it started to spin him.

"Ulec!" both Seacra and Almas cried in alarm.

"Impressive, but I've made my decision," the Lich Lord said, and with a flick of his staff the wind lifted Ulec high into the air over the heads of his sister and friend, flinging him far over the edge of the cliff.

Seacra screamed her brother's name as he flew over but before she could see her brother's fate, Almas' voice shouted a warning next to her, "Seacra, look out!"

Seacra turned back to the Lich Lord just as a bolt of magic fired off from the Lich Lord's hand right at her. Time seemed to stand still as the bolt came at her. The lich had said he wanted her and now he was trying to kill her! Right before the bolt hit her, she felt strong hands push her out of the way and heard someone shout. She was halfway down the cliff before she realized Almas had pushed her over the edge and yelled at her to fly. She turned into a hawk but only managed to flap her wings a couple times before plunging into the icy river.

Chapter 3

"MY LORD LICH-EL, YOU'RE back! Where have you...What happened to your arm?"

"Nothing that won't regenerate in a few days. Do not concern yourself with it, Deleta. I simply went to give a message to an old friend. Unfortunately, she didn't appreciate it. Her injuries might have been less severe, but they will take longer to heal."

"Her? You fought Lady Alixia?"

"Yes."

"And you both survived?"

"Well, the fight was dragging on so I mentioned that I wanted to hurry so I could get back here before Tornal got back from his expedition to Aguerius Forest. She left in quite a hurry after that."

"Is Tornal in danger?"

"Only if he takes too long... or if he succeeds. Either way I wouldn't be able to protect him. Not from her when she's enraged. Oh, how I can hardly stand the suspense."

SOMETHING HAD HAPPENED. All activity in the forest had suddenly stopped. The path in the forest Gidon and Teaneas had been following remained, but the forest had gone completely silent. Teaneas hoped that Alixia had reached the children.

The elf's worrying was interrupted by a sudden bright light through the trees that lasted a couple of seconds then disappeared. Gidon running just behind Teaneas, swore when the light appeared, adding quietly, "I hope that wasn't what I think it was."

As soon as the light faded, the forest was filled with a huge roar. Gidon stopped and hesitated a moment, but Teaneas quickly motioned for him to continue following. "That was my wife... and she didn't sound happy. Hurry!"

After a few moments they came to a clearing in which Alixia was kneeling near a cliff over the river. She was holding somebody that he promptly recognized as Ulec, and he spotted Seacra sitting next to her, holding her knees to her chest and crying.

Alixia was talking to Seacra as she bandaged Ulec's shoulder. She noticed Gidon and Teaneas approaching and as soon as they were in speaking range spoke to Teaneas. "He has a deep cut on his shoulder, and it looks like he was hit hard on the head. I arrived just as Tornal used Cyclone to fling him off the cliff. I had to quickly catch him. He must have passed out as he fell. Once I had him and returned for Seacra, I just caught the gate closing. It took me a moment to realize Seacra was in the river and hadn't been taken. I collected her and came here only moments ago."

"And Almas?" Gidon asked hopefully.

"I couldn't find him." Alixia answered without looking up from bandaging her son's wounds, "I think Tornal took him."

Gidon looked stricken and Teaneas moved to steady the large warrior, but Gidon waved him off and said, "I'll be fine. Lady Alixia, do you have any idea what this attack was about?"

Seacra, who had said nothing, spoke up, "He wanted me," she sobbed.

Teaneas knelt and held his daughter, "What do you mean?"

Seacra hesitated a moment, then explained, "He said he was looking for an elf and a shapeshifter was too good to pass up. Ulec attacked him but got swept off the cliff. He fired a magic bolt at me, but Almas pushed me out of the way and over the edge. I don't know what happened after that."

Gidon bit his lower lip and Teaneas started, "I'm sure he–"

"I'm sure too," Gidon interrupted. "He'll be fine. I'm going to see if I can find any clues as to where they might have taken him from the remains of the revenants."

With that Gidon began walking off. Teaneas started to follow him when Alixia put her hand on his shoulder. "Let him go. We have things to discuss."

IT SEEMED MOST OF THE revenants never left the forest. Fallen branches and trees along with various animals took their claim. Ulec had set the entire forest against the undead invaders and made them pay dearly for invading his sanctuary. It was just east of where they had found Alixia and the two children that Gidon found the spot Ulec had first fought the revenants.

Gidon had just begun using tracks to reconstruct the fight when he heard a whimper near the edge of the forest.

"Crusty?" Gidon called out. After hearing another whimper Gidon followed the sound to some bushes behind which he found his son's pet wolf. Lodged just above the wolf's hind leg there was an arrow and wrapped around both the arrow and the side of the wolf was a slime. After a brief moment of panic Gidon realized the slime was Ulec's pet, Metal. The slime seemed to be putting pressure on the wound to slow the bleeding.

Moving slowly to avoid startling Metal, Gidon knelt by the wolf and addressed the slime. "Okay Metal, I need to see the wound, so I'd appreciate it if you didn't give me an acid bath."

Gidon nudged the overgrown slug and Metal just oozed off the wolf. Gidon focused himself on bandaging up the wolf in an attempt to distract himself from the feelings of frustration, helplessness and fear that were building up in him. As he worked a horn sounded nearby in the forest. Gidon picked up his own small horn hanging from his belt and gave an answering call.

Gidon put his hands over the bandages and focused some healing magic into the wound. It was a Paladin spell. Paladin magic was created by selfless service and could only be used by those of the Aguerius bloodline. It was a gift given to his ancestor before the War of Destruction by the gods.

As he finished working on Crusty, he heard the sound of two large animals approaching from the forest. Soon two forest dragons carrying two riders came out of the woods. The first was his own mount with his son Creetan riding. The second was Jerad, the captain of his men and his best friend.

"What happened!?" Jerad called as he came to a stop and began to dismount.

"I'm still trying to put it all together," Gidon responded as he finished bandaging Crusty. "Best I can make out is some Lich Lords and revenants attacked Almas and his friends."

"Where's Almas?" Creetan asked.

"Taken, it would seem," Gidon said, staring off at nothing.

"What!?" Creetan cried.

"How!?" Jerad asked.

"It was Tornal," came a voice from behind. "And from what my daughter described, Keshen was with him," explained Teaneas, walking up to the group.

Jerad, not noticing Teaneas arrive, instinctively gripped his battle axe. "Who? Where did you–"

"It's okay," Gidon interrupted, "he's a friend. It was his children that were with Almas."

Jerad relaxed but kept his eyes trained on Teaneas. "I'm sorry, I didn't notice your approach. I wasn't expecting an...elf?"

"It's alright," Teaneas reassured. "As I was saying, Keshen attacked first..."

Teaneas was stopped short by another horn sounding, this time to the east.

Jerad responded first. "That would be from the scouts I sent to find the missing men."

"Go to them and find out what they found," Gidon ordered, "then come back here. I need to look around here more."

"My Lord," Jerad nodded to Gidon, returned to his mount and left, giving Teaneas only a moment's further glance as he left.

"I'm sorry for the interruption. Please continue, Lord Teaneas," Gidon apologized.

Teaneas went on to explain all that Seacra had told him about the attack and everything the two Lich Lords had said. After Teaneas finished they began to carefully load Crusty onto Gidon's forest dragon. Jerad returned with three other men wearing leather armor bearing the Aguerius symbol over the left side of the breast. They escorted another three men with their arms bound.

"What do you have for me?" Gidon asked them.

"We found these men on your land who fled when we tried to question them," one of the three newcomers said. "We caught them, and at first, we thought they were poachers. Then we found this."

Taking the first of the bound men he pulled up the sleeve on his right arm, revealing an image of two bone spikes crossing each other on the back of his forearm.

Gidon looked at the tattoo, then at the bound man.

"Three Kadus Knights, servants of the Undead, this close to an undead attack. Would you like to tell me what you were doing out here and why a couple of Lich Lords came all the way out here to attack my son and his friends?'

None of the three Kadus Knights made any attempt to answer and after a few moments Gidon motioned to his men and said, "Tie them to that tree."

Gidon then went over to his forest dragon and unrolled a blanket attached to the side of the dragon's armor. Rolled inside the blanket were a dozen or so weapons of various types. He removed three bronze daggers and took them over to the three Kadus Knights.

"What are you doing?" asked one of the knights as Gidon dropped a bronze dagger in each of their laps.

Gidon responded, "Since you don't want to speak with us, we are done here. Get an arm free; you can use the dagger to cut yourself loose or use it to defend yourself from hungry animals. Personally, I'd hurry if I were you," Gidon said, finishing with a glance off to his left.

The three knights followed Gidon's glance and noticed Metal oozing toward them.

"Great god Snipies, that's a slime!" one of the knights exclaimed, suddenly alarmed.

Teaneas took his turn to respond, "For starters, great may not be the best word to attach to Snipies the god of Chaos. He may have created the human race, but he was definitely not holy. Second, that slime is named Metal and is my son's pet, one of the children your masters tried to murder. I'm sure it slipped Lord Aguerius' mind that Metal's favorite food is bronze."

Gidon didn't respond and silently began unpacking various weapons from bundles and bags tied to his mount. The three Kadus Knights squirmed as Metal drew closer, but Gidon continued unpacking from his mount and repacking into some travel bags.

Finally, as Metal approached one of the knights, he called out, "Okay I'll answer your questions!"

Gidon called back, "I'm listening," as he continued packing but made no movement to stop the slime.

The knight began speaking franticly as Metal approached a couple inches from his feet, "We were supposed to investigate rumors about a forest spirit and draw it out. Chel is a ranger. He noticed the boy in the tree when the forest turned on us and put a magic mark on him. Then we reported his location to Tornal."

"Where did Tornal go from here?" Gidon asked, still occupying himself with packing weapons.

"It'd be suicide to try to go–"

"WHERE?" Gidon commanded, turning to face the knight.

Metal was now crawling up his leg almost to the dagger and the man yelled, "Demon Mountain! We have a forward base in the caves under it!"

Gidon nodded to Teaneas who stepped forward and scooped up Metal in one hand and the dagger with the other hand and dropped both a few feet away. After only a couple of moments, the air filled with the smell of slime acid on bronze. Ignoring the smell, Gidon turned to his men and motioning to his two scouts, instructed," You two take these three to town and lock them up."

Then turning to Teaneas, he addressed him, "Lord Teaneas, you can–"

"Go with you? Certainly," Teaneas interrupted.

"Thank you, but you should see to your family."

Teaneas just shook his head and said, "Alixia will see to the care of the children. I need to see to the young man that saved my daughter's life and find out what Tornal is up to. The Kadus Knight is right. Going to one of their strongholds is suicide. I may be able to get us in without a fight. I knew most of the Lich Lords when they were still human. I think they will listen to me."

Gidon thought this out for a moment. "Okay, Teaneas and Jerad are with me, Creetan and Mogen take the dragons and take Alixia and the kids back to the house and let my wife know I'll be back in a few days with Almas."

"Father... I want to go," Creetan pleaded.

"Cree, I need you with the family," Gidon answered.

"Frankly, my lord," Mogen countered, "I'm with Creetan. Choice between fighting some Undead and explaining all this to Lady Izybel; I think I'd rather face the Undead."

"You all have your orders. I expect them to be followed," Gidon said, then turning to Teaneas continued, "Any weapons you need off the dragon before I send it back?"

"I have all I need."

"You have nothing," Jerad muttered.

"Lord Teaneas is a hero of the War of Destruction. If he says he has all he needs, then he has all he needs. Let's get these horses loaded and get moving," Gidon answered.

After quickly loading their gear on the horses the threesome took their leave from the others and rode off toward Demon Mountain.

WHEN ULEC WOKE UP HE knew he was in a strange place before he opened his eyes. Even with his head pounding and arm throbbing, he immediately knew he wasn't outside in the forest. The place he was lying on was too soft and the air was still and didn't smell right; he'd never slept in a bed before but figured he must be in one.

His first instinct was to open his eyes and look around, but he resisted the impulse. There were two voices in the room that he quickly identified as his mother's and the voice of Almas' mother, Izybel. He stayed still and gave no sign of being awake. He had learned long ago that adults tended to be less careful of what they said when they thought the child present was asleep.

As he listened, he stretched out his mind to nearby animals. All he could sense close were some mice, some birds, a couple cats, and Crusty. He was relieved to feel Crusty there, apparently not too bad off despite being wounded. He was kind of worried that he couldn't sense Metal nearby. Last he knew his pet slime wasn't in danger and was taking care of Crusty.

"...trusting the words of those Kadus Knights. They can't even be sure the Lich Lords are there, or if they are walking into a trap," he heard his mother say.

Crusty was sleeping so Ulec had to rely on the other animals to help him gather information about what was going on.

Izybel responded to his mother saying, "Gidon is more than capable of tracking him down. What do you think they should've done? Stayed and done nothing?"

Getting help from the nearby animals was difficult. The mice were too timid and afraid of him; the cats for the most part didn't care or refused to show they cared. The birds seemed most cooperative. From the senses of the four birds and only one mouse, he determined that Seacra was on the back porch of the house sitting quietly on the stairs, and Giddy, Creetan and Cady were all fussing over Crusty.

"I should have gone instead. No one attacks my children. I should go and leave a crater where that mountain stands," Alixia ranted.

Ulec had his animal eyes and ears search further out. Aside from some of Lord Gidon's men, he couldn't find anyone else nearby. A knot started to form in his stomach. Where was his father and Almas?

"Look at yourself. You are hardly in a condition to go fight Lich Lords. And don't you forget for a second my son is likely in that mountain you want to destroy," Izybel said, her voice and temper rising.

Ulec's blood suddenly went cold as the conversation started to make sense to him. They had taken Almas. After all he had done, he completely failed to protect his friend.

"Mind your tongue human. Do not forget who you're talk-... Ulec! How long have you been listening?" Alixia demanded.

Ulec sighed, taking a moment to compose himself. Then opening his eyes, he answered, "Not long. I just woke up."

"How are you feeling dear?" Izybel asked, "Can I get you something?"

"I can manage caring for my own son. You may leave now." Alixia interrupted.

"Mother, please don't speak to her like that," Ulec said softly but with a slight warning in his tone. How he wished his mother could just once make a good first impression.

"I will not let some human interfere in our family affairs. She would do well to mind her own family," Alixia responded.

Ulec sat up quickly, anger flashing in his eyes," Don't speak...like...that," he started to yell but as soon as he was in a sitting overcome by a surge of pain and nausea, and barely ...st couple words before collapsing back on the bed.

...lec!" Izybel cried and stepped forward, but Alixia beat her to Ulec's side.

"Careful, my son. You have a concussion. You shouldn't make sudden movements like that," Alixia soothed. She then hesitated and turned to Izybel, "I... apologize. I'm not accustomed to feeling so helpless."

"We've both been feeling a lot of that today. I should leave you both to talk. I'll go see how the other children are doing," Izybel said quietly before leaving the room.

Before Alixia could say anything, Ulec asked, "What happened?" Then lowering his voice asked, "What happened to Almas?"

"After Tornal swept you off the cliff, he attacked Seacra. Almas pushed her off the cliff and she fell into the river. I was busy catching you as you fell and by the time I got back, I only saw Tornal's magic gate closing. There was no sign of Almas, so we assume Tornal took him. Lord Gidon and your father have gone to try to find him."

Ulec took a moment to take in the information. He then opened his mouth to ask another question when the door burst open and Seacra ran in.

"Ulec! Are you alright?!" she asked as she rushed to his bedside.

That was the problem with using Natela magic. It alerted every nearby elf that he was awake.

"I'm fine," Ulec answered, then turned to his mother, "What happened to Metal? I can't find him."

Seacra answered before Alixia could answer, "Father took it with him."

"Oh," Ulec wondered what his father was up to. He'd have to think about that. Speaking again to his mother he said, "You should go help Father and Lord Gidon find Almas. Seacra and I are safe here."

"As much as I'd like to, Lady Izybel is right. I'm not in good enough condition to fight right now. I should be focused on making sure my children will be okay."

"But Mother–"

"Don't argue. Now, I can see how tired you are, and you need rest to heal. So get some sleep."

"Mother, I know how you feel about humans, but he's my friend," Ulec finished as he closed his eyes. His mother was right about how tired he was, but he had one more thing to do.

As he heard his mother and sister wordlessly leave the room, he reached his mind far out and searched among the minds of the animals until he found a familiar one. He found it far to the east and using the familiar mind as an anchor, he pulled his own awareness to it.

Metal was upset, but not because he didn't trust Ulec's father. The slime trusted Ulec's father as much as Ulec did himself. Metal was upset at being out of contact with Ulec and not knowing what was happening.

Ulec calmed the slime down and took note of the slime's location as best he could. Being in the shoulder bag, Metal knew little of what was going on outside the bag, but Ulec knew all he needed for the moment. Ulec closed down his connection to Metal and the other animals and was soon sound asleep.

Chapter 4

"I GAVE ONE ORDER, AND you couldn't even do that right?"

"I was able to save him."

"He wasn't supposed to be injured to begin with, Tornal!"

"How was I supposed to know he'd jump into my attack?"

"The boy is an Aguerius; self-sacrificing for others is bred into the Paladin line. Why do you think after over a hundred years, Gidon and his children are all that's left of it?"

"I think you're forgetting about your 'pet.'"

"He abandoned that line years ago and the line has abandoned him. But he isn't what we're discussing. I'll be taking the boy into my personal custody from this point. I expect that is fine with you?"

"Yes...yes Lord Lich-El."

ALMAS AWOKE WITH A start. He'd been having a nightmare but couldn't remember a single thing about it. He didn't take much time trying to remember it as he looked around and realized that he was still in the nightmare that his life had become.

He could remember the Lich Lord's attack. He could also remember the helpless feeling he had had as he watched his best friend get swept off a cliff. When he saw the attack on Seacra, everything had gone to slow motion, and he had acted almost on pure instinct. He never even saw if Seacra made it or not. All he saw after pushing her off the cliff was the magic bolt coming right at him, a flash of pain, and then waking up here.

Here... Where was here? He was in a cave; the rock walls and cold musty air said that much. Light came from torches on the wall. He also took a moment to look himself over. His shirt was burned and torn where the magic bolt must have hit him in the chest, but he couldn't find any trace of what had to have been a serious injury. In a moment of panic, he felt for a heartbeat, and he looked for small bones sticking out of his arms.

His heartbeat was strong, and everything else seemed normal. He wasn't a revenant. The only thing that was weird was a creepy feeling he felt there in the cave. He couldn't really explain it, but the place felt like death.

"Everything in working order?"

Almas spun around to face the source of the voice. Sitting at a table behind him sat a Lich Lord that looked far older than the two that had attacked him in the forest. Even though he looked old and seemed to have a number of old wounds, including a missing hand, there was nothing frail about him. His build was more or less the same as Almas' father, which meant his build was more or less the same as a bear. The Lich Lord sat with a relaxed posture, but Almas took note of the sword strapped to his side and the largest war hammer he had ever seen sitting on the ground next to him, the handle leaning against his leg.

The Lich Lord regarded him for a moment, then spoke, "I must apologize; Tornal was under strict orders not to harm anyone in your family. So, when you were accidentally injured, he had no choice but to bring you here so we could heal you. How are you feeling?"

Almas said the first thing that came to his mind and answered, "Scared out of my wits," as he tried to stare coolly at the Lich Lord.

The Lich Lord chuckled and responded, "I'd almost forgotten the Aguerius humor. It's nice to see that after a hundred years it still breeds true. I've been rude; I should have introduced myself. I am Lich-El, and I assure you your safety while you're here. Please come closer so we can speak more comfortably."

Almas didn't move an inch. Lich-El was the leader of all the Lich Lords, and he hadn't left the eastern wastes in nearly 75 years. Either Almas was very far from home or something very serious was happening.

"Come, come now," Lich-El beckoned. "Come have a seat and play a game with me."

Almas noticed for the first time sitting on the table was a Chintal board set up and ready to go. Almas took a tentative step forward and hesitated. He couldn't trust a Lich Lord, especially their leader.

"Do come and sit. If we intended any harm, it would have already been done. I simply wish to speak with you over a friendly game of Chintal. I understand you're quite good."

Before he could do anything, Almas had to ask, "What happened to my friends?"

Lich-El smiled and responded, "They are both no worse for wear I assure you. They will be quite alright, in part thanks to you. You serve your friends well. Now sit, for goodness' sake."

Almas took a step towards the chair. He was still scared to death and in no way trusted Lich-El, but the rational part of his mind was telling him that offending an old, super powerful Lich Lord was a bad idea. Tentatively he took his seat.

"Guests go first," Lich-El said politely.

Almas moved a piece in the center of his ranks forward with a classic opening move, then looked up and asked, "Why are you doing all this?"

"Doing all what?" Lich-El casually asked as he made his own move.

"Everything, the attack on my friends and me, bringing me here, healing me. All you liches do is murder people and yet here I am alive. Why?"

Lich-El thought a moment as they continued to take their turns moving pieces. Finally, he answered, "The politics of war are far more complicated than most people, particularly children, understand."

"Try me," Almas responded.

"To explain I'd have to start from the beginning. What do you know of the War of Destruction?" Lich-El began.

"Well," Almas started, "our ancestors came from another land, but it was destroyed by an evil god called Destruction. Our ancestors agreed to help the other gods and the elves to fight him, so we were given this land to live on."

"Not bad," Lich-El responded. "Hundreds of kingdoms of men and only one agreed to stand and fight. While the armies of the other kingdoms fled or fell upon their own swords, your ancestor made a deal with the gods that his army would stand and fight to slow Destruction down. In return he asked that the families of those that fought would be taken to safety and given lands of their own. Even with that deal only twenty thousand of us agreed to fight."

"Twenty thousand of us? You fought in the war of Destruction?"

"Yes," Lich-El answered. "We fought and bought two months for the elves and the gods to prepare a defense on this continent. Of the 20,000, only 50 survived to be brought here. All 50 of us volunteered to fight here in the final battle. That turned out to be the turning point that won the war. After the battle was over, Destruction's demonic armies were defeated, and he was sealed away."

"Good for you. What does this have to do with what you're doing now?"

"Everything. Destruction was sealed away, not killed, which means one day he may return."

"How can that be? Lord Teaneas and my father told me he was sealed away with a blood seal. The only way to break a blood seal is with the blood of the sealer. Mundial, the god of life, sealed himself with Destruction. The only key is also sealed away."

"Just because there isn't a way to unseal Destruction now doesn't mean one day a way won't be found. During the war I met a race of elves known as Desert Elves. Their ancestors had once made a pact with the Fates and received great powers. I, along with many others, decided to visit the Fates and ask for the power that could defeat Destruction should he escape."

Almas focused a moment on what Lich-El said about the Desert Elves. He remembered that Seacra had told him her mother was half Desert Elf. Almas had often wondered why Lady Alixia seemed more powerful than Lord Teaneas. Perhaps some of what Lich-El said was true, but what parts?

Lich-El continued, "The Fates agreed to grant us our request. The result was to turn us to what we are now."

"How is turning you into blood thirsty, murderous monsters supposed to help you defeat Destruction should he come again?"

"At first, we remained the people we always had been inside. We returned to our old lives, but no one in the kingdom was comfortable with what we had become. So, they asked us to leave. We traveled east and built a home for ourselves. We kept in contact with the king for twenty years. The king slowly began to lose trust in us, for after the twenty years he sent an army to destroy us."

Almas sat up, "Wait, you're saying we attacked you first?"

"Yes."

Almas couldn't believe this. All he had ever heard about the Undead was that they were the ones constantly attacking and invading. It couldn't be possible that they were victims. They were the monsters here.

Lich-El smiled and began speaking again, "We won the battle and drove them away. After a few months they attacked again. We again drove them off, but this time we were so angry we pursued them. We decided that if they wanted a war, we'd give them a war. We drove your people back as far as Aguerius Forest. I gave the order to move over the north of the forest and attack the Forjad province and bypass the Aguerius province."

"Why? I mean, why bypass Aguerius?" Almas asked, suddenly even more confused. "It would take you far out of your way and would leave you wide open for attack from the Warriors Guild."

"Lord Aguerius and his people had refused to participate in the two attacks on my people. So, I convinced the others to leave them alone and bypass the area."

"But my great grandfather did fight you and won," Almas interrupted.

"It was a great battle, with many losses on both sides. It seems while your grandfather didn't attack us, he also wouldn't stand by and let us attack the rest of the kingdom. The battle ended in an agreement that we would return to the east and they would leave us alone. The treaty lasted 30 years,"

Lich-El stopped a moment and stared into space. Almas began to feel uneasy. Lich-El looked like a lifeless figure. Then suddenly he came to life and began speaking again, "My comrades here never forgave the attacks on us. They began to pressure me to allow them to go finish the war that had ended with a draw 30 years previous. Finally, after a while, I allowed them to go to war under certain conditions."

"Which were?"

"Mostly that they would be on their own. I wouldn't go with them. Second, that they were not to harm those of the Aguerius family. Conditions they have come to hate."

"I keep hearing about orders to not harm my family. Why?"

"Many reasons, first the Aguerius family has never participated on an attack on us. They have only fought defensively. Second, I am still under oath to the Aguerius family as a retainer. I am honor-bound to protect the family."

"Retainer?! How? When?"

A retainer was a noble's most trusted officer. That position was not lightly given, nor their oaths broken.

"High Lord Morin Aguerius was royal strategist at the time of the beginning of the War of Destruction. He was the one that made the agreement with the gods and elves to let the families that fought settle here. I fought by his side and protected him in every battle. He was the most brilliant strategist ever to live and also the first Paladin. We fought side-by-side till the last battle. It was there that I failed to protect him. Your move."

Almas was so taken aback he had forgotten about the game. He knew the story of Lord Morin. He had even heard mention that his retainer was a powerful warrior, just never that his retainer became the leader of the Lich Lords.

Almas made his move, his head still swimming, and Lich-El continued, "Of twenty thousand men I alone returned to my family. I had a daughter. She was my only family. I also continued to protect and care for my Lord's widow and son. Many people resented the fact that I alone returned while their own loved ones didn't. After a number of years, Lord Morin's son married my daughter. He was a capable warrior and a strategist nearly equal to his father. I decided at this time that it was best to leave and began my quest to find the Fates with those who wished to follow me."

"Wait... If your daughter married Morin Aguerius' son, then would that make you..."

Lich-El smiled what was possibly the most sinister smile Almas had ever seen when he said, "Yes, your great grandfather who stopped our invasion over seventy years ago was my grandson, which would make you my three-time great grandson."

Almas was speechless at this point. What Lich-El had said was one part of his family history that he had been failed to be notified of. It had to be a lie. How could he possibly believe any word that came from the Lich Lord's mouth? How could the blood of something so evil be found in the blood of the Paladin line?

Lich-El continued, "It's been rather fortunate for your family that I've been able to protect it for so long. Many of the other Lich Lords would have liked to have destroyed the Aguerius line long ago. With the line not having the strength it once had, it would have been destroyed long before your birth."

Almas' astonishment began to fade as it was replaced by a hotter emotion, "What do you mean, 'not having the strength it once had'?"

"Earlier generations stood shoulder to shoulder with elves and even with the gods. Even the Desert Elves fell by the hundreds. Few of my Lich Lords could have lasted more than a few seconds against such power. Now only my protection allows your bloodline to continue. Your family today lacks in both the power and the wisdom it once had."

Now there was a fire blazing inside Almas. To insult his family, especially his father, was unforgivable, yet even worse, with everything Lich-El had said, Almas could see enough truth that he wondered and feared that the Lich Lord might be speaking the truth here. It also made him furious that he, too, was powerless to do anything. So, he said the only thing he could in retaliation, "Chintal."

Lich-El looked at the board. Almas had only a few pieces left, yet looking at the board it was clear he had positioned them so that Lich-El had no way to win.

Slowly a grin spread across the Lich Lord's face and looking up at Almas, he spoke, "Even with my attempts to distract you as we spoke, and all the things I said to surprise and astonish you, with minimal attention you still beat me. Perhaps there is hope for our bloodline."

While his anger remained strong, he also began to feel uneasy; partly from Lich-El's use of "our line". Second was the way Lich-El now looked at him. His Grandpa Cree often gave him a similar look after Almas played the harp for him. Lich-El was looking at Almas like a proud grandfather would look at his favorite grandchild. Almas began to feel sick.

He sat staring at the game board. Lich-El was pure evil and nothing he said could be trusted. Almas couldn't believe how easily he'd been drawn into Lich-El's lies, and hated himself for how easily he had begun to believe those lies.

Soon Lich-El broke the silence, "Almas you are an impressive young man. As a reward I have decided to give you a choice, a chance to decide your own destiny."

Almas looked up at Lich-El suspiciously and said, "If I get to decide my destiny, then my choice is to go home."

Lich-El sighed, "Things change, and I'm afraid this land is soon to undergo a big change. I could let you go home, but things will change far quicker than you can imagine. No, I'm afraid there are two choices. You've lived happily for twelve years, surrounded by those who love you. If you are satisfied with that life and wish to avoid the coming change and all the horrors that will come with it, then you can choose to have it all end here."

Almas stared at Lich-El not sure if he was understanding, "Have what end here?"

"Why... your life. Compared to some things, death is preferable."

Almas felt his blood turn to ice and his voice squeaked a little when he asked, "Wh...What is the other choice?"

Lich-El smiled another sinister smile and answered, "To simply live as best as you like and do me a small favor."

"What favor?"

"It involves your friend Ulec. I need you to keep him alive."

"What?"

"I owe Ulec's father a debt left over from the war. If you keep him alive for me then my debt will be paid."

"So, all I have to do if I want to live is make a promise to keep my best friend alive?"

Lich-El nodded, "Yes, but think it through. Once you decide, there will be no changing it no matter how hard you try."

Almas was incredulous, "Think about it? There's nothing to think of. I don't want me or my best friend to die."

Lich-El again sighed, "Very well, it is my command that you live and protect Ulec's life whenever the occasion commands it. Now I will have someone take you to a room where you can rest."

Almas caught a hint of a smile when Lich-El mentioned a room. Somehow Almas felt he wasn't going to like the room he would be sent to. "Can't you just let me go home?"

"All in good time."

Lich-El said nothing more and Almas was about to ask when the "good time" would be, when a door opened and a man entered and addressed Lich-El, "You summoned me my lord?"

The man who entered wore a uniform with the symbol of the Kadus Knights on it. He was younger but still had a warrior's build. He seemed like a normal young warrior except for one thing that Almas found eerie, his face had an uncanny resemblance to his brother, Creetan.

"Please escort our young guest here to stay with our other guests," Lich-El ordered.

The man casually looked Almas over then did a double take looking at the melted remains of Almas' Crest that still hung on his neck. The look that crept onto the man's face afterward could only be described as pure hate.

"He's an Aguerius, isn't he?" The man asked as his right hand started for his sword but stopped short and dropped back to his side.

"Yes," Lich-El responded matter-of-factly.

The man looked at Lich-El for a moment then said with clenched teeth to Almas, "Please follow me."

Almas hesitated. This man had a simply murderous look on his face. He glanced at the Lich Lord and wondered if he was being sent to his death after all.

"You may feel safe to leave with him, dear boy," Lich-El said with a smile, "Deleta may be the leader of the Kadus Knights, but he would not disobey my order to not harm members of the Aguerius family, especially his own cousin."

"Cousin?" Almas asked in disbelief.

"Yes. This is Deleta Aguerius, your cousin. Now please follow him to our guest quarters."

ALMAS WAS STILL TOO dumbstruck to move; Deleta pulled him up roughly from his chair and said as he began pushing him towards the door, "When Lich-El commands you to do something, you need to obey immediately!"

Almas took one last look at the leader of the Lich Lords as he was ushered through the door. Lich-El simply sat at the table watching Almas leave with a look of amusement on his face. Then Deleta shut the door and he was alone in a cave-like corridor with his older cousin.

Deleta, still tightly gripping Almas' arm just below the shoulder, dragged him down the corridor at a brisk pace. With his short legs and body twisted by Deleta's grip, Almas walked along uncomfortably with the Kadus Knight. After a minute he complained, "I can walk on my own. You don't have to drag me."

"I don't care," Deleta responded without loosening his grip even slightly.

Almas looked his cousin up and down; he may have resembled Creetan in his face, but his build was more like his father's. This meant there was little chance of shaking loose of him by strength. He needed another plan.

"If you're my cousin, how'd you become a Kadus Knight?"

Deleta again responded without looking at Almas, slowing down, or loosening his grip, "My uncle murdered my father 13 years ago and Lich El took me in."

"Your uncle? Who's–" Almas suddenly understood the implication and tried to stop walking. "Now wait one minute! You're not saying my–"

Almas was interrupted by Deleta shoving him hard against the stone wall. "I saw it! I know what I saw!"

Almas' head was pounding, and he thought he felt a trickle of blood moving down the back of his neck. This conversation wasn't heading in a good direction. Glaring at his cousin he responded, "I'm sorry to upset you. I failed to introduce myself. My name is Almas Aguerius."

"What?" Deleta said with disbelief in his eyes, and momentarily loosened his grip. "I can't believe he'd name you after my father."

"Well, he did."

Deleta seemed to think a moment, then his face seemed to turn to stone, "It doesn't matter, I still know what I saw."

Deleta pulled Almas off the wall and began moving through the corridors again, although he didn't handle him quite as harshly.

After a number of turns they reached a door guarded by two revenants. Deleta opened the door and ushered Almas in. It was a large, open room, most of which was behind large thick metal bars.

Behind the bars were about 30 people, mostly women and children with a few men here and there. They were seated in small groups, heads turned down, and silent. Only a few lifted their gaze as Deleta opened the gate into the cell.

Deleta apparently realized he hadn't roughed up Almas as much as he had wanted and pushed Almas hard into the cell and said, "Enjoy your stay."

Almas lost his footing instantly, fell down and rolled a couple of times before coming to a stop on the floor. He heard the cell door slam as he sat up and saw Deleta leave the room.

"So much for cousins," he muttered under his breath and started to brush dirt off his pants then decided it was pointless. All of his clothes were dirty, torn and burnt. Hardly anyone in the cell still looked at him, although one large man who appeared to be missing an arm came over to him and offered his one hand to help Almas up.

"Okay there, young man?"

Almas looked at the large man. Despite his huge size he had a gentle face. He wore a uniform with a soiled emblem of the Aguerius family on it, which meant he was one of his father's men.

Almas took the man's hand and answered as the man pulled him to his feet, "I'd like to say that I've never been better, but I'd be lying."

The one-armed man gave Almas a strange look when he heard Almas' response and looked him up and down. Almas was about to ask if something was wrong when the man looked him in the eye and asked, "You're Lord Aguerius' son, aren't you?"

That statement immediately got everyone's attention, and suddenly Almas had every eye on him.

"Yes, I am... How did you know? What's left of my crest was hidden."

The man smiled, "Your face, the way you talk, even the way you stand is just like your father."

Everyone in the cell started talking at once:

"Have they invaded the Aguerius province already?"

"No, they were going to sacrifice us before that."

"Will Lord Aguerius come for his son and save us, or is he dead?"

"Ask the boy!"

As the room went silent, Almas noticed everyone in the cell was looking at him expectantly. He started to panic. Son of a high lord or not, they surely couldn't expect a 12-year-old to know what to do about being stuck in an Undead dungeon.

Before he could say anything a man in the corner of the room apparently heard his thoughts because he laughed and said, "Yes, that's right. Let's pin all our hopes on some snot-nosed kid because his daddy's 'important.'"

The man who spoke was missing a leg and his clothes were as tattered as anyone else's, but he could still make out that he was wearing a ranger's uniform. The crest of Leflion could be seen clearly. Almas wasn't surprised at what the ranger said. For one thing it was true. Secondly, the Ranger Guild had never been friendly towards the Warrior Guild or the Aguerius family. However, the ranger's next comment began to anger Almas.

"If the Aguerius family was worth a tenth of what you people think they are, the Undead would've been destroyed long ago. Not only are the undead still here, but Lord Aguerius can't even protect his own family apparently. I'm sorry, but if we leave it to him this whole kingdom is going to end up like the Vatan Province."

"Shut up!" Almas had had enough. That was the third time in the last hour that someone had insulted his father. He didn't care if the guy was an adult or if he sounded like a petulant child. He wasn't going to let anyone get away with it anymore.

"If you think you can do better, then you break out of here and go save the kingdom!"

The ranger only smirked and said, "But I'm not anyone 'important.'"

Almas was about to explain to the man exactly how unimportant he was when the one-armed warrior put his hand on his shoulder and said, "Let it go. He isn't worth your attention. Come over here and have a seat, we can talk."

He introduced himself as he led Almas over to a section of the back wall as far away from the other people as they could get.

"My name is Bosha."

"I'm Almas."

"It's an honor, Almas. Now don't let that ranger, Lemuem, get to you. He's just bitter about losing his leg; even though losing it is why he's still alive."

"How is that?" Almas asked, confused.

Bosha answered, "Revenants, unlike Lich Lords, don't regenerate limbs back. So, missing a leg made him unfit to be a revenant. So, he was put in here with the rest of us that are thought to be unworthy to be Undead."

"So why are they keeping all of you?" Almas asked.

"Sacrifices."

"What?!" Almas asked, alarmed.

"Undead get their power from the energy released by death. If they kill all of us right before battle, then they have that much more power at the start of it."

"That's terrible." Almas had never heard of any such thing from his father. Most of his war stories were about his victories. While he often mentioned that the Undead did many horrible things, he never went into detail about what those things were. The more Almas learned, the more he understood why his father avoided telling some of the details, and hoped he could avoid learning any more.

"Yes, it is," Bosha agreed to Almas' last statement, "but as long as we live it gives us time to find a way to continue living."

"So have you tried anything to escape?" Almas asked.

"I tried a strength burst to bend the bars, but they are thick and magically reinforced I'm afraid."

"Has anyone else tried anything?"

"I don't know. Most of us came from Noneh Village that got raided two nights ago. I was the only survivor with magic training. There were ten people here already when we arrived, but I haven't gotten any of them to talk, unless you count insults from our ranger friend as talking."

"In other words, they aren't much help?" Almas asked.

"I don't know about that," Bosha replied. "Shall we go try to talk with them? Maybe they'll respond to you."

"Me? I'm 12. That guy may have been a toad, but he was right about me. There isn't anything I can do," Almas said.

"Maybe. Maybe not," Bosha said with a shrug. "Sometimes all that is needed is for you to just be you. Your name got more responses from them than I've seen since I got here. If you do nothing else but be a symbol to unite us, then it could be enough to save us all."

Almas looked at the floor. Lich-El had told him he would live and eventually be released. If he was telling the truth, then all he had to do was wait. But these people would all die if they didn't escape. His father wouldn't leave them here to die. Despite all the insults and accusations Almas had heard, he knew his father wouldn't rest till all these people were safe.

Ulec would also do what he could to rescue these people. He had, after all, risked his life to save Almas before they had become friends.

Suddenly a thought hit him like a lightning bolt. They would be coming for him. His father and his friend would stop at nothing to rescue him. If Lich-El knew his father and best friend as well as he seemed to, then he also knew they would come for him.

Could he be bait for a trap? Did Lich-El lie about everything? Almas couldn't see any point in lying to him if it was a trap. Regardless of whether any of what Lich-El said was true or not, he was up to something, and Almas just couldn't figure it out. How can you choose what to do if you can't figure out what is going on?

Frustration and fear finally got the best of Almas. Leaning his back against the wall he slid down and collapsed into a sitting position, hugging his knees, and let all the built-up emotion flood out.

Bosha, taken aback by the sudden breakdown of emotion, tried to comfort him. "Hey, I'm sorry. I shouldn't have put everything on your shoulders like that."

The warrior sat down next to Almas and placed his hand at the base of Almas' neck in a comforting manner. Meanwhile Almas let the tears and sobs flow freely.

Despite being around people and Bosha's best effort to comfort him, Almas hadn't felt this terrified and alone since the time he had been lost in the forest. He had been attacked by a forest dragon and almost killed back then. This experience was far worse because not only was he terrified for himself, but he could see now the danger his loved ones were in and realized for the first time that he feared more for his family and friends than he did for himself.

Lich-El hadn't said anything specific, but he had seemed to have hinted at both threats to his family and toward his best friend. He had watched Ulec nearly get killed; he still wasn't sure how he'd survived. And if Ulec could be beaten so easily, then he realized his own father could be beaten.

Now that he could better see the depth of evil and power the Lich Lords possessed, he suddenly had all those nightmares and fears come back that he had had whenever his father left for a battle. Only now his better understanding just increased the fear not just for his family but for everyone he cared for.

Almas was beginning to see why his father had always taken such lengths to keep his family safe. Ulec had mentioned once that the number of scouts was increased when he was in the forest playing.

Scouts... Some of the revenants that had attacked him had been some of his father's scouts. They had been out there to protect him and were murdered and raised as revenants. His father had told him many times they were heroes for risking their lives to protect them, but Almas had still always taken them for granted. One of them he had recognized a few times delivering reports to his father and once in town with his family. Almas' worst fears were now a nightmarish reality for that family; their father wasn't coming home. He had died protecting him and he didn't even know his name. How many had died for him that he never knew?

Anger began to replace his fear as he began to understand better the depth of pain and suffering the Lich Lords were responsible for. He'd find a way to stop them. He was done standing back and just watching as others risked and gave their lives for him.

Almas hadn't realized he had stopped crying. But Bosha apparently had and felt he could speak again.

"Don't worry about what I said before. We adults shouldn't pass the responsibility of escape to the young. You're our responsibility."

Almas shook his head. "No, you were right before. If we are going to get out, we all need to do what we can."

Bosha still looked worried and asked, "Are you sure?"

"Yes. It's time I go introduce myself to my roommates."

Chapter 5

"IS YOUR COUSIN COMFORTABLE in his accommodations?"

"Why is he here?"

"He quite bravely stepped in front of one of Tornal's attacks to save a friend. He needed immediate care, and no, letting him die wasn't an option. He's family and you can't punish him for events that happened before he was born."

"I'll accept your words and decisions, but I don't have to like it."

"You aren't required to. But keep in mind the boy's bloodline alone could make him a valuable ally against our enemies."

"I don't need help against my enemies."

"If you say so. What I need now is for you to take some knights and scout out the area west of here. Lord Aguerius won't be happy about us taking his son and I need eyes out there."

"As you wish."

GIDON, JERAD AND TEANEAS rode quickly all night stopping briefly at sunrise to eat and for Gidon to use his signal horn to signal his men in the area they were approaching.

Shortly before noon they were joined by one of his scouts. Enas had been on his way to Morenville when he heard Gidon's signal. He brought news that Noneh Village had been wiped out by the Undead.

Gidon then promptly recruited Enas to take them to Demon Mountain by the shortest possible route. After all no one knew the regions of the Aguerius Province better than the scouts assigned to that region.

As the sun began to set, Demon Mountain was in full view. Gidon ordered a stop for camp. They had been traveling a full night and a day without rest. As much as Gidon wanted to hurry, he knew he'd be no help to his son if they approached an undead stronghold ready to drop from exhaustion.

Gidon pulled out a small, black box and opened it. Inside were two spindles: One pointed north and the other pointed towards Demon Mountain.

"What's that?"

Gidon turned to find Teaneas standing near him. Putting the box away, Gidon answered, "Four years ago after Almas got lost in the forest, we realized how close we came to losing him. So Izybel made a new crest for each of the kids and made compasses with a spindle magically linked to a crest. This one is linked to Almas' crest. It's pointing directly at Demon Mountain."

The two were silent for a couple of minutes, then Gidon began speaking again. "I was doing archery practice with Creetan when I was notified that some of my scouts had failed to report in. I could've gone home, retrieved this and followed it right to the kids. But I decided it would be faster to try to go find him right away. I thought I was just taking a precaution. I never thought the enemy could get so close so quickly."

"There is plenty of blame to pass around," Teaneas started. "My son's protection of the forest made it seem that nothing truly evil could penetrate it. I grew too complacent. For now, what we need to do is to focus blame on those most responsible, those that invaded our children's sanctuary."

"Speaking of which," came a voice behind them. They both turned to see Jerad, who continued, "Do we have any kind of plan on how we are going to get Almas out of an undead forward base?"

Teaneas and Gidon looked at each other for a moment. Then Teaneas turned to Jerad and answered, "Gidon and I will go in and negotiate the boy's release."

Jerad's eyebrows shot up. "You're just going to go in and ask for him?"

"Yes, they will not attack Gidon as long as he's accompanied by a neutral party."

"What happens if they decide you're not neutral? Tornal didn't seem to think your kids were neutral," Jerad responded gruffly.

"I knew most of the liches when they were human. They were children when I gave their parents this land, and they should know me well enough to know that to attack me would be...unfortunate... for them"

"Unfortunate? Who do you think you are? Planning to take Lord Aguerius into an Undead base unarmed and–"

Jerad was suddenly cut off as Teaneas suddenly extended his right arm towards him. As his arm rose a sword materialized in his hand, the point of which stopped, pressed against Jerad's chin.

As Jerad tried to stutter a response, the elf answered, "I am Teaneas, Lord of Telaxia; third son of Dunas, Lord of the Elves. I am knight and retainer to Mundial, God of Life, and a veteran of the War of Destruction, and I am never unarmed.

"If the Undead choose to attack us, then I can guarantee that they will regret it. Beyond that I guarantee nothing."

Gidon decided this might be a good time to interject. "That's enough, both of you. We have a hard day ahead of us."

Teaneas lowered his arm and the sword disappeared. Meanwhile Gidon continued, "I don't have much trust in the Undead. Yet I don't see us being able to sneak in, and fighting our way in and out would require a large force and would put Almas in danger. It's better to try some diplomacy."

"This still feels like suicide," Jerad grumbled as he stalked away.

After a moment of silence, Teaneas spoke. "I apologize. I was completely out of line."

Gidon rubbed his temples and responded, "We are all tired and on edge. I wish I had been allowed to let him know about your family earlier. I'm sure he feels a bit mistrusted. I'll try to soothe things over with him when I get a chance – for now let him walk it off. Once we get some sleep, we'll all be a little less cranky."

Enas, who had kept a discreet distance till that moment, stepped forward. "I'll take first watch. I'm far more rested than you three."

"Thanks, Enas," Gidon said, then headed to bed. As he did, Teaneas let Metal out of the shoulder bag before retiring for the night.

IZYBEL HAD YET ANOTHER sleepless night. When Almas was lost in the forest, she at least knew enough that he was in protected land. Now one of her babies was in the hands of some of the evilest creatures in existence. Meanwhile all she could do was stay at home and argue with the most intolerable woman she had ever met while she waited for a son and husband that might never return.

She had tried to busy herself by helping to see to Ulec and Seacra's injuries, but Lady Alixia quite rudely refused any and all help. How she was able to raise such sweet children while possessing the personality of a viper was beyond her. Giving up on any hope of sleep, Izybel got up to check on Crusty. It seemed that as far as Lady Alixia was concerned, the wolf was the only one injured that she was qualified to nurse back to health.

After checking the wolf's bandages, Crusty let out a faint whimper. Izybel sighed and comforted her son's pet.

"You did really well the other day. Don't worry. Almas will be back soon. Till then just work on getting better."

She patted the wolf on the back and then stood up. She started to head out to the kitchen when she heard a soft voice, almost a whisper, behind her.

"Mother?"

Turning, she found her daughter standing in the doorway. "Cady? What are you doing up this early?"

"I heard you and thought you might have been Seacra."

"Seacra? She should be in bed sleeping," she said with some concern.

Cady shook her head and said, "She isn't. She's been gone a real long time."

Izybel felt concern and a fear growing. Walking briskly past her daughter, she went straight to Ulec's room. She quietly opened the door and peered inside. The bed was empty!

She turned to wake up Lady Alixia only to come face to face with the elvish lady.

"Oh," Izybel gave a small shout of surprise. How could these elves move around without making a single noise?

"What's going on?" Alixia demanded immediately.

"You startled me," Izybel said catching her breath, then added, "Cady came and told me she couldn't find Seacra. So, I came to check on Ulec, and he's missing too."

As Izybel jumped aside, Lady Alixia rushed by her into Ulec's room muttering a word in a language Izybel didn't understand but was sure it was probably not a word she wanted spoken in front of her daughter.

"Lady Alixia, please calm down. I'm sure they are safe–"

"Curse it all! That boy will be the death of me!" Alixia said as she came back out with a small piece of paper. "That boy is far too much like his father. He's going to get himself killed."

"Cady, wait here," Izybel ordered her daughter, then ignoring Cady's protests, followed Alixia and asked, "What does the note say?"

"He went with Seacra to help Teaneas rescue Almas," she answered stepping out the door.

Once outside and before Izybel could say another word, Alixia transformed into a bird and fluttered away. After picking up both speed and height, she transformed again into a mountain dragon and rapidly flew off.

Izybel watched her fly away as Creetan appeared next to her followed by Giddy and Cady.

"Mother, what's going on?" Creetan asked.

"Complications... Complications I hope your father can handle," Izybel answered.

Chapter 6

"I THINK IT'S TIME WE find a new leader."

"You're speaking treason, Dilfer."

"Come on Tornal, his protection of the Aguerius family is nothing less than treason. They are the enemy and yet he ties our hands concerning them."

"You've seen him fight. Trying to dethrone him would be our death."

"I've been speaking with others. He's only as strong as his weakest point, which happens to be the Aguerius family itself. Lord Aguerius will come for his son. If we have him, we can easily take the rest. If we have power over that family, we'll have power over him."

"You'll have to take care of that yourself. He's keeping me far too close for me to do anything. But let's say I wouldn't mind it if he was no longer meddling with my experiments."

"Soon. If we stand united with his precious descendants in our possession, nothing will be able to stop us.

GIDON HAD EVERYONE up and camp broken before the sun rose. Everyone was more or less rested, even Jerad who had taken a one-hour walk to calm down after his exchange with Teaneas.

After nearing the mountain Gidon announced that he, Jerad and Teaneas would continue on foot and Enas would stay behind with the horses. Gidon didn't want to risk losing the horses to any Undead scouting parties. Plus, Enas could bring them quickly when signaled.

As they neared the mountain, Gidon started using his compass more and more. He could tell he was getting close by the way the pointer became more and more unstable. From far away they could walk a little off course and the pointer changed little. Now if the path was just a little off the pointer it started to rotate.

"You're being tracked," a voice in Gidon's head spoke.

Gidon's bow, a fielis named Sacred Knight, hung on his shoulder. Like all fielis, Sacred Knight could only see what was in view, but could see in great detail.

Gidon responded in his mind, "*Where and how many?*"

"Two that I can see, 200 feet to our left and slightly behind us."

Gidon stopped. Teaneas and Jerad stopped right behind him, Jerad asking if something was wrong. Gidon made a subtle gesture indicating two enemies and the direction. Jerad gripped his axe, ready to bring it to bear. Teaneas only nodded and whispered, "Are you ready?"

Gidon responded, "Now is better than later."

Teaneas nodded once again, and then turning to face the direction of the undead scouts loudly announced, "I am Lord Teaneas of the Elvish Realm. I wish to speak with he who is in charge here."

At first Gidon saw nothing, although Sacred Knight assured him they were coming. Shortly after, he caught movement in the brush and greenwood. The flashes of movement soon began to take the form of two revenants.

As the pair of undead creatures came close, Gidon motioned to Jerad to take no action. Jerad nodded but he kept a tight grip on his axe, ready for anything. Gidon couldn't blame him for being edgy; he was feeling edgy himself.

The revenants stopped about ten feet away and one bowed and said with a lifeless, hissing voice, "Lord Teaneas."

Teaneas, keeping a constant and dignified posture, addressed the one that bowed, "I would like to see who is in charge here as would these two men under my protection to negotiate the release of a child by the name of Almas Aguerius."

The revenant again hissed its answer, "Audience and safe passage granted. Follow."

Both revenants walked past Gidon, followed by Teaneas who nodded to him indicating he should follow. Gidon sighed and turned to Jerad, "Shall we?"

"After you," Jerad responded, and the two men fell in behind Teaneas.

The revenants continued to lead them towards the mountain till they reached the base. They stood before a wall of rock with an opening. On either side of the opening, a revenant stood at guard. Their escorts led them into the opening. After a short corridor a chamber opened up with a large metal door in the back. The revenants stopped at the door, and one turned around and addressed them.

"Leave weapons."

"You want us to go in unarmed?" Jerad asked, raising his eyebrows.

"Safe passage," the revenant hissed as his reply.

"Guess we better do it," Gidon said and began unstrapping all of his various weapons.

"You're seriously going in unarmed?"

"Yes, Jerad, I am. Everything will be fine," Gidon assured him, glancing at Teaneas. The elf was putting down Metal's bag, undoing the knot but not opening it. He did not remove his ring, but the revenants didn't seem concerned about what appeared to be a normal ring.

Jerad sighed and put down his battle axe and also his supply of lightweight throwing axes. Gidon also dropped a small arsenal as he pulled weapon after weapon out of hidden spaces in his armor.

Once the Undead were satisfied they were unarmed, they unlocked and opened the metal door at the end of the room and led the threesome deeper into the caves.

"OK, I THINK WE HAVE everything. Now we just need to figure out when to escape and what we're going to do once we get out of this room." Almas looked at the instruments of their escape in his hands. If someone told him a week ago that he'd be planning to break out 30 people from an undead dungeon cell with a couple of turkey bones, he'd have died laughing at the person.

Admittedly, they were useless without the magical talents of various prisoners. And while he was fairly certain the plan could get them all out of the room, they still couldn't figure out how they would find a way out of the caves.

"So, any ideas?" Almas continued.

Bosha and the others gathered around him all shook their heads at a loss. Almas was about to recommend that they should sleep on it when he heard the last voice he expected to hear speak up.

"I can lead everyone out but only on one condition."

The speaker was Lemuem, the one-legged ranger that had mocked Almas when he first arrived in the dungeon. His statement raised a number of eyebrows.

"You?" Bosha asked. "You've done nothing but speak ill of us this entire time. You wanted nothing to do with this."

"I wanted nothing to do with you or the kid. As much as I'd hate to give you credit, I think your plan has a chance. And I can stoop to work with you if it means getting out of here."

"And how do you plan on leading us out?" Bosha asked.

"Don't you take me for some novice ranger. I've tracked every revenant, lich, and Kadus Knight that has entered this cell. By tracking their movements, I have constructed a nice map in my head. I know the path out of here."

Bosha was about to say something, but Almas spoke first. "What is your condition?" His father had once said that the rivalry between the Warrior's Guild and the Ranger's Guild was as big as a threat to the kingdom as the Undead. Almas was beginning to understand why.

"Only that we go right now," Lemuem answered.

"Now?!" Almas and Bosha said in unison. A few people nearby started murmuring at once, and Bosha continued, "Why now? We need at least a little time to rehearse."

"Just about every revenant, lich, and man I'm tracking are gathering in the main chamber. The path out is as clear as we can hope for. Not to mention they've never gathered together like this; it might not mean anything good for us."

"If this is the start of the invasion, then yes, the next step would be to start sacrifices. But why would they gather the revenants also? They have no mind apart from the lich that created them," Bosha observed.

"Whatever the reason, I doubt we will have another opportunity like this," Lemuem insisted.

"Well?" Bosha directed his question towards everyone present.

"I say we trust him," Almas answered. "I'm ready to leave now. This place feels like death and a change would be nice."

Everyone else nodded in agreement and Bosha conceded, "Alright then. Let's get everyone ready and get to work."

JERAD AND THE OTHERS were led through a maze of tunnels. It seemed that they had gone deep underneath the mountain when they came to a huge chamber filled with revenants, Kadus Knights, and Lich Lords. The ceiling was high with huge stalagmites hanging from it.

In the back of the room was a large throne that appeared to be made of stone. Sitting on it was the oldest looking Lich Lord Jerad had ever seen. Although he looked old, it'd be wrong to say he looked weak. In fact, Jerad wasn't sure he had ever seen a stronger-looking warrior. Other than looking Undead, his body appeared to be in top physical form. He also seemed to radiate both confidence and power.

They were brought before the Lich Lord, who broke into a cold smile and said, "Teaneas, my old friend welcome. And Lord Aguerius, I'm honored to finally meet you, my boy."

"Thodien," Teaneas responded coldly.

"Lich-El, if you please."

"As you wish," Teaneas responded. "I have come here to ask about a crime committed by one of your company and inquire after the fate of one of the victims."

Lich-El smiled pleasantly and answered, "If you are referring to Lord Gidon's son, I am pleased to inform him that the boy is here and quite safe. He will be returned to you immediately."

Gidon gave a sigh of relief while Teaneas continued, "We are relieved to hear that. Perhaps you could enlighten us as to why it was felt necessary to attack three children and abduct one of them."

"Tornal was investigating rumors of a strange spirit in Aguerius Forest. He was under strict orders not to harm any of the Aguerius family. The boy was injured during a small fight, and it was necessary to bring him here to heal him," Lich-El answered.

"And where is Tornal now?" Teaneas asked.

"Tornal is being punished for disobeying my orders."

"And just what," Gidon asked, "is his punishment?"

"How I choose to punish him is my concern," Lich-El's response came.

"Your concern?" Gidon said with anger clearly growing on his face. "Tornal murdered two of my men!"

"Gidon..." Teaneas warned. "Not here."

Many of the liches stepped back as Gidon continued despite Teaneas' warning, the air around him beginning to glow with sacred magic, "... he attacked my son and my son's friends..."

"That's enough," Lich-El warned, his face growing serious for the first time.

"...then injured them and brought my son here! And you dare say–"

Lich-El stood up and tapped his war hammer on the ground, and at once all around Gidon a circle of long stone spikes shot up from the ground at an angle that pointed the tips at Gidon's head.

Before Gidon could react, they stopped less than an inch from piercing his skull.

Gidon stood wide-eyed and shocked. His head only was visible above the stone pyramid. Jerad reached reflexively for his axe that wasn't there. Teaneas grabbed his wrist and whispered for him to wait.

How could he wait? His lord and friend was just about decapitated.

"That," Lich-El spat, "is enough. I have granted you safe passage, but do not forget that our peoples are at war. I, as your enemy, am not responsible for the wellbeing of your children. That is your responsibility as a father, a responsibility you failed to fulfill and would have cost you your son had I, your enemy, not intervened.

"You claim to be a protector of your people. Yet you know as well as I that your people would've been annihilated years ago for their crimes against us had I not been merciful and held back my armies. As you are now, you are powerless to protect anything. You and your people live by my mercy. But I have done my last favor for your family and your kingdom. Go collect your son, and then I suggest you find the power within to protect him and the rest of your family and people."

Gidon stared open-mouthed at Lich-El. He dared not move with the ring of sharp rocks pointed right at the base of his head. Lich-El tapped his war hammer once more and the stones receded as he sat down. Gidon, now free, was still speechless. Teaneas, however, was not.

"The other two children Tornal attacked were mine. And we are not at war," he said.

"Ahh, but we are," answered Lich-El. "I tried to warn your wife, and she rewarded me with lies and attacked me. That is a declaration of war. If she had listened to me and left at once, your children would have been safe under her protection. Instead, she did this."

Lich-El raised his left hand, revealing three missing fingers, and continued, "They will finish regenerating in the next day or two, but I will not accept unprovoked attacks on my people or on myself."

Teaneas nodded, not losing his composure for a moment and answered, "I see. If that is how things are, then I thank you for your audience and will leave just as soon as we collect Lord Gidon's son."

"Wait," Jerad spoke up, "that's it?"

"Yes, it is," Teaneas answered. "We came to find and secure the release of Almas. We've accomplished that so it is time to leave."

"I agree; you should leave before the tension grows anymore," Lich-El said. "Dilfor and Solis will take you to Lord Aguerius' son and retrieve him for you. Goodbye and take care."

Lich-El waved for them to follow two liches near the room's only exit. Teaneas bowed his head respectfully towards Lich-El and followed the pair of liches out of the room. Gidon and Jerad followed a step behind him.

ALMAS WATCHED ANXIOUSLY as the older woman dipped the pointed end of the turkey bone in the blood on the tip of her finger, and then continued to use it to draw cracks on the bars of the cell.

The woman was a member of the Artist's Guild and had been taken prisoner by the Lich Lords four years earlier when the Undead had wiped out the Vatan Province. She had been stuck in various dungeons since. Almas couldn't imagine being trapped in dark cells for that long, which was longer than he had even known Ulec, and hearing her story deepened his resolve to get himself and everyone else out.

The woman had been trained in artistic magic which meant she could work magic through her art. Right now, he was using that ability to weaken the bars.

Once she finished drawing cracks on the bottom and top of two bars, she took a step back. Now it was his turn.

Almas glanced back at Bosha, who seemed to be meditating. Then he turned to another woman with a little girl who would be his helpers.

"Okay just like our short practice," he said, after which they placed their hands on the bars.

The plan was for them to move their hands as he hit the bars with the larger turkey bone, changing the tones and allowing him to use bardic magic to further weaken the bars. Almas hoped that the little music training he had gotten from his uncle and his mother would be enough.

Almas started beating out a tune on the bars with his helpers, and after a moment started humming an accompaniment to it. They continued like this for a couple minutes, hands working the bars to get the right tones and Almas humming and pouring as much magic into the bars as he could.

Soon the older woman helping Almas work the bars said, "Okay, get ready. On the count of 3. 1...2...3!"

On the last count Almas and his two helpers jumped away from the bars and Bosha leaped forward. With a yell he hit the bar from the side with his hand and broke it off and smashed it into the second bar, which also broke off right where the cracks were drawn.

Bosha took one of the bars and stepped out of the cell and nudged the other one to fall into the cell where Lemuem caught it and used it like a crutch to follow Bosha out. No sooner were the two men out then the door to the room swung open and a revenant came in.

Bosha wasted no time throwing his bar, pointed at one end where the break followed the cracks drawn on it, which struck the revenant in the chest like a javelin. The undead creature crumbled to dust, and Bosha stepped forward and collected his make-shift javelin. He then glanced at Lemuem.

"We are clear for now," Lemuem answered Bosha's unspoken question.

"Alright," Bosha said looking at everyone in the cell. "The lich that the revenant belonged to knows what we are doing, and we can count on him spreading word fast. So Lemuem has point and will lead us out. I'll cover our backs. Follow Lemuem."

"Right this way everyone," Lemuem added as he helped some of the children out of the cell and then started down the tunnel at a surprisingly quick pace for someone missing a leg.

Almas moved up and down the line of people seeing if there was anything he could do to help but found there wasn't much he could do now. Lemuem seemed to have been right about the way being clear. There didn't seem to be any opposition at all. He could only hope their luck lasted.

GIDON AND THE OTHERS had only been following the pair of liches for a couple minutes when the pair and the revenants with them suddenly stopped. Gidon watched them for a moment in silence as the liches gave each other confused looks. He was about to ask if something was wrong when they took off at a run with their revenants close behind. Gidon swapped some confused looks of his own with his comrades for a moment, and then Teaneas said, "We'd better follow and see what's up. Just be on your guard."

Teaneas took the lead and the three followed the Undead down a few passages. Soon they caught up to the Undead as they were looking into a room.

The lich that Lich-El had called Solis turned to Gidon and accused, "This is your doing!"

"I don't know what happened, but I assure you I've done nothing beyond what we discussed with Lich-El," Gidon answered.

"You came here and drew our forces away from the cell so the prisoners could stage an escape!"

"Prisoners?" Gidon questioned. He had been so preoccupied with his missing son he hadn't even thought that there might be others held here.

Teaneas responded quickly, "You would best use your time recovering your prisoners than wasting it hurling baseless accusations. Just direct us to Lord Gidon's son and we will leave you to that task."

"We will recover them just as soon as we deal with you!" Solis shouted as he drew his sword; Dilfer and all the revenants following suit.

Teaneas took a step back as the Undead approached and complained, "We were granted safe passage by Lich-El."

The revenants advanced as the two Lich Lords hung back and Dilfer answered, "Lich-El's time is about up and his orders will no longer hold meaning, once we have all of you."

Teaneas stepped between the approaching revenants and Gidon and Jerad. The revenants raised their weapons to strike Teaneas, but with one lightning-quick swing of his arm the two nearest revenants disintegrated as a sword appeared in Teaneas' hand.

"Can you two find your way outside?" Teaneas called over his shoulder as he dispatched two more revenants.

"I think so. We passed the passage leading back the way we first entered a little while back," Gidon answered.

"You two go and find the escaped prisoners. Almas might be with them. I'll cover your withdraw and catch up."

"There's too many of them. We should stay together."

"No, please trust me and do as I ask!" Teaneas commanded, fending off five revenants.

Gidon hesitated a moment. Teaneas became more and more surrounded as he slowly moved back. Gidon's instinct was to stay, get a hold of one of the revenant's weapons and help. But then Teaneas had far more experience in battle than Gidon did. Plus, if the legends about him were true, then Teaneas was far from boasting when he said he could handle it.

Signaling Jerad to follow, Gidon started back down the tunnel. After running a few yards, he stopped to give one last glance at the fight behind him–a move that almost cost him his life.

Just as he turned to look at Teaneas, there was a flash where Teaneas stood, then the entire tunnel was enveloped in flames and heat. Even as far back as he was, Gidon was knocked back by the force of the heat. Gidon started to get up but realized the brush with the flames had set his tunic on fire. Jerad was by his side in an instant and helped pat out the flames as he pulled him back.

While he was being pulled back, Gidon looked back to see if he could find the source of the explosion. He found it standing in the tunnel.

Teaneas' cloak was engulfed in blue flames and everything within 15 feet of him was either burning or already ash, Solis, Dilfer, and the revenants Teaneas had been fighting being the latter.

"Get going!" Teaneas called stepping further down the tunnel away from stone walls that were beginning to melt.

Gidon nodded and stood up. No Undead could get close enough to Teaneas right now to hurt him. He'd be safe for now, and now it was time to find his son.

Chapter 7

"THIS IS GETTING OUT of hand, Lord Lich-El."

"The prisoners are of no concern."

"Solis and Dilfer were both just killed."

"Teaneas wouldn't break the truce unless he was attacked first. They should have thought out their plan to use the Aguerius family against me better. Oh well, it saves me the trouble of executing them for treason. Hopefully it will serve as

an example of what happens when one plots against me. Don't you think so?"

"Yes...my lord."

"Getting the prisoners back is now in the hands of our scouts. And the fate of the Aguerius family is now in their own hands. My protection for them is ended. As soon as the situation is resolved, we'll abandon this base."

ALMAS WAS WITH BOSHA when he realized their escape had hit its first obstacle. They caught up to the group gathered in front of a large metal door.

"It's locked," one of the women said in despair.

"Snipies!" Bosha swore. "Where is Lemuem?"

"I...don't know, he was just here!"

"He left us!"

Almas searched the room while walking to the door. It was a small room with two passages going out of it, not counting the door. Had Lemuem abandoned them by going out the other passage? He checked the door, but it was locked and looked far stronger than the bars on the cell. Breaking it down wasn't an option.

Almas was sure that this was the door to the exit – a fortified gate that trapped them in as well as keeping the liches' enemies out. He was looking at the lock when he noticed a familiar smell. He didn't have much time to think about it because he heard footsteps running from the other passage.

At first, he thought it might be Lemuem but realized immediately that he couldn't be running. It turned out to be Deleta, who appeared at the entrance with his sword drawn. He smiled in triumph once he saw all the escaped prisoners.

"Going somewhere?" he asked in a gloating voice.

"Yes," Bosha answered, "we decided it's time to leave. Now kindly unlock the doors and we'll leave you alive."

Deleta laughed at the threat, "I have a better idea. All of you go back to your cell now and you might live to the end of the day."

Things were about to get bloody. If his suspicions about the smell were correct, then all they needed was a little more time. It was time to stall and see how strict the rule against killing him was. Taking a deep breath, Almas stepped between Bosha and Deleta.

"None of us are going back so if you are going to start killing people, you will have to start with me."

Almas watched Deleta's face as Bosha protested Almas' interfering and demanded him to step back. But Almas didn't move. Deleta hesitated with doubt passing momentarily across his face. Then he smiled and said, "In your case I only need to make sure I cause no permanent damage."

Well, so much for that idea. Deleta took another step forward while Almas searched his mind for another idea. Bosha stepped in front of Almas and raised the bar he held, ready for a fight. However, the fight never came. Deleta was hit by another bar from behind without warning. He crumpled to the ground and revealed Lemuem standing behind him.

"Lemuem!" Almas exclaimed, "We thought..."

"I had left you all?" He grinned, "When we hit the locked door, I knew this one would catch up, so I had to find a hiding spot and plan an ambush quick."

Using his bar for support, he lowered himself and took Deleta's sword and dagger from him. He fastened the dagger and sheath to himself and standing back up he held the sword over Deleta to finish him off. Almas, realizing what he was doing, stepped forward and grabbed his arm before he could strike, yelling, "No, wait!"

"He's a Kadus Knight," Lemuem responded calmly.

"He's also my cousin," Almas whispered back, then he added, "Please leave him and let's just go."

"We still need to get past that door," Lemuem reminded him.

"I think that's being taken care of. Bosha, would you give it a try," Almas responded.

Lemuem reluctantly put the sword away and kept guard on the two rear entrances while Almas and Bosha went to the main door. As Bosha used a strength burst to open the door, he heard a loud snap on the other side, and it opened.

"How did...?" Bosha started to ask as Almas helped open the door and found a slime attached to the outside of it over the lock.

"Metal!" Almas exclaimed and began pulling the slime off the door.

"Do you know that thing?" Bosha asked, eyeing the slime as Almas finished pulling it from the door.

"It's my friend's pet. Let's get everyone outside," Almas answered.

"Must be an interesting friend," Bosha replied as he motioned all the other escapees to follow him.

Everyone followed Bosha to the outside as Almas scanned the room beyond the door. Metal was here but no Ulec. He quickly spotted Ulec's shoulder bag and went over to retrieve it. Why would he leave Metal in the room and not be nearby?

As Almas put on the bag, he was only slightly aware of the rest of the prisoners leaving when he noticed a pile of weapons in the corner nearby. The pile consisted of various swords, daggers, axes, and a bow. They looked familiar so he stepped over to them. He picked up the bow, which looked like his father's. It was the one that he nearly always saw his father carry, he was sure of it. The battle axe nearby looked like the one belonging to his Uncle Jerad. If they were also here, why did they leave their weapons here? Were they captured or in trouble?

Almas felt panic rising when suddenly a voice came to his mind, "*Your father and friends are fine. You need to leave now!*"

Almas gasped and dropped the bow. It was a fielis! His father's bow was a fielis!

"Come on Almas, we're the last ones!"

Lemuem grabbed Almas with his free hand and moved towards the entrance with the speed of a whole man.

"But–" Almas started to say but he couldn't find the words to protest as Lemuem pulled him outside. Almas had once found a fielis, a magical object with a soul of its own. Though the one he had met had the worst personality.

Reaching the outside Almas heard Lemuem mumble a curse. Becoming alert to his surroundings, he saw the other prisoners heading west along the mountainside while revenants were coming out of the forest from the east and south.

"Quickly go with the group," Lemuem said as he pushed Almas in the direction the rest of them were going.

"Wait, what about you?"

"I'll slow them down. You go help Bosha get the others out of here."

Almas hesitated. He couldn't possibly leave a cripple to face revenants alone. The first revenants were reaching Lemuem, who pulled out the dagger he had taken from Deleta and lifted the bar he had been using as a crutch and balanced himself on one foot. Almas then saw the most amazing thing. Hopping and balancing with just one foot, Lemuem fought with just as much speed and nimbleness as a warrior that wasn't crippled.

He hopped, dodged, parried, and struck without once losing balance, slowly giving up ground. But more and more revenants were surrounding him, and Almas knew he would soon be overwhelmed by sheer numbers. It was then that Ulec arrived.

Lemuem had moved back under a tree and Ulec just noiselessly landed next to him, pulled Deleta's sword from the scabbard Lemuem had strapped to his side, dodged the ranger's startled counterattack, and with lightning speed took out two revenants.

"Ulec!" Almas shouted.

"Where did you come from!?" Lemuem demanded instantly, going back to his fight with the revenants.

"He's a friend, don't worry," Almas responded.

"I figured that out. I asked where in the demonic pit he came from! No one's ever snuck up on me before!"

Ulec ignored Lemuem and shouted to Almas, "Take Metal to where the others are. The revenants have us surrounded."

"But..." Almas started to protest.

"Go now!" Ulec insisted.

Almas turned and ran. Ulec was right. Bosha was protecting a couple dozen people by himself so he could use all the help he could get.

He didn't have far to run before finding Bosha swinging his bar like a madman with the rest of the prisoners 20 feet behind him at the base of a cliff.

Bosha was taking down revenants with each swing but just like Lemuem was before, he was getting mobbed quickly, and this time he was sure Ulec wouldn't be dropping out of any trees.

Almas reached a spot between Bosha and the rest of the escaped prisoners, thinking quickly about how he could help. Two revenants broke off and started towards him. Remembering what Ulec had done a few days earlier, Almas grabbed the bottom of Metal's shoulder bag and whipped the bag in front of him, flinging the slime at the nearest revenant. The revenant raised its sword, but Metal was already spraying a stream of acid at the revenant's head. The revenant crumbled to dust and Metal shot another stream of acid reducing the second revenant to dust also.

"Almas! Go help the group!"

Looking to the source, Almas saw Bosha completely surrounded by over a dozen revenants. He was purely on the defensive using the length of the bar to keep the revenants as far from him as possible.

Another group of revenants were moving in on the remaining prisoners from the side. Almas looked around desperately for ideas, but he knew they were hopelessly outnumbered, and he had no weapons. His heart sank as he realized he had failed these people. He had brought them hope only to get them all killed. Then he heard a hawk shriek.

Looking up, he saw a hawk diving at the group of revenants heading towards the prisoners. It landed right in front of the advancing Undead and changed into Seacra, who shot one of the revenants with a magic bolt from her hand and yelled something at them in elvish. Then as the remaining revenants closed in on her, she turned into a forest dragon. Before they could react, she knocked the undead creatures aside with one sweep of her tail, banging them hard into the side of the cliff.

Almas cheered, "That's it! Go Seacra!"

"Almas! Move, curse it all!"

Bosha had broken free of the group of revenants and was slowly retreating towards Almas and the others.

"How'd you break free?" Almas asked as he started backing up.

"The slime attacked from the bushes. That's one clever little – watch out!"

Almas looked to his left and found three revenants only a few paces from him coming at him with raised swords. Almas only managed to take a step back when a voice behind the revenants called out.

"Almas, down!"

Almas knew that voice well and responded more out of reflex than anything else. He just let himself drop to the ground and a golden blade of magic cut down two of the revenants and passed over him. Meanwhile the third revenant fell forward with a throwing axe sticking out of the base of its neck.

Looking up Almas saw his father and his Uncle Jerad jogging up to him.

"Father!"

Jerad spoke first, jogging past Almas saying, "Sorry about that. Those three got away from us."

His father bent down and helped Almas up as Jerad went over to Bosha to help out.

"Nice party you have going on here, son. Mind if we play too?" Gidon asked with a smile.

"Father you're... you're... smoking!?"

Almas could see his father's clothes were singed and there was some light smoke coming off of them.

Gidon didn't miss a beat and responded, "Thanks, you should've seen Ulec's father down there. He was really on fire. Now go over to where everyone else is. We'll take it from here."

GIDON DIDN'T WASTE any time. He sized up the situation and started giving orders.

"Seacra seems to have the west side taken care of. Jerad has southwest, I have south, Bosha has southeast, and Lemuem take the east. Where is Ulec?"

"That would be anyone's guess. I tried to put a magic mark on him to keep track of him and ended up tracking a tree stump. That kid is like a ghost or something," Lemuem answered.

"Is that him by the dragon?" Bosha asked.

Sure enough, there was Ulec right by Seacra and fought a few moments with her right before she turned back into an elvish girl and collapsed for no reason he could see.

Gidon cursed and prayed that the girl was ok. He tried his best to keep tabs on everything as he took down two revenants with his sword and three more with a blast of holy magic. Stealing a glance over to where the two elvish children were, Gidon saw Ulec was fighting off the revenants Seacra had left; meanwhile Almas had dashed over there and was pulling Seacra out of danger, giving Gidon the dilemma of praising his son for bravery later or knocking him upside the head for putting himself in danger.

Gidon cut down another group with another blast of magic, but it seemed for every revenant they took down three more arrived. One bit of good news was they were not using the bones growing out of their arms. It would seem they were interested in taking them alive rather than turning them into revenants.

Glancing at the others, he figured they were seconds from being completely overwhelmed. He needed to buy time.

"Everyone, pull in close around the non-combatants," Gidon ordered.

"Do what!?" Lemuem asked incredulously.

"Just do it," Jerad barked back.

Everyone started retreating back and Gidon ordered everyone to get as close together as they could. Just as everyone came together, Gidon knelt on the ground, thrust his sword into the dirt and bowed his head. Instantly a transparent golden dome appeared over everyone. Some of the revenants attacked but were repelled and burned by the dome.

"So, this is the Paladin's Holy Shield," Lemuem mused. "How long can you hold it up?"

"Not long," Gidon muttered, already feeling his magic reserves getting low. Protecting so many at once helped slow down the drain, but he couldn't hold long. Hopefully Teaneas was as powerful as legend said, and hopefully he'd catch up soon.

The revenants stopped attacking the shield which also helped slow the drain and Gidon saw a Lich Lord approaching through the revenants. Seeing he had a few seconds, he quickly asked, "What happened to Seacra?"

"She used a lot of magic flying us here. She was supposed to rest; not fight. She over did it, but I think she'll be ok," Ulec answered.

Gidon nodded and said, "She saved a lot of lives here. She's a brave girl."

The Lich Lord approached close enough to address the group, "That was a bold attempt, but I think it's time this ended. Put your weapons down and submit."

"No, thanks," Gidon answered with a smile. "We're quite comfortable right here. Was thinking of building a homestead, maybe a workshop over where you're standing."

"You're wasting your wit on the wrong person. We both know you can only keep that shield up for a few moments longer. If you expect help from your friend inside, I wouldn't count on him getting out any time soon."

Was it possible they got Lord Teaneas? From the stories told about him, Gidon thought it unlikely, but he couldn't be sure. What he was sure of was the liches would eventually kill everyone here whether they surrendered or not. If Teaneas wasn't coming, they would be overwhelmed easily unless he could kill the lich and in so doing all the revenants belonging to it. But the lich was no fool; it kept a wall of revenants between them.

Gidon was thinking furiously when he heard Ulec utter an "oh no" behind him. At first, he was concerned something might be wrong with Seacra, but looking at the boy he saw Ulec's gaze was focused upward.

"What is it, Ulec? More trouble heading our way?" He asked.

"Yeah, big trouble. For me anyway."

Another hawk swooped down between the revenants and Gidon's shield and changed into Lady Alixia as it landed. She stepped forward towards the magic shield, her eyes a storm of rage. She raised her hand to the shield and with a burst of light from her hand, Gidon's shield shattered and Gidon was thrown back feeling like he had just got hit by a tree. Jerad caught and steadied him. Everyone, including the lich, stared in shock as Alixia walked up to Ulec who had handed Seacra over to Almas and faced his mother with an impassive face.

"How dare you sneak out and disobey me! You are in no condition to be out and about, let alone be fighting. What happened to your sister?"

Ulec glared at his mother for a moment then answered, "She over-exerted herself magically, but I think she'll be fine. Father is still fighting down the tunnel east of here if you care at all."

Alixia's hand moved faster than Gidon could track but Ulec staggered and red marks from where his mother had slapped him began appearing instantly. For an instant Gidon saw the same shock on Alixia's face as on everyone else. Almost instantly she composed herself. And apparently so did the Lich Lord.

"If I'm not interrupting, I was demanding a surrender."

Alixia answered without even turning her head to the undead army behind her, "Rynos, take your abominations and leave."

The revenants raised their weapons and began to advance as Rynos started to say, "Do you really dare to dictate to m–"

Alixia's form changed to that of a male elf and tapped the toe of her right foot behind her left foot. A small crack shot out from the spot she tapped, went under the advancing revenants right to Rynos, who only had time to take a surprised step backwards before the crack reached him and he disappeared in a pillar of magical energy that erupted from the ground under him.

In a moment the Lich Lord was gone, and the revenants crumbled to dust. Alixia resumed her natural form and shaking her head said, "His father was a fine warrior who would've been sorely disappointed."

Alixia then brought her focus back to Ulec and said, "Your arm is bleeding again."

"It's fine," Ulec responded, only glancing a moment at the bandages on his shoulder that was now turning bright red.

"What's more, you haven't recovered completely from your concussion. You could have passed out."

"I said I'm fine!" Ulec growled.

Alixia just sighed and said, "Gidon, I suggest you take your people and leave. I will take care of things here," as she turned and started towards the entrance to the Undead base.

"I'll stay with them while you get father," Ulec stated matter-of-factly. "We'll see to Seacra, too."

Alixia stopped a moment then without looking back answered, "Very well," and continued.

As she walked away Ulec turned to Gidon and said, "We need to go now." and then taking his shoulder bag from Almas, went over to some nearby bushes and picked up Metal out of them and dropped the slime into the bag.

Gidon took the moment to do a quick examination of his son. From the condition of his clothes. He should've had a serious injury to his chest but there wasn't even so much as a scar on him. He'd have to question why Lich-El had spared his son later. Right now, he was just relieved to have him back. Standing up, Gidon ordered Jerad to take Seacra and told everyone else to follow him.

THEY HAD ONLY GONE a couple hundred yards when roars began filling the air. Glancing back Almas saw thick, black smoke rising from the direction of the cave entrance, along with a small burst of flame appearing in the smoke. Turning to Ulec who was beside him, he mumbled, "Is she helping your dad or trying to kill him along with the Undead?"

Ulec said nothing, but Almas' father a few steps in front of them answered, "From what I saw earlier I don't think we have to worry about Lord Teaneas. I'm beginning to see how they were so successful fighting together in the War of Destruction. Their abilities complement each other. What was in your father's cloak that burned like that?"

"The same stuff that dragons make to breathe fire – only concentrated. My father's magical gift is power over fire. So yes, he's the only one able to fight near my mother without risking his own life. Her attacks aren't very selective."

"I've noticed," Gidon responded.

Ulec then whispered to Almas, "If you're worried about the Knight you left in the tunnel, he made it to safety."

"How did you know about him?" Almas asked in a whisper.

Ulec smiled and responded, "I have my sources."

He then looked down at one of his pockets and Almas, following his gaze saw a small mouse climb out and scamper away."

Almas had wondered about Deleta but wasn't about to mention him in front of his father. He didn't think this was a good time to bring up his newfound cousin.

Suddenly the ground started shaking but it was over before most of them realized what was happening.

"What was that?" Jerad asked.

"I think," Ulec began slowly, "I think it was a cave-in in the tunnels."

"What about your parents?" Almas asked, noticing that the flames and roaring stopped with the earthquake.

"They're fine. The liches sealed the entrance as soon as my father was out. They should be here in a few seconds."

Sure enough, Almas could already hear the sound of large beating wings. Soon the form of a mountain dragon could be seen through the trees. Hanging from one of the dragon's legs was Teaneas.

Teaneas dropped to the ground nearby and then the dragon landed next to him and changed back to Alixia. Teaneas strode up to Gidon and asked, "Is everyone alright?"

"Yes," Gidon answered. "Lady Alixia's timing couldn't have been better. We are indebted to the both of you as well as your children."

"I'm happy all are well," Alixia said promptly. "Now it is time for us to leave. Teaneas, take Seacra. Ulec, let's go."

Go? Almas had a feeling she didn't mean go home or go for a walk. "Where are you going?"

"Away," Alixia answered. "I will not allow such an attack on my children again. It is no longer safe here."

"I'm not going," Ulec said softly.

"Nonsense. Now let me see to your shoulder and we will be off."

Alixia stepped towards Ulec, but Ulec grabbed his bandaged shoulder and raised his voice, "Don't touch me!"

Alixia stopped, which was less a reaction than everyone else showed who took a step or two away from Ulec. Along with his raised voice and fierce look in his eyes, Almas could suddenly feel magic around Ulec stronger than he had ever felt before. For just an instant Almas thought he might have seen a look of fear cross Lady Alixia's face.

Finally, Alixia responded, her voice softer, "You don't understand."

"I do understand some things better than you," Ulec responded, his voice also softer but still radiating power. As Ulec continued, Teaneas stepped up to his son who offered no protest as he began fix the bandaging on Ulec's shoulder.

"I can see clearly, Mother, what is coming. The Lich Lords are not doing one of their raids. I can see them now gathering in dozens of locations. They are getting ready for something big, and it looks like they will do it soon. I will not leave while they kill my friends. I also have a responsibility to the forest. I can't just leave it in a war."

Ulec seemed to be in a trance now. He often gathered information from the plants and animals of the forest, but Almas had never seen him look so distant.

Alixia now looked a little worried. "Calm down son. You will hurt yourself."

"I'm not leaving."

"War is no place for children. And this is not our war."

"Alixia," Teaneas had finished adjusting Ulec's bandage and stepped towards his wife. "A moment please."

Alixia gave Teaneas a foul look but followed him a few paces to speak with him. Meanwhile Ulec seemed to calm down. The magic that had seemed to surround him before disappeared, and he suddenly looked tired.

"Are you okay?" Almas asked him.

Ulec nodded and answered, "I'm fine."

Almas thought he still sounded tired but didn't argue with him. After a few moments Seacra, who was still being held by Jerad, started to stir. Ulec was to her first as Jerad gently put her on the ground.

"What happened?" she asked sleepily.

"You overdid it and collapsed. I told you, you needed rest," Ulec reprimanded.

"Almas?"

"I'm here."

"We are all here safe because of you," Gidon added. "You were very brave and saved my son's life and the life of others. I'm indebted to you."

"He saved me first," she murmured, still not fully awake.

"I think we should let her rest some more," Gidon said as he patted Almas on the shoulder and pulled him into a one-armed hug.

Normally Almas would have been embarrassed by the show of affection in front of everyone, but this time he didn't care. He couldn't think of anything better than knowing his dad was proud of him.

The sound of Alixia clearing her voice brought their attention back to her.

"After discussing it with my husband, I've decided that Seacra will come with me as I attend to some business elsewhere. Ulec may remain with you if he chooses for the time being as long as Teaneas stays with him."

"Then I choose to stay," Ulec said.

"Let me finish," Alixia said giving her son a scolding look. "You may stay till my business is done. Then we will discuss where to go from there. You will mind your father in all he decides."

Ulec thought a moment and answered, "Alright."

"It is settled then. We will accompany you back and once Seacra has recovered completely, we will go."

As soon as Lady Alixia finished, it was Ulec's turn to collapse. Lord Teaneas gently caught him and picked his son up.

"Is he okay?" Almas asked with alarm.

Lord Teaneas smiled at him and answered, "He'll be fine, although it wouldn't surprise me if he slept a day or two. He was most certainly pushing his limits. Just let him rest a bit."

"Okay," Almas responded. Part of him was glad that Ulec was staying, but he couldn't forget what Lich-El had told him. He just had this feeling that something horrible was waiting in the future. Maybe it was just the creepy, death-like feeling he had felt since he had been taken, but he wanted to believe that things would work out now. He was, after all, back with family and friends. Things would be better once he got home.

"Well, if everything is settled, shall we get going? This place feels creepy, and I'm ready to get home."

Escape through the Sacred Forest

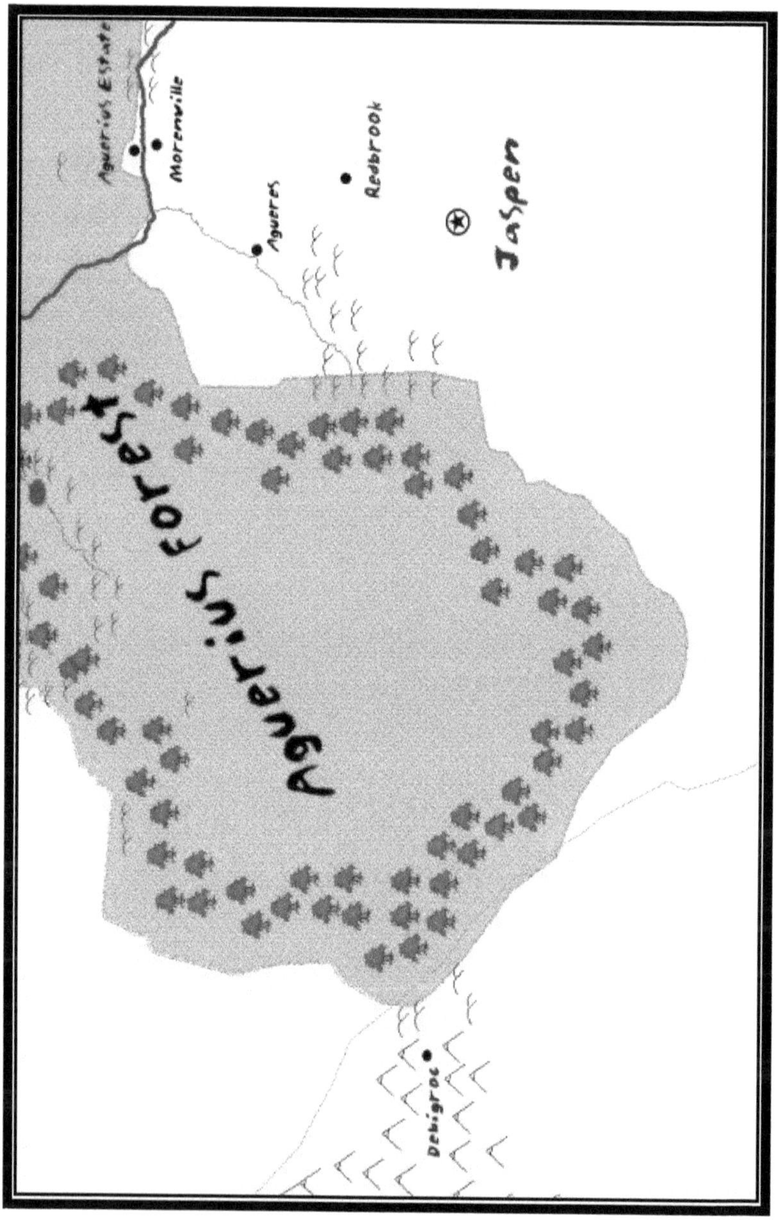
Aguerius Estate
Morenville
Redbrook
Agueres
Jaspen
Aguerius Forest
Debigroc

Chapter 1

"LORD AGUERIUS MUST not be allowed to take command of an army."

"He can't if he is dead. Such a small force shouldn't be that hard to wipe from the face of the land."

"Do not underestimate him or Lord Teanas. Simply delay him. First, we will destroy his army, then we can worry about the more difficult tasks."

CREETAN FELT HIS STOMACH twist into a knot as he pulled back on the arrow that he had notched into the string of his bow. Just a week earlier archery had been nothing more than an activity. Now he found himself in a line of fellow archers; spread out and watching a force of undead revenants approaching.

He resisted the urge to once again look behind him to where his mother and siblings were taking shelter with the rest of the non-combatants – wishing for all he was worth that he was a couple years younger and could be cowering with them.

It had only been a few days since his father had returned from Demon Mountain after having rescued his younger brother, Almas, from the Lich Lords. One of his scouts had sent word ahead of the imminent attack and, as soon as his father and brother arrived, preparation had been made for everyone in the town of Morenville and the Aguerius estate to begin their journey for the protection of the city of Jaspen, capital of the Aguerius Province.

The day before they had been joined by refugees from the towns of Redbrook and Aguares bringing the number of the company to several hundred, but with only a few dozen guards to defend them.

It was only a few minutes ago that Ulec, Almas' elvish friend, had alerted them of the undead's impending attack. Creetan's father had only taken a few seconds to put together a defense and assigned positions to everyone trained with a weapon.

"Archers take aim!" He heard his father call out. Creetan glanced down the defense line and saw his father mounted on the back of his armored forest dragon that he used as a war mount, aiming his own bow. His father was the only archer without any guardsmen; but then, being a weapons-master, he could handle himself just fine.

Creetan's hand shook badly as he waited for the order to fire. Suddenly a calming feeling came over him; his hand stopped shaking and he found himself able to focus better.

He then noticed the harp playing faintly behind him. That would be Almas. Their uncle had taught him to play, and more recently how to work magic through the playing of music. Creetan could see that the music had a similar effect on the other defenders and standing there, waiting for the order to release his arrow to begin the battle, he suddenly had a whole new appreciation for music.

"Release!" Creetan heard his father command.

Releasing his arrow, he watched it shoot out with arrows from the other archers before finding its mark and causing one of the revenants to crumble to dust. Out of the corner of his eye he saw a beam of light erupt out from where his father was mounted and disintegrate a whole line of the undead attackers. His father's powers as a paladin were also useful.

Nocking another arrow, he quickly shot it at one of the revenants approaching him and his guards. He took out four more before the pair of swordsmen assigned to protect him were forced to meet a group of three. Creetan continued firing at other groups of advancing creatures until he suddenly felt a wave of heat crash into him from behind. Glancing back, he saw a pillar of fire rising from behind the hill where the non-combatants were taking refuge.

That would be Lord Teanas, Ulec's father, ambushing the large group of undead that were trying to sneak up on them. While Ulec could speak to animals and plants, his father had the power to control fire. It looked like he had unleashed a flaming whirlwind on the undead on the other side of the hill.

"Creetan look out!" A voice near him warned.

Turning around he found a revenant right next him moving to strike! Creetan barely dodged as he struggled to pull out his short sword. He got it out just in time to block a second strike which knocked him off balance and he fell backwards to the ground. Looking up he saw the revenant holding its sword above him ready to finish him when suddenly it began to crumble to dust. The sword dropped but a hand caught it before it could fall on him.

"Get up and pay attention to the battle before you, not the one behind."

This was Ulec. As usual the elvish child had come from nowhere. While he looked to be no older than his twelve-year-old brother, Creetan knew the boy was over a hundred years old and had the fighting skills to go with decades of training. As was his custom he wore no shoes and even in battle he had his shoulder bag in which he kept his pet slime, named Metal.

Using the sword, he had caught he took out two more nearby revenants with lightning speed before flinging the sword into a revenant that was about to kill one of Creetan's guards. A stream of acid came from his shoulder bag, into the face of yet another undead which began to instantly melt. He then pulled a knife from the sheath that another revenant was wearing as it fought Creetan's other guard. Striking the revenant, he again caught a falling sword and tossed it to the first guard as he got to his feet.

Ulec then took off through the crowd of fighting men and monsters looking like a child running through a crowd at a fair, only everywhere he went revenants would start tuning to dust as he ran past them.

Embarrassed, Creetan scanned the battle nearby. The undead that had made it pass the line of defenders were being intercepted by a few warriors mounted on forest dragons, keeping them away from the women and children.

Creetan spotted two revenants pass by his guards and head his way. This time he was better prepared and had proper footing as the creatures attacked; he blocked the strike from the first one to reach him and stepped around the revenant in order to keep it between him and the second one. This allowed him to get two quick strikes in; the first one being blocked and his second finding the creature's head and reducing it to dust.

The remaining revenant attacked through the dust of its companion and Creetan felt its sword graze his leather armor as he side-stepped the attack. He countered with his own sword and the creature joined the first as a pile of dust.

Scanning the battle, he saw the undead creatures pulling back.

"Warriors, hold your ground; archers, fire freely," Creetan heard his father order.

After sheathing his sword, he picked up his bow from where it had fallen and dropped three more revenants before they were out of range.

It took a few moments for him to realize that they had won and were safe. There was silence except for the sound of his brother's harp which then faded. A cheer went up from the defenders but as soon as the music stopped the fear and uncertainty Creetan had felt before the battle returned. He dropped to his knees, fighting to keep his last meal in.

"Creetan!" He heard someone call. Looking over he saw Almas running towards him and Creetan instantly had mixed emotions, embarrassment that all the focus and ability he showed in his first battle was because of his brother's bardic abilities, and also gratitude for the fact that those abilities probably saved his life.

"Are you okay?" Almas asked as he approached and offered Creetan a hand to help him to his feet.

"I'm fine...and thanks," Creetan responded as he took his little brother's hand and stood up.

"For what? All I did was play my harp and try to help everyone focus," Almas said.

"Well, it worked. I couldn't even string my arrow right, my hand was shaking so badly before you started playing," Creetan responded.

"You still did very well for your first fight," a young voice piped up.

Creetan jumped a little at Ulec's voice. The elvish boy was standing right next to him and as usual with Ulec, he hadn't noticed him until he spoke.

"Right, I was a half second from getting my head chopped off. One fight and I already owe my life to two children who don't even come up to my shoulders."

"At least you didn't twist your leg, almost get eaten by a forest dragon and get your life saved by a slime and a human infant." Ulec said matter-of-factly, referring to his own first life or death fight.

"Hey, I was eight, not an infant!" Almas retorted.

"To an elf, you're still an infant."

"Don't forget that this 'infant' is an inch taller than you."

Ulec gave Almas a mischievous grin but then his face grew serious as he turned towards a group of guards several hundred feet away. "Two of the guards were hurt pretty bad, I think they'll make it, but they are in a lot of pain."

"Who?" Almas asked with sudden concern.

"Jestin and Torley."

"I should see if there is anything I can help with," Almas said as he hurried away.

Creetan marveled at the change in his younger brother in the past couple of weeks. Almas had barely noticed the guards around the Aguerius estate before he was kidnapped by the Lich Lords; now in just a few days he had learned each of their names and most of the names of their family members. He spent all his time as they traveled getting to know them.

Ulec seemed to read his mind and commented, "He blames himself for the death of the two guards that were killed the day he was taken by Tornal."

The sound of Almas' harp could once again be heard coming from where the injured men were being tended to. Creetan felt all the aches and pains from the scratches and bruises he got from the battle instantly disappear.

After listening to his brother play for a moment Creetan started to say something about the deaths not being Almas' fault when a horn in the distance started to sound a series of short and long bursts.

"I never did figure out your father's code. What are they saying?" Ulec asked.

"Jaspen is under attack," Creetan answered dazed. Jaspen was the only fortified city in the area, and with undead forces attacking it, they were trapped!

Chapter 2

"LORD LICH-EL WARNED you not to underestimate them!"

"They will pay for this; I will go myself and personally watch the life drain from their faces!"

"Lord Lich-El's orders were..."

"Lord Lich-El isn't here! He went to deal with Jaspen. I am in command here now. We will leave immediately."

"We?"

"Yes, you and some of your men. What better way to kill an Aguerius than with an Aguerius?"

"WE CAN'T TAKE OUR WIVES and children into the middle of a battle!"

"We can't leave them out here in the open either, and we have nowhere else to go; we are completely boxed in!"

High Lord Gidon Aguerius had called a quick meeting of all his men after the horns had alerted them that Jaspen was under attack. He was letting his men give their opinions as he tried to determine his own.

If it was just them, he would have led them right to Jaspen's aid, but they had several towns' worth of families with them, depending on them for protection. On the other hand, they were completely exposed where they were.

"Our only option right now is to find a defensible position, dig in, and hope the siege is broken," Gidon said.

"That won't work," a young voice spoke up.

Everyone turned to the source of the voice to find Ulec sitting on the ground, with one leg extended and the other folded against his chest, right at the outskirts of the group of men. Next to him was a gray puddle happily making a meal of a revenant's sword. Almas could be seen several feet back at a more respectable distance with an uncomfortable look as he watched.

"Almas!" Gidon's second-in-command, Jarad spoke sharply, "Please take your friend and leave–"

"It's fine Jarad let him speak," Gidon interceded as he nodded to Almas to also approach; both boys while young had fought or acted bravely in battle and had earned a spot in the planning.

Ulec continued immediately, "The city's walls were breached badly a few minutes ago. The city is being overrun as we speak. The defenders are engaged in a fighting retreat towards the keep."

"They couldn't have breached the walls so quickly!" one soldier exclaimed in disbelief while another demanded to know how he knew.

Ulec's father spoke up, "My son has far reaching vision, and he was the one that alerted us to the recent attack. As far as the wall being breeched, Lich-El could easily bring down those walls in moments."

Ulec nodded in confirmation, then looking at Gidon said, "Your men there are going to use the passage to evacuate everyone taking refuge in the keep."

"What passage?" Another soldier asked.

"After the fall of the Valen Province I ordered secret escape passages from all major cities and towns in this province. It should give the people a chance to flee. Sadly, we don't have one here and our position is even more perilous. We are completely alone now and surrounded," Gidon answered.

"Cross the forest into the Forjad Province," Almas spoke up for the first time.

"Sorry Almas," Teanas responded immediately, "but the southern part of Aguerius Forest is strictly off limits, the forest won't tolerate trespassers here as it does in the north.

Almas looked nervously at Ulec who seemed withdrawn. After a few moments Ulec looked up to Gidon and said, "If everyone stays together, and on the path provided, then they will be permitted to enter long enough to cross over to the city of Debigroc; but anyone leaving on their own, or that goes out of sight of the path, would do so under pain of death. I wouldn't be able to save them."

"Ulec, I don't think this is a good idea," Teanas cautioned his son.

"Tornal attacked the forest, as well as Almas, Seacra and me while under the forest's protection. Because we all have a common enemy, we can allow this under the conditions given," Ulec responded and looking his father in the eye said with authority, "It's my choice to make."

Almas' eyes grew wide and even Gidon raised an eyebrow. In all the years he had known Ulec, this was the closest to disrespect he had ever seen the young elf show towards his father.

"Very well," Teanas said not showing any acknowledgement to Ulec's tone.

For the first time ever, Gidon realized that Ulec, despite his age, had supreme authority over the sacred forest. Even Teanas deferred to his son's decisions concerning it. Was it the boy's power over living things that gave him such authority? Gidon felt there was much more to this than was apparent. All these years he had known them there was still so much he didn't understand.

Suddenly Gidon realized all eyes were on him waiting for his decision. He would have to consider these things later.

"I think crossing the forest is the only choice we have. Notify the families under your care and make sure they all understand the rules Ulec gave us. We head west in twenty minutes."

"You might want to leave sooner," Ulec said looking as if he had come into himself again, "A large force of revenants and Kadus Knights are marching from the same direction as the last group, and I think they are headed towards us.

Chapter 3

"IT SEEMS THAT LORD Gidon has learned from the past."

"The people in the keep?"

"Gone. Everywhere we go the people seem to melt away. Lord Aguerius was ready; not to fight us, but to run and hide."

"The coward."

"Believe that and you will deserve your fate. Where is he now?"

"Heading west; towards the border of the forest."

"Really? Then he is out of our reach for now."

"Maybe not, Ormeun has gone after him."

"Ormeun should pay better attention to his enemies. Gidon knows you never fight your enemies on their terms."

ALL GIDON'S EXPERIENCE told him to find another defensible position and fight off the pursuing undead. Right now, they were just a long line of exposed people moving at the best pace the old and the young of the group could muster.

Ulec insisted that if they continued as they were that they would reach safety in time, but the woodland began to thicken as they approached the border of the sacred forest, and he couldn't help but worry.

As Gidon helped the line of refugees move forward he found Ulec leaning against a tree watching the road weary people pass by. He had what most would describe as a sullen expression, but Gidon knew the young elf well enough to know that it was the expression he had whenever his mind was elsewhere among the plants and animals.

Almas was pacing nearby showing the anxiety that his friend didn't. Gidon felt a pang of sorrow at how his second born seemed to have aged several years in the past week. The worries of a man now creasing his face. Yet he couldn't dwell on it. Right now, the physical safety of his children was more important than the emotional. He could worry about healing those scars when his family was safe.

"Ulec," Gidon addressed the elvish boy, "my scouts report that the undead forces will overtake the rear of our column before they reach the border of the forest."

Ulec didn't even look up as he answered, "I know–I'm working on it."

"Working on what?"

"Slowing them down," Ulec said with a smile slowly spreading across his face. Finally looking up he added, "We were caught by surprise last time. This time the forest will be ready. The front of the column is getting close to the border, we should move up the line."

Ulec turned and walked off at a quick pace towards the front of the line of refugees. Gidon glanced at Almas who just shrugged and went to follow. Gidon couldn't help but ask himself why elves had to be so mysterious all the time.

As he moved to catch up with the boys, he heard wolf howls, and it was only a few moments later he caught a glimpse of a large pack of wolves running in the opposite direction of the refugees.

"Are those dire wolves?"

Gidon looked back and noticed Lamuem nearby shepherding a group of children. The ranger had taken it on himself to keep an eye on the large group of children rescued from Demon Mountain. Izybel had fitted him with a peg leg a few days ago and the ranger was already walking without crutches and as fast as any man still with both legs.

Before Gidon could respond to the man's question; Almas, who had stopped to watch the wolves pass, asked, "Dire wolves?"

Nodding, Gidon answered, "Dire wolves are also called wolf lords. They are largest and smartest of all wolves. The god Mundial created animal lords to rule over the different kinds of animals. Most animal lords live in or near the sacred forests."

"They look like Crusty, just bigger."

Crusty was Almas' pet wolf that Ulec had given him to raise four years earlier. Almas had raised the wolf and it had been a constant companion to the boys along with Ulec's pet slime, Metal which the elf kept in his shoulder bag.

"That's because Crusty is a dire wolf. He's just a lot younger than those you see there. Come on, we need to catch up with Ulec."

Lemuem raised an eyebrow as they continued walking, "Your son has a pet dire wolf?"

"It's a long story, but yes, he was injured defending Almas; he went back into the forest right after we got back. I'm sure his pack in that part of the forest is taking care of him."

Walking at a brisk pace that forced Almas to part walk, part jog to keep up with his shorter legs, they soon reached the head of the column.

Ulec was ahead of the column with Lord Teanas standing near a wall of vegetation with a tunnel-like opening. Gidon motioned to several of his men to follow him and hurried ahead to where the two elves waited by what could only be the entrance to the sacred forest. He noticed that Lemuem and his flock of children kept pace behind them.

Ulec addressed Gidon as they arrived, "My father will lead the way. This is the most sacred part of the forest so make sure that everyone understands that they cannot leave the path. If anyone moves beyond sight of the path or the group, they will lose the protection granted them."

"Where will you be?" Gidon asked.

"The back of the column, the closer I am to the animals slowing down the revenants, the less strain the connection I have with them takes on me."

"I'll go with you," Gidon stated, and as Ulec nodded in agreement Gidon continued speaking before his son could ask the question he knew was coming, "Almas, you stay up here and help Lord Teanas and your mother."

Almas looked like he was about to argue but seemed to stop himself and simply nodded.

Gidon gave his son an appreciative nod before leaving with Ulec back towards the end of the column.

After walking in silence for a few minutes, Ulec spoke up, "Deleta is with the force attacking us."

Gidon sighed, he had only recently learned that his nephew was not only alive but was currently the leader of the Kadus Knights. They were living people that, for whatever reason, had pledged loyalty to the lich lords.

"Is there anything you can do for him?" Gidon asked.

"I can't stop the forest from defending itself. As long as he is fighting for the Lich Lords he is in danger–but I will do what I can."

They passed the end of the column and, far sooner than Gidon was comfortable with, he began to hear the sounds of wolves engaged in battle.

Gidon began moving more cautiously but Ulec continued to move with complete confidence. In no time they came across the scout that had been assigned to keep sight of the enemy.

"My lord," the scout said in surprise, "They are just beyond that grove of trees! You shouldn't be this close!"

"Thank you for your concern," Gidon said, "Report."

The scout gave a quick bow and reported, "They seem to be bogged down in the shrubbery, the wolves and other animals seem to be able to move almost unimpeded; which is taking a toll on the Lich's forces, but they just keep cutting their way through."

Gidon nodded and turning to face Ulec began, "What would you suggest–"

Of course, the elvish boy had slipped out of sight when he hadn't been looking. Gidon sighed and returned his attention back to the scout.

"Can you show them to me?"

The scout led him to a nearby mound with several trees. The spot provided both an elevated view and enough cover to let them view the approaching enemy without much risk of being spotted.

Both revenants and Kadus Knights were using swords to cut through thick shrubs. Gidon caught glimpses of movement under the cover of the plants and saw both a revenant and a knight suddenly drop out of sight and not return.

Gidon smiled–this was costing them, in both time and numbers.

Suddenly all the undead turned sharply to their right. Looking ahead along their path he saw Ulec's head above the top of the vegetation in the center of a group of five...wait, now four undead.

He couldn't see what Ulec was doing but within a few moments all the revenants nearby were gone and Ulec began to retreat back away from the undead and knights now converging on him.

The very fact that he could see him moving back told Gidon that Ulec was purposely drawing the enemy off.

"I think I've seen enough," Gidon said, "let's get heading back."

"Will the boy be okay?" Asked the scout with concern.

"As long as he doesn't have to worry about us, he can fade into the woods at will. Let's catch up with our people."

ALMAS HAD ALWAYS THOUGHT he knew Aguerius Forest. It turns out the small portion of the forest that had been his childhood playground was the most normal part of the forest. The western leg of it was nothing like what he was familiar with.

Shortly after entering the forest, it turned dark and scary. Both sides of the path were lined with brier bushes taller than Almas and the trees had almost no visible leaves.

Almas had seen Ulec make the forest look scary before, but this part was the creepiest woodland he had ever seen.

Then suddenly the forest seemed to open up and he saw another amazing sight. A grove of massive trees. They were tall with thick trunks and unbelievably thick branches. The branches stretched out and intertwined with branches and trunks of nearby trees.

Many of the intermingled branches were thick enough you could comfortably walk along them from tree to tree. In fact, the path they were following led right up to one such branch that had bowed down to the ground. The branch was wide enough that even the wagons could roll right up the branch, and with clusters of smaller branches lining the side of the large limb, they formed a kind of guardrail. Almas realized that this branch was part of the path.

He followed Lord Teanas up to where the path led onto the branch. The tip was buried so it made a perfect ramp that the wagons would have no trouble rolling onto.

Lord Teanas addressed Jarad, "Make sure everyone understands that from this point we must stay on the branches, if anyone falls off onto the ground it will be certain death."

Almas looked at the ground under the latticework of branches and noticed that just behind where the branch touched the ground that there was nothing on the forest floor. Aside from the trees, nothing grew; no plants or shrubbery. He couldn't even see so much as a fallen leaf or branch; just dead earth.

"Is there some kind of magic there?" asked Jarad.

"No those are firewater trees."

The speaker was Lemuem, but he didn't get a chance to say any more before Lord Teanas spoke up.

"We don't have time for further explanation. We have to get the people into the branches as quickly as possible."

With that he led the way up the branch. Jarad ordered a few men to spread warning about staying off the ground and then followed the elf lord. Lemuem told a few of the older children he had been taking care of to take the younger ones ahead and then he stood at the end of the branch as people and wagons began passing by up the branch.

"You're staying here?" Almas asked.

I think I know what your elf friends are planning and there is no way I'm missing this."

"What do you think they're planning?"

Lemuem flashed Almas a mysterious smirk, "Can't spoil a good surprise. Just wait here a bit.

Soon everyone had passed by except the rearguards who were just starting to insist that he and Lemuem move along after the rest when Almas saw his father, Ulec, and the remaining scouts arrive.

"They're only a few minutes behind us. Everyone hurry along," Almas' father said and then looking pointedly at his son asked, "Why are you still here?"

"That doesn't matter right now," Ulec interrupted, "Everyone on the branch."

Ulec was the last onto the large limb and had everyone move several feet up the branch while he stood on the end and closed his eyes.

Almas was worrying about how Ulec seemed to be getting paler and sicklier looking with each passing hour when he felt the ground underneath him suddenly yet slowly start moving. To his astonishment he realized the branch was beginning to rise.

It was slow at first, but the ground at the spot where the huge limb disappeared into the ground broke apart, as several feet of the branch that had been buried rose at an increasing rate.

"Now that's a trick," exclaimed Lemuem as the wood creaked and cracked its way higher and higher.

Soon the branch was high above the ground and beyond reach of the approaching undead and knights. Ulec turned around and motioned everyone to move back and soon they were all above the barren ground surrounding the enormous trunk of the tree. That was where Almas' friend leaped over the side of the branch that was turned upward making a natural guardrail.

Ulec landed on a small limb jutting out of the main branch and taking a few steps out stood balancing effortlessly facing back in the direction they had come.

Almas peered over the side and asked, "What are you doing?"

"I don't like watching people die without at least giving them a warning," Ulec responded.

Chapter 4

"THEY HAVE ENTERED THE forest."

"Then they are out of our reach for now."

"The children weren't out of my reach in the forest.

"Think of the losses you suffered in the most tame and tranquil part of the forest. They have entered Mundial's most holy land. During the War of Destruction, an entire fleet of Sky Chariots were sent to the heart of the sacred forest; none returned. The same will happen to anyone and anything that enters without permission."

ALMAS, LOOKING BACK, could now see forms approaching from amongst the vegetation. His father suddenly appeared right next to him partially blocking his view. A glance revealed his father looking down at him and the High Lord said in a serious tone, "Keep your head down."

Almas nodded and then peeked around his father and watched as the first of the revenants approached the boundary of the vegetation and the barren ground.

Before any could step over the boundary, Ulec called out, "That is far enough. You are commanded to proceed no further."

Amazingly the revenants stopped. After a moment of the undead army gathering behind the first line of still revenants, Almas noticed one moving through the crowd that was different.

Even from this distance Almas could see this one didn't have the same vacant look in its eyes that the rest had. This one had intelligence in them.

The Lich Lord moved its way through the army of revenants and knights, but stopped a few rows back from the front line, keeping several of its revenants between itself and the refugees in the tree.

"Who are you to command us?" The Lich bellowed out, eyeing the small elvish boy standing above it in the tree.

"I am the Guardian of the holy forest of Mundial. These people have been given sanctuary and you have been forbidden to enter," Ulec declared with surprising authority.

The Lich Lord smiled and answered, "Mundial is dead...and it will take more than you and a few animals to stop us."

"If you approach any further you will be destroyed," Ulec stated flatly and continued, "This is your last warning."

The Lich Lord said nothing. The only response was that the army resumed its march into the clearing.

Almas' father leaned a little more in front of Almas and Ulec just bowed his head and shook it sadly with his eyes closed.

Almas knew that once the undead reached the trunk of the tree they would be able to march right up the huge mound that made up the base of the tree right to the huge branches they and the other refugees were perched on. He was about to ask if it was wise to just be standing there when Lemuem spoke.

"That's it for them."

"What do you mean?" Almas asked.

Lemuem gave an evil grin and answered, "Just watch."

He turned his eyes back to the approaching army and saw the front lines stopping just at the edge of archery range; some were beginning to string their bows while the rear of the column was just crossing onto the clearing.

Suddenly, the Lich Lord got an alarmed look on his face and turned to look towards the back of the column. Almas looked just in time to see the back row of revenants suddenly crumble into dust. He also heard a muffled cry as one of the knights disappeared from view.

The army moved forward away from whatever was taking out the back rows as the second and most of the third row vanished.

"What's going on," Almas asked with some sense of alarm. The throng of undead and humans blocking his view of the back of the army.

Lemuem answered, "Look at the ground around the base of the tree and around the edge of the clearing."

Almas did and saw a dark shadow spreading outwards from the base of the tree and another one spreading inward from the outside edge of the clearing. As the shadow coming from the edge of the clearing reached a revenant or knight, they would in moments collapse in pain or crumple to dust.

"What is that?" Almas asked.

"Those," Lemuem said, "are ants."

"Ants?" Almas asked incredulously.

"Firewater Ants," Ulec confirmed as he looked down sadly at the doomed army below, "They will strip just about any animal to the bones in seconds and eventually the bones themselves in about a minute."

"I think we've seen enough", Lord Aguerius said as he started to turn Almas away.

Almas knew that by "we" his father was speaking about his son, that he had seen enough; and in this case he agreed. He started to let his father turn him away when he saw something, or more accurately he saw someone below he recognized.

"Deleta!"

He was near the lich lord gathering his knights away from the advancing shadows. Meanwhile the revenants were trying to use the flats of their weapons to try to sweep a path through the ants back to the edge of the clearing, but the ant's march was too swift. Dents made in the advancing insects' line filled almost instantly in and, more often than not, they overtook the revenant destroying it within seconds.

"Ulec!" Almas started.

Ulec just shook his head, "There is nothing I can do. Once the ants sense something on the ground above them they come out in a frenzy. I can't control them."

Suddenly all the revenants crumbled all at the same time and Almas realized that the lich lord, having his attention on the ants approaching from the edge of the clearing, had failed to notice the ones coming from the base of the tree which overtook him. With only time for a quick shout of surprise he was gone. Now only Deleta and a few of his knights remained.

Some tried to make it across the mass of ants by making long leaping steps out of the clearing, but the insects were too fast and even the few moments contact with the ground was enough for the ants to attack their feet and cause them to trip in pain to be swallowed up instantly by the shadow.

Deleta watched and with only seconds left yelled something to his remaining knights that Almas couldn't make out. Then, with what running start he could get, in the little room he had left, he leapt over the mass of ants. As he started to come down from his leap, he pulled his feet up under him and slipped his shield under his feet. He landed on the shield and slid a few moments before making another great leap off the shield and landing with a roll just outside the clearing onto safe ground.

One of his knights didn't leap far enough and another lost his balance on the shield, but three others made it to safety. Deleta checked on the other three survivors before looking up at Almas' group with a look of pure hatred. After a few moments' wolves could be heard howling nearby and at the insistence of his men he turned and fled with them towards the boundary of the forest.

"I'll give him this," Lemuem said, "the young man is smart. Few people have ever wandered under a firewater tree and lived to tell about it."

"How do you know about them," Almas asked.

"I've seen a few," Lemuem said with a shrug.

"The Ranger's Guild built their capital city in the trees of a firewater forest," Ulec stated as he rejoined the group on the main branch.

Lemuem glared. "No one outside the Ranger's Guild is supposed to know that."

Ulec shrugged and said, ignoring Lemuem, "We should catch up with the rest of the group. I shouldn't be too far from them.

Chapter 5

"CONGRATULATIONS ON surviving your visit to the forest of death. You seem a little more subdued than normal, your first close brush with death?"

"No, my lord, it's just that Ulec was with them, I had almost forgotten about him. Father had just told me about him and his family right before he died. We had started to become friends, I can't believe he was with them, that he actually tried to kill me."

"Do not mistake Ulec's ability to speak to the forest as being able to control it. Do not mistake the forest's action as his. Soon they will leave the forest and you will have another chance. Clear your mind, I will have a special task for you."

"Will I like this task?"

"No, my boy, I think you won't, but you are the only one I trust."

"SO, ALL THESE TREES have millions of ants under them?" Almas asked Ulec.

All the power Ulec had been radiating had faded and once again he seemed pale and frail–the strain on the elvish boy was obvious.

"They need each other," Ulec answered still a little out of breath, "The tree roots provide a source of food for the infant ants and the ants bring nutrients down to the roots."

"Why do they call them firewater trees?" Cady asked. She and Giddy had been walking with the two boys since they had caught up to the main group.

"The Ranger's Guild named them that because the sap of the tree catches fire as soon as it touches the air," he answered.

"Really?" Giddy exclaimed. "Wouldn't that catch the tree on fire?"

Ulec laughed, "Not easily. The bark is fireproof."

The refugees had been following the network of branches over the nearly barren ground among the enormous firewater trees for hours now. Almas was starting to wonder if they would have to camp for the night among the branches. He had asked Ulec if that would be the case. His friend had shaken his head and told him they would come out of the firewater trees a couple of hours before sunset.

So, they had continued mostly in silence. The exhaustion clear on the face of almost every refugee and soldier. When they finally stepped off the branch road onto solid ground, most people wanted to set camp right there. Ulec, however, recommended that they go just a little further, so no one accidentally wandered onto the ants' harvesting ground.

When they did set camp, most ate a small meal and went right to sleep. While Ulec assured Gidon that they were safe he still set up a watch around the camp. Wanting to maintain discipline.

In the morning Ulec showed the refugees a grove just outside the camp that was full of fruit trees and berry bushes. After eating their fill, they recommenced their journey.

Every time Almas thought he had seen the most beautiful part of the forest, he came to a newer and even more spectacular part of it. The lushness and colors were breathtaking. Again, the path they followed seemed to open before them and close behind them. The path itself was covered with soft grass that cushioned their aching feet, and yet allowed the wagons to roll freely.

Everyone seemed to be traveling much easier. Everyone that was except for Ulec. The elvish boy seemed paler and slower than he had before. He also seemed to be constantly out of breath. All the Aguerius children asked him several times throughout the day if he was okay, to which he responded he was just tired.

They stopped early that day. Ulec told them there would be another firewater tree grove coming up before they left the western part of Aguerius Forest and there would be no access to water if they camped further down the path.

That night Almas was wondering among the refugees as they were finishing supper. The people sat and ate in silence. They were tired, scared, and broken despite the beauty and safety that they were, for the moment, surrounded by.

"They need something to raise their spirit," he heard Ulec's voice next to him.

Almas turned to face his best friend. "What do you suggest we do?"

"We?" Ulec asked with a raised eyebrow. "I'm not the one trained as a bard here."

Almas sighed. He wished his uncle, an accomplished bard, was here. His friend was right, the people desperately needed the service of a bard. Sadly, he as an apprentice bard was the best that they had available.

Going back to his own family's campsite he quickly retrieved his ocarina. It and his lap harp were the only instruments they had brought with them.

"What are you doing?" Giddy asked as he started walking away with the ocarina.

"We need to get some life back into the people here. We need some music," he said.

He took a few more steps before he stopped. An idea had come to him. Turning around to face his younger brother and sister.

"Would you two like to help?"

Cady looked at him a little suspiciously. "How?"

"Remember that dance Uncle Marpel taught us last time he was here?"

"A little," Giddy answered not sounding very sure he liked where this was going.

"That's okay. I remember it and I can guide you both through the music if you let me," Almas said.

"I don't know," Cady said. "In front of everyone?"

"Look at them all," Almas said, "They need something to lift their spirits. Help them forget about our situation for a bit and remember what it's like to live. They need this."

The two children looked around at those families camping nearby. They looked at their bleak faces and with resigned looks they both nodded.

Almas found a small clearing on the edge of camp and took a couple minutes to plan out how he wanted everything to go. Once he had everything planned out in his head, he began playing his ocarina.

It was a slow peaceful tune, and, in the music, he put feelings of that peace and also hope into the music along with an invitation to come listen.

The music flowed out and the refugees responded. Some alone and some with their families or friends, but the music brought them.

After several minutes he finished the song. Seeing that most of the camp was there and not seeing any more coming he turned to Cady and Giddy.

"Alright, just let the music guide you and I'll take care of the rest."

His younger siblings both nodded nervously and went and hid in some bushes out of view. Once they couldn't be seen Almas put the ocarina to his lips once more. This time he started playing a playful, mischievous song.

Giddy skipped into view and once he got to the center of the clearing switched to doing cartwheels. He then moved seamlessly into spinning with his arms stretched outward and a look of carefree childish joy on his face.

Giddy continued to dance around the clearing swinging himself from low branches on the edge of the field, jumping like a frog over rocks and being the very image of a small boy playing in the woods.

Then the tune changed to a sterner sounding tune and Giddy flipped himself over a rock and hid behind it as Cady came into view moving from spot to spot as if she was searching for someone.

Whenever she turned away from Giddy's hiding spot the boy would roll, skip, cartwheel, or flip himself with a mischievous grin to a new hiding spot. Cady continued searching, always just missing catching a glimpse of her brother. At one point Giddy was behind a rock with Cady right on the other side looking for him. Almas hit a high note and magically prompted Giddy to rise at the same time Cady looked away. He then played a low note as Giddy ducked and Cady turned just missing sight of her brother. Almas alternated between the two notes as Giddy kept looking over the rock as Cady looked away and then ducking with each low note as his sister kept just missing sight of him.

This drew a laugh from the audience and Almas continued the song. He moved between the mischievous tune and the stern tune as the two children continued their antics and the crowd responding with more and more laughter and cheers. They continued with this for several minutes to the delight of the crowd.

Almas reached the last part of the song where Cady finally caught sight of Giddy and the tune changed to a faster pace to match the chase that the two siblings were enacting. Cady trying to lay hands on her brother as Giddy dodged, rolled, and used branches to swing away from his sister all the time smiling and laughing.

The song was supposed to end with Cady getting a hold of Giddy's arm and in time with the final staccato notes pull him to face her and in the last two notes first place her free hand on one shoulder and then with her other hand release Giddy's arm and grab his other shoulder firmly capturing him on the last note.

As Almas reached the last part of the song, another idea came to him. His siblings had given almost all control to him through the magic he was putting into the music. They could resist his magical suggestions but right now they were purposely letting him control them. So, as the last few notes played out, when Cady pulled Giddy to face her, Almas altered the end just a little. As Cady put her firsthand on Giddy's shoulder, Giddy raised his hand up to his face and plunged his finger into his nose. Then before either child realized what was happening Almas played the final note prompting Cady to grab her brother's other shoulder and prompting Giddy to remove his finger from his nose and smearing everything he pulled out of it onto Cady's shoulder with a grin.

As he realized what he had done, a look of embarrassed horror came over Giddy's face as Cady stared at her little brother first in shock and afterwards disgust. Then seeing Giddy's expression, she figured out what happened at the same time as Giddy. They both angrily turned to face their older brother and together yelled, "Almas!"

Almas was already fleeing at his fastest sprint, and with threats and promises of what they were going to do to him they took off in pursuit.

Throughout it all the audience roared with laughter and cheered. That sound, of happy people, sounded better to Almas than any music. It was definitely worth the bruises his siblings would undoubtedly inflict on him.

Chapter 6

"WHERE DID LICH-EL GO?"

"He left to keep track of Lady Alixia."

"He left as we are preparing to press our attack into another province?"

"Yes, he gave us our orders, and it wouldn't be good if she returned as we are approaching victory."

"Still, he has a way of vanishing right before battles."

"Would you like to trade jobs? Would you like to deal with Alixia?"

"No."

"Then go do your job."

CADY COULDN'T SLEEP. There were birds chirping loudly and apparently, they preferred to spend the night singing and keeping poor young refugees awake all night.

The chirping was at least pretty, but they had another day of walking ahead of them. Where was Ulec and why wasn't he telling them to be quiet? What good were elves that could talk with animals if they couldn't even get the creatures to keep the noise down?

"Almas are you awake?"

Cady was sleeping on her mat between Almas and Giddy. Almas had been having trouble sleeping since being kidnapped and then rescued from the Lich Lords. What little time he seemed to spend sleeping he was always tossing and turning and jerking awake from a nightmare he always said he couldn't remember. Oddly enough he never seemed tired despite his lack of sleep. That was why she was surprised when he didn't answer.

Sitting up she looked over at her brother. He was sleeping the most peaceably she had seen him do for days. How he, or anyone in camp for that matter, could sleep with the noise coming from the trees above was really weird.

Sure enough, Giddy was also sound asleep. When no one in her family awoke when she called them, she started to get scared. Looking around the camp, she saw nobody up and around.

Cady was about to go over to her father and try to shake him awake when she noticed movement out of the corner of her eye. Someone was near the edge of camp walking towards the trees.

It took her a moment to figure out why that was even stranger than the apparent sleeping spell affecting the whole camp. In all the years she had known Ulec, she had never seen him arrive or leave. He always seemed to appear or disappear when no one was looking.

As he walked away, she had a strange calm urge to follow him. Because it was Ulec, and she knew him, and this whole situation with the birds fit him–she got up and followed him.

She saw him leave camp and walk right next to one of the sentries. When she reached the guard, she found him to be asleep while standing. She only stopped a moment to look at the odd sight before continuing after Ulec.

She entered the forest; Ulec ahead of her but still in sight. After following him for just a couple of minutes she saw Ulec stop and just stand as if waiting. She had covered most of the ground between them and was about to call out to him when she saw something else moving.

Cady wasn't prepared for what came out of the forest and walked up to Ulec. It was a beautiful white horse with a long horn coming out of its forehead.

She had heard of the Unicorn before. Ulec had once said it was the soul of the world; that the very life of the world was connected to the Unicorn.

And there it was right before her eyes! She cautiously approached as Ulec began to stroke her shining mane.

"She's beautiful," Cady said breathlessly.

Ulec didn't turn; he just continued to stroke the Unicorn's mane as he said, "Only a handful of mortals have ever seen her. Meeting you is one of the reasons we were allowed to enter this part of the forest."

Cady gaped at Ulec and asked in awe, "She wanted to meet me?"

"She can see, even better than me, everything that happens here in the forest. She has watched you and your brothers. She knows you are someone she can trust and has a favor to ask you."

"From me? What is it?"

"The Unicorn only appears to those she has chosen to be one of her guardians. If you're willing of course," Ulec added with a smile.

"I don't think I understand. What would she need me to do?" Cady asked.

Mostly you save people's lives by keeping them away from this forest. Also, if she needs your help, you will hear her voice in your mind."

"You mean I'd be like you?" Cady asked hopefully.

Ulec smiled but also shook his head, "Not quite like me. You would only be able to hear her voice. My ability to communicate with plants and animals is something unique I was born with.

"Oh," Cady said still a little confused, "but why me?"

"Because she needs someone to trust. Who can she trust more than a paladin?"

Cady felt the look of confusion cross her face as she said, "But I'm not a paladin, my dad is the only paladin."

Ulec smiled as he said, "Yes you are. The sacred magic swirls around you even if you don't know it. You simply need to learn to use it. Trust me, you have both the heart and the power needed."

Cady looked at Ulec in astonishment. Could it be true? She had never even considered that she might have her father's gift. As far as she knew only men had been paladins. She'd have to ask her father about it.

After letting Cady be alone with her thoughts for a few minutes Ulec asked, "Would you like to touch her?"

Cady looked up and saw him motion her to come closer. She timidly came forward and lightly put her fingers on the Unicorn's neck. She stroked the beautiful creature's mane for a couple of minutes with eyes full of wonder and then became somber as one more thought hit her. Facing Ulec she asked, "Why would she need me to be a guardian when she already has you?"

Ulec took a deep long breath before responding, keeping his eyes locked on the Unicorn. "I might not be able to continue as guardian for much longer and she'll need someone."

Cady faced Ulec and looked at him. He was the palest and frailest looking she had ever seen. She was afraid to ask but still did.

"Why not?"

Ulec closed his eyes and bowed his head as he answered, "Because I'm dying."

Chapter 7

"I SAY WE ATTACK THE moment they leave the forest."

"That wasn't Lich-El's plan. We are only to amass our army."

"Why put our trust in a traitor if we don't have to."

"Because lately those that have disobeyed him have come to bad ends. Let's wait to see where they exit the forest, then we can decide what to do."

IT WAS GIDON WHO HAD to break the news to the rest of his children the next morning. Cady was still asleep, or at least was pretending to be asleep. She was taking the news hard–just as Almas was right now.

"What do you mean he's dying? How?" Almas asked, his voice rising.

Gidon took a deep breath and answered, "The weapon his shoulder was wounded with was cursed. The wound won't close or heal. The bandage he has on keeps him from bleeding to death, but it isn't stopping it from getting infected."

Creetan then asked, "Can't your healing magic do anything?"

Gidon shook his head, "The curse blocks all healing. We must remove the curse before I can do anything. Lady Alixia is looking for a way to do it, which is why she and Seacra left."

"So, there might be a way to save him?" Creetan asked hopefully.

Gidon glanced at Almas who was quietly staring at the ground. Several emotions seemed to be fighting for control of his face.

Still watching his second born, he answered, "It's possible, but he is running out of time. I'm sure you've all noticed by now how pale and weak he seems to be growing."

Almas suddenly looked up and asked, "You said the dagger the Lich Lord cut him with was cursed right? If it was magical then it was a fieles. Shouldn't there be a fieles that can lift curses?"

"That's one of the things Lady Alixia is looking into. All we can do is wait and hope she finds something and gets back to us," Gidon answered.

Almas suddenly turned and stalked off. Gidon fought the urge to go after him knowing his son needed time alone to work through his emotions. Of all his children he knew Almas would have the hardest time with this. He hoped Lady Alixia hurried–for the sake of both Ulec and Almas.

ALMAS WENT TO THE WESTERNMOST side of camp and once he was away from everyone that was busy breaking camp he called out, "I know you're out here. Come out where I can see you."

The answer came from high to his left, "You had been nearly killed and then taken prisoner by the Lich Lords. I didn't want to add to your worry."

Looking up he saw Ulec sitting on a branch a good 12 feet above the ground.

"I could still tell something was wrong, even if I didn't know what it was. And the fact you weren't telling me what it was made me worry all the more–you should have told me!"

"I'm sorry. How do you tell your best friend you're dying?"

"You're not..." Almas paused. He was about to say, 'because Lich-El ordered me to save you,' but he stopped himself.

Where did that come from? It had to be him wanting to save Ulec because they were friends. Lich-El's orders had nothing to do with anything. Almas continued, "We'll figure something out."

Ulec gave him a tired but sincere smile, "I've learned to never underestimate you. Now try not to worry too much. I have some time left. You should go get ready to leave. We have to cross another firewater tree forest today."

Almas gave his friend a long look before nodding and heading back into camp. He didn't feel comforted. Nothing felt right.

Most of the day was spent traveling among the giant branches of the firewater trees. Almas stayed by his friend's side and traveled for the most part in silence; frustrated that he couldn't think of a single way to help him.

Now many of the other refugees were starting to notice that their guide through the forest was obviously becoming ill. So it was that the good mood granted to them the night before gave way to a more subdued mood when they came out of the firewater tree branches and set up camp just a little further past them.

After helping set up his family's campsite, Almas found that Lord Teanas had already prepared a campfire for their family and was sitting on the ground near it. Ulec was also there lying on the ground asleep already, his head resting on his father's lap.

Almas tried to read Lord Teanas' stoic face but couldn't read much in it, so he asked, "How is he doing?"

Lord Teanas looked over to where Almas was sitting down near the fire. He smiled warmly and answered, "He's exhausted but he's hanging on. Luckily, he has his mother's strength...and her stubbornness."

"Do you think Lady Alixia will find a way to heal him?" Cady asked, also taking a spot by the fire along with the rest of the family.

"As I said she is stubborn. She won't give up until she does, and neither should we," Lord Teanas answered.

"We should wait for her. We should be trying to figure something out," Almas cut in.

"But if Father and Lord Teanas can't do anything, then what can we do?" Cady cut back.

"You would be surprised at what even those as young as you can do. Kingdoms have been saved in the past by ones younger than even you," Lord Teanas added.

Cady looked at him doubtfully and asked, "How?"

Lord Teanas took a moment to consider, then smiled and started, "Many years before the War of Destruction I once traveled to the old Aguerius Province as an emissary for Mundial.

"There was an orphan boy there about Giddy's age. He was considered to be a lunatic. He saw things that weren't there and talked and played with people who didn't exist. Not simple childhood fantasies mind you; he really saw and heard them in his own mind.

"Now I was there to meet with the lord of the province and the King of Yucaipa. There was a horde of barbarians preparing to invade the kingdom and I was there to advise them.

"Sadly, the horde moved quicker than we expected and launched a surprise attack. There were so many that we had no choice but to try to flee. Sadly, we were overtaken and captured."

"They even captured you?" Giddy exclaimed in shock.

Lord Teanas smiled and said, "Yes, even I couldn't stand against such a numerous army, but as the barbarians argued over who would take credit for capturing us, this small boy came running into the clearing where we were, screaming in terror that something was chasing him. One of the barbarians grabbed him and demanded to know what he was screaming about. The boy yelled that the king had released his screeching mind drinkers."

"Screeching mind drinkers?" Cady asked.

Creetan snorted, "And they believed the boy?"

Lord Teanas continued, "They probably wouldn't have except for the fact that as soon as he said it, the forest in the direction the boy came from suddenly filled with the sounds of screeching.

"The barbarian holding the boy was so astonished that he lost his grip on the boy, who fled the clearing screaming that they were going to drink their minds.

"Now these barbarians weren't the kind that got scared and ran. They craved glory and most drew their weapons and charged in the direction of the screeches, lusting after the glory of killing these monsters.

"Meanwhile I suddenly felt someone behind me cutting my hands free. I looked behind me to find the boy moving down the line of prisoners freeing their hands also, all the while arguing with someone who wasn't there about the wisdom of helping us. Once we were free, we quickly overpowered the few barbarians left to guard us."

"But what was making the screeching?" Almas asked.

"That is exactly what the king asked the boy. The boy answered that the mind drinkers did, as if it was obvious. It was at that moment we heard the voice of Snipies, the God of Chaos."

"You met Snipies?" Giddy asked wide-eyed.

"Many times," Lord Teanas answered, "But those are other stories. Snipies explained that the boy was using magic to make those around him experience his delusions. He further told us that the part of the boy's mind that made dreams was so strong that it made dreams even while he was awake."

"But why did Snipies appear? I thought the gods didn't appear to mortals very often," Creetan asked.

Snipies was the god of chaos; he told us the confusion the boy deliberately caused while suffering from his own confused mind had attracted him. He had come to give the boy a gift. He then handed the boy a flask of Kaynarian Blood."

Giddy interrupted again to ask what Kaynarian Blood was. His own father answered him.

"The gods who created this world called themselves Kaynarians. Their blood was said to be a source of pure magic. Giving so much magical power to a confused boy who could spread that confusion to others is something only the god of chaos would think wise."

"So, what happened," Cady asked.

Lord Teanas continued, "As soon as the boy touched the flask the blood inside disappeared. With so much power, he didn't just make others see his delusions, he made all the fantasies of his mind become real."

"So, the mind screechers or whatever they're called, became real?" Almas asked. Not quite believing it.

"Yes, but the barbarians made short work of them; but more than the monsters, he had in his mind an entire world that existed outside our own. We were able to pass through this world to escape the barbarians and put together an army to repel the invaders."

"He made his own world? What happened to the boy?" Giddy asked

When he touched the flask and made his fantasies real, it healed him of his confused mind as part of that. After that he could always see clearly what was real and what was not. He still had a great imagination and the ability to make his stories seem real to those that heard them. The high lord of the Aguerius Province, having no children of his own, adopted him. The boy later became your ancestor, High Lord Morin Aguerius."

"Lord Morin was the boy?" Almas asked incredulously. Lord Morin was the most famous of the Aguerius line, and the first paladin. It had been his plans that had won the War of Destruction; but he had never heard any stories of his childhood before. He had never known he had spent his childhood as both a common orphan and sick in the mind.

Lord Teanas simply nodded in response to his question, while Giddy asked, "What about the world he created?

"Lord Morin and Mundial sacrificed themselves to imprison Destruction within that world, and seal him away forever; so not only did he save the kingdom while still a boy, but he also paved the way to save us all. So, I end this story to tell you again to never think you can't make a difference simply because you are young."

Almas looked down on Ulec's sleeping form. He vowed silently to himself right there that he would find a way to save his friend. They had been through too much together to let some stupid curse take him away.

Chapter 8

"YOU'RE A FOOL TO DO this."

"We can't pass up this chance to end Lord Aguerius once and for all. I will only send my revenants and some Kadus Knights. We will never be in danger. Just do your part, Tornal, and open the way."

THIS WOULD BE THE DAY they would leave the forest and enter the Forjad Province. Giddy was excited; his grandfather Cree Forjad was the high lord in this province, and he hadn't seen him since he was little. He knew his grandfather lived on the far side of the province but there was always a chance he could be visiting nearby; even in his old age.

In his excitement he didn't really notice the nervousness of those around him. They would be leaving the safety of the sacred forest and make a dash for the city of Debigroc. It was a few hours travel from where they would leave the forest; they would be on their own once again until they reached the safety of the city walls.

So, as he was waiting for everyone to finish breaking camp, he was trying to find ways to amuse himself. He was looking at some rocks, looking for any he might be able to make something out of. He noticed one interesting looking stone that was roughly egg shaped with red swirls mixed into the otherwise grey stone.

He had only studied the stone for a few moments when he heard the horns signal everyone that it was time to begin the day's journey.

Slipping the stone into his pocket for future study he scurried down the forming line of refugees to where his family was standing and speaking with Lord Teanas and Ulec.

"What do you mean you're staying here?" Giddy heard Almas asking the two elves.

Ulec looked sicker than ever and had a tired voice when he answered, "I've gone as far as I can go; right now, the forest is strengthening me. If I leave, I won't last very long."

The line of refugees was passing by them and Giddy wondered who was leading them since his father and both the elves were still back here. He didn't see Uncle Jarad, maybe he was leading them, although he wondered how he knew where to go.

Giddy's father was speaking now gently to his brother, "Almas I know you're worried about him, but this is the best place for him. He'll be safe here and won't overwork himself. We on the other hand need to get going."

Almas turned to his father and asked, "Can I at least wait here with him till the end of the column passes?"

Cady piped up with a quick, "Me too?" and Gidon seemed to think a moment before his wife intervened.

"It's okay, I'll wait here with them and make sure they come."

Gidon nodded to his wife, turned, and bowed to Lord Teanas and Ulec before leaving towards the front of the column.

Giddy noticed Creetan was also staying and decided to wait with his mother and siblings.

Almas again started speaking to Ulec, "So what are you going to do?"

"All I can do is wait here for my mother to find a way to lift the curse," Ulec answered with a shrug.

"What if she can't find anything in time?" Almas asked sounding a little frantic.

Ulec smiled and said reassuringly, "As long as I stay here and rest, I'll hold out long enough. Don't worry."

The end of the column was passing by and the guard in charge of making sure none were left behind stood at a respectful distance waiting for them.

"Almas," his mother gently spoke, "We need to go. Say your good-byes."

Almas didn't seem to know what to say or do. Cady had no such problem, like the typical girl she was, she stepped forward and gave Ulec a big hug. The elvish boy, as pale as he had been the past few days, still managed to turn a shade of red and Giddy couldn't help but feel sorry for him.

She finally let him go and stood back staring at her feet and obviously trying to keep the tears in her eyes from spilling out.

Almas still stood there not seeming to know what to do. It was Ulec who stepped forward and placed his hands on top of his best friend's shoulders.

"Don't worry about me. There is nowhere safer than here, and we'll find a way to get rid of this curse."

Almas looked like he was about to cry but managed to place his own hands on Ulec's shoulders and said with a nod, "Okay, you take care of yourself, and we'll see you soon."

Almas took a step back and they parted. Creetan gave Ulec a pat on his back and their mother also gave him a hug. As they started to leave Giddy, suddenly not sure what to do himself, awkwardly waved and simply said, "Bye."

Almas and Cady walked slowly. Slow enough that they were falling way behind the rest of the refugees. Mother and Creetan walked with them along with the rear guard.

They were still talking about Ulec. In fact, they were so focused on their discussion that they didn't even notice passing the border of the sacred forest. One moment they were in a tunnel of dense trees and bushes and the next it was like coming out of a cave into just a normal forest.

Giddy hesitated just a moment there; in the sacred forest they had been safe and protected. Now they would be on their own, and now without Ulec or Lord Teanas.

His parents had told him it would take weeks for the undead to march around the southern tip of the forest and reach them in the Forjad Province–and that would be marching unopposed. Yet it was still scary leaving.

Tired of moving at such a slow pace, Giddy moved ahead to catch up with the rest of the refugees.

He had pulled a few dozen yards ahead of his slower family members when he suddenly felt his leg get hot. Startled, he stopped and reached into his pocket and pulled out the stone he had found earlier. It was growing uncomfortably hot. He quickly dropped it to the ground and spun around when he heard a strange humming sound behind him at that same moment.

There was a pillar of light just a couple of feet from him. Taking several startled steps back away from the light he called out a frightened and drawn-out, "Mom?"

A figure emerged from the light. The pale rotted skin and spikes of bone coming out of its arms made it clear it was an undead creature.

Giddy shouted a much louder and more frantic, "Mom!" as a second form emerged from the light. He quickly backed away from the new threat as the pair of undead creatures both looked right at him.

He watched the two start to approach him as more figures emerged from the light, and right then he tripped backwards over a root and fell backwards to the ground. Getting himself quickly up to a sitting position he saw the undead drawing weapons as they approached. He was about to scream for help again when he heard a loud thud as one of the creatures stumbled forward and instantly started to crumble to dust. As it crumbled, he saw his mother's hatchet fall to the ground inside the growing cloud of dust. There was another softer thud as the second undead also stumbled forward with an arrow in its back.

Back at the pillar of light Giddy saw Creetan, bow in one hand and his short sword in the other, attacking the creatures still emerging from the light. His mother ran past the combat right to Giddy and in a voice filled with worry asked, "Are you alright?"

Giddy only managed a frightened nod as his mother pulled him up. Looking back to the fighting as his mother hurriedly retrieved her hatchet, he saw his brother and the guard quickly being surrounded by the still emerging undead. Meanwhile Cady and Almas were still far beyond the light running to catch up. Suddenly Almas grabbed Cady's arm and pulled her to a stop. Giddy realized immediately why they stopped–they were cut off.

Creetan and the rearguard were being surrounded and with mother on this side of the light there was no one between them and the growing army of undead.

"Mom!" Giddy called out the warning and pointed, "Almas and Cady!"

His mother, having picked up her weapon, looked to where her son was pointing and seeing the situation heard his mother mutter an exclamation that he never imagined his mother could say. Holding the hatchet in one hand she pulled her blacksmith hammer off her belt with her other hand and yelled over the sound of battle, "Almas! Back to the forest!"

Almas looked past the battle, locked eyes with his mother for a moment, and nodded. Still clutching his sister's arm, he turned and pulled her with him as he began to run. Several undead noticed them and began pursuing them.

"Giddy," his mother snapped back to him, "Go get your father!"

As she gave the order, she pressed a button on the handle of both her hammer and her hatchet and both handles suddenly extended with the sound of a spring releasing.

She looked back at Giddy long enough to shout "Now!" and that was all Giddy needed. He turned and started running as fast as he could in the way he had last seen the refugees go.

He had only gone a short distance when he heard a blast from a horn behind him. Glancing back, he saw the rear guard blowing his signal horn as he stood behind Creetan and his mother who were shoulder to shoulder holding off the undead as he blew a warning.

His mother was now holding what amounted to a war axe and war hammer with their extended handles. They were both slender weapons but to Giddy's astonishment his mother was cutting down undead with a skill second only to his father. He had never known his mother could fight.

The sound of other horns answering the first reminded him he was supposed to be getting his father and he took off again.

He only ran about a minute when he saw several of his father's men ahead running right for him. He noticed a moment later his father wasn't far behind them.

His father had caught up to the others by the time they reached Giddy.

"What's going on?" His father demanded.

Giddy breathed out, "A light appeared and undead started coming out of it. Mother and Creetan are fighting them."

"Where's Almas and Cady?"

"They got trapped on the other side of the light. A bunch of them chased them back towards the sacred forest."

Hearing that, Giddy's father picked him up and handed him over to one of his men.

"Take him back and tell Jarad to find a defensible position and get everyone there. Every available man we can spare needs to get over here and help slow them down. Now go!"

The soldier took Giddy, flung him over his shoulders and took off back towards the refugees.

Chapter 9

"CURSE IT ALL! SOME boy moved the stone. We lost our element of surprise!"

"No time to worry about that now! Hurry and move your army through, before they have time to react!"

ALMAS COULD RUN FASTER; Cady could not. Luckily, they both were smaller than the revenants chasing them. They were able to dash between trees that were too close for their undead pursuers to get through.

They made it to the border of the sacred forest, but the revenants were right behind them. The whole time he was running he kept expecting the forest around them to come alive and defend them–but it stayed eerily quiet. What was Ulec doing? Surely, he had noticed they were in trouble? Maybe he had fallen asleep?

Even the path they had used to leave the forest was gone, which might actually be working to their advantage. While he and Cady were scampering through the thick branches and trees the revenants were having to use their swords to cut through some parts. Sadly, it wasn't enough to help them lose the creatures.

Suddenly Cady grabbed his arm and pulling him to the left said, "This way!"

Not being able to waste a moment in argument Almas followed immediately but did manage to huff out, "This isn't the way back to Ulec!"

"Trust me!" Cady responded.

Suddenly the thick foliage gave way to a clearing; in the middle of which stood a firewater tree–complete with its circle of barren ground.

Cady pulled him towards the tree and Almas looked all around for any branches bending down to the ground, but he didn't see any. They would have to go around.

They got to the edge and before Almas could say anything Cady pulled him to the left and said, "This way, under that branch!"

She pulled him under a branch that extended far past the border of the barren ground but much too high for them to reach.

"We need to stay away from the blossoms," Cady said in a voice that didn't sound very sure.

Glancing up he saw blossoms sprouting from the branch several feet away.

"What's going on? How do you know?" Almas asked.

"The Unicorn told me," was all she said before they heard hacking at the edge of the clearing and saw the revenants cutting themselves out from the thick foliage. There were five of them.

Almas instantly saw that the revenants would pass under the blossoms as they approached and asked Cady, "I'm guessing we're supposed to stay right here?"

Cady gave a worried nod as the revenants came closer, weapons in hand.

"Hope this Unicorn knows what it's doing?"

"Me too," Cady agreed.

As the revenants got close to where the blossoms were Almas glanced up and to his amazement saw the flowers moving. They looked like they were turning to face the approaching undead. Not only that, but the back of the flowers seemed to be swelling bigger.

Suddenly each blossom ejected a glob of liquid at the revenants and each glob seemed to instantly ignite as it shot towards the undead; turning into small fireballs that splattered flames all over the revenants, quickly reducing them all to ash.

Both Almas and Cady stared as the flames began to die down. Almas broke the silence.

"I think I know why they call them fire water trees."

Cady just gave a shocked nod.

Almas finally snapped out of his shock and said, "We need to find Lord Teanas. If a whole army comes out of that magic gate, then the whole province could be in danger, not just Mother and Father and the rest of the refugees."

"This way, but I can't run anymore," Cady indicated.

"Walk fast," Almas ordered and then asked, "and what's this whole 'Unicorn' thing."

IZYBEL, CREETAN, AND his rear guard, Poxan, had broken off fighting and were fleeing with an undead army right behind them when Gidon reached them with four more of his men.

Gidon sent a wide arc of holy magic into the line of pursuing revenants. The first few rows were blasted into dust and all eight of them began a fighting retreat. He had Creetan fighting on his left and his wife on his right.

"Where are Almas and Cady?" He asked Izybel.

"They got cut off from us. I told them to run back to the forest, a few revenants followed them. I don't know more than that," she answered nearly sobbing.

Gidon felt a sudden surge of fear and anxiety for his two young children. He inwardly cursed his current helplessness.

He could only hope Ulec and Lord Teanas would see their plight.

More of his men kept arriving, but the number of revenants seemed to be ever growing. If they didn't turn and flee soon, they would be flanked shortly.

Finally, one of his men came up behind him and reported, "My lord, we found a hill with only one side that is ascendable. Thick trees on that side make it a very defensible position. We have the refugees on the hill, and we have the archers positioned a hundred yards back to cover your retreat."

"Our war mounts?"

"Also in position."

"Signal the retreat then." Gidon ordered

The soldier behind him immediately put a horn to his mouth and blew a signal. A moment later a barrage of arrows flew overhead as Gidon's entire line of warriors turned and fled. Everyone except Gidon.

Spreading out his arms he erected a holy shield spanning the entire line. He would only be able to hold the shield a few seconds, but it would give his people a head start. As the shield began to falter, he heard heavy thundering footsteps behind him.

He dropped the shield and tuned around. Behind were three forest dragons, all with heavy armor and riders. He dodged a swinging tail that flung the first line of revenants, that had surged forward, away; then he leaped up onto the dragon's back, taking a seat behind the rider holding the reins, and they were off. Now it was a matter of his men being faster than the revenants.

Chapter 10

"CAN YOU FEEL THAT?"

"Yes, magical pressure building, something immensely powerful is getting close to death, something near the battle."

"Should we pull back?"

"No, let's see what happens, it may be to our advantage."

EVER SINCE HE HAD WOKEN up as a prisoner of the undead, Almas had had this strange creepy feeling. It felt like death; which considering he was around or being pursued by undead all that time wasn't all that surprising.

As he and Cady neared the place, they had parted with Ulec and Lord Teanas, he felt that creepy feeling suddenly intensify. It startled him and he looked back at the way they came. He didn't know how but he knew the feeling came from back where the undead were attacking the rest of the refugees. Something bad was happening back there. Also, ahead of them the same creepy feeling seemed to be intensifying.

"What's wrong?" Cady asked with concern.

Almas glanced back at the way they had come again and shaking his head answered, "Just a bad feeling. We need to hurry and find Lord Teanas."

"I think they are close," Cady said and started moving quicker, "Come on."

They found them in a small clearing. Ulec was laying on the grass. Lord Teanas was sitting next to him with his son's head on his lap letting him use it as a pillow.

"Lord Teanas!" Almas called and ran up to them.

Lord Teanas looked up startled and Almas came to an abrupt stop. Was he crying? Could an elvish lord cry?

Dread filled Almas as he looked down on his best friend. Before he could ask the question Lord Teanas answered it for him, "He's alive, just sleeping for now. Why did you come back?"

Keeping a worried eye on Ulec, Almas answered, "We were attacked by revenants just outside the sacred forest."

"What?" Lord Teanas exclaimed with a shocked expression.

Almas quickly explained what had happened. As Lord Teanas listened to his account his expression went from shocked to stricken.

Never had Almas seen so much emotion from the elf lord. He watched as Lord Teanas looked down into his son's face.

"I'll need both of you to stay here with Ulec. I need you to give him what care you can."

"He's dying now, isn't he?" Almas asked.

Lord Teanas nodded, "He was sustaining himself with magic. He wanted all of you to leave with hope. Now he's fading quickly."

Lord Teanas' voice caught a little as he spoke the last few words. He took a moment to compose himself before continuing, "Please stay with him. I have to go help your family."

Lord Teanas gently moved Ulec's head from his lap and carefully laid him on the grass.

"What can we do for him?" Almas asked Lord Teanas as he quickly gathered his weapons.

"Stay with him and keep him as comfortable as you can. I'll return as soon as I can."

With one last look at his son, he turned and dashed off.

Almas watched him go then looked down on his dying friend. Ulec was asleep, drenched in sweat, and the palest Almas had ever seen him.

There was also a feeling coming from Ulec that Almas couldn't quite grasp. It was similar to that creepy feeling he'd been having since being captive in the undead's base, but it was like it was building up in Ulec.

Almas' mind was on this when he heard his sister ask in a frantic voice, "Isn't there something we can do?"

"I don't know," Almas answered sitting down next to his friend, "If I were paladin like Father, then I could try to heal him...but if Father couldn't do it, then what chance is there I could?"

Cady knelt beside Ulec across from her brother. She tentatively put a hand on Ulec's chest and closed her eyes.

"What are you doing?" Almas asked

"Ulec told me I had the power of a paladin–I just need to learn how to use it!"

Almas just stared a few moments shocked; his sister could use paladin magic? Ulec told her? Almas felt a moment of jealousy before pushing the feeling away. Cady was also Ulec's friend and now wasn't the time to dwell on negative thoughts.

Cady knelt there for a few minutes looking more and more frustrated till finally she shook her head and cried, "I can't; I just don't know how."

Almas had watched his father use healing magic and had asked him about it to learn a little about how he did it. He took a moment to compose his thoughts before trying to help.

"Clear your mind and just focus on Ulec; on your connection to him. Now with that connection think of his injuries healing and try to use your heart to push those injuries to heal and his infection to fade."

Almas saw his sister's hand start to glow with a faint golden light and excitedly exclaimed, "That's it! You're doing it!"

Cady didn't respond right away. She sat concentrating a few moments before shaking her head with a troubled expression and said, "I think something's wrong. It feels like something is blocking the magic."

The glow around her hands started to fade as she began lifting her hands from Ulec's chest. Almas was about to say something along the lines of it being a good try when Ulec suddenly made a long raspy sound as he breathed out. Then there was nothing.

"Ulec?" Almas asked in alarm. Ulec's chest had stopped moving up and down and that strange feeling began to intensify even quicker. It was like the dam keeping his friend's life force in him was beginning to burst.

"No, Ulec!" Almas cried, beginning to shake him, "Try it again Cady! Please keep trying!"

Cady, with an expression of pure panic, put her hands back on Ulec and the glow returned. Almas stopped shaking his friend and watched intently for any reaction. The creepy feeling was so intense it was like he could almost see it...in fact, when he focused just right, he could–and more.

In a moment a whole new world seemed to open up to him. He was suddenly completely aware of all the magic around him. It was as if all his senses were focused on it. He could sense perfectly Cady's healing magic trying to enter and heal Ulec. He could also sense the curse in Ulec's shoulder snaking out a tendril and blocking her magic.

He could also sense how other magics around him worked. There was a life force in all the living things around him. That must be the magic Ulec's sister had called Vithal that the desert elves used. Some of that magic seemed to radiate out and become another kind of magic, most likely Natela, the magic used by the elves and shadow elves. Many other kinds seemed to flow tightly around his sister, the strongest of them being her paladin magic. These must all be the magic created by humans; Trabar Magic. In dead things like fallen leaves that life force changed into yet another type of magic that Almas recognized as the source of that creepy feeling he had been having. He didn't know if this magic had a name or not; he had only heard that the Lich Lords used magic from death. This must be that very magic.

There was one more kind of magic that Almas could sense. This one came from Ulec and combined with his life force, his Vithal, made him the most powerful source of magic of all. It seemed to be contained in Ulec's blood.

Almas noticed all this in just a moment but didn't have time to contemplate most of what he sensed at this time. What took all his attention was Ulec's life force–it was rapidly changing into the magic he could sense coming from things that were dead.

He was watching his friend die. Cady was desperately trying to save him, but the curse blocked every effort. He had to do something now.

Without even knowing what he was doing, as if some other force was controlling him, Almas somehow grabbed hold of the curse with his own mind and pulled hard.

The curse seemed to resist a moment before suddenly releasing its grip on Ulec and jumping right into Almas.

He gave a cry of surprise and fell backwards as intense pain exploded in his own shoulder.

Cady looked up in concern at him but before she could ask what happened Almas shouted, "Don't stop! Heal him now!"

She brought her attention back to Ulec and cried out, "It's working!"

Pushing aside the pain in his shoulder, Almas watched Cady as she healed his friend. He saw the healing magic move throughout his body wiping out infection and repairing damage. Suddenly Ulec gasped and started breathing hard and Almas saw his life-force begin returning to normal.

Both he and Cady sighed in relief and Almas told Cady to keep the healing up as long as possible.

Cady did as she was told but gave her brother a worried look and asked, "What happened?"

The pain in his shoulder had become a sting. Looking at it he could sense the curse there; it had transferred over to him. Looking up to his sister he simply said, "I was able to remove the curse. It didn't want to go easy."

Chapter 11

"WHAT WAS THAT? SO MUCH death energy on the pinnacle of being released, then it was gone. Was that a god?"

"It must have been one of the elves, but I never dreamed they held so much power in them, just waiting for death to release it to us."

"Pay attention to your revenants! There is still a battle to be won."

CREETAN FIRED ARROW after arrow into the gaps between trees but to little effect. The same trees that were protecting them also gave the undead protection from his arrows. He had to keep telling himself to calm down and take care to aim, he hit far more targets when he wasn't shooting arrows off in a mad panic.

He paused to survey the battle. His father was in the forefront of the battle with a short sword in each hand. The smaller weapons allowed him to fight and move more easily in the close quarters of the trees. His Uncle Jarad similarly was using a pair of hand axes right alongside his father.

Glancing along the lines he spotted a revenant knock one of the guards down. In one fluid motion he sent an arrow into the creature before it could finish the man off. He hadn't even thought about what to do, his training had acted before he had had a chance to second guess or worry about it. He called out to a nearby guard to go assist the man and once he was back on his feet Creetan began scanning the front line for more targets. He was still terrified but maybe if he tried to clear his mind of worries and let his training take over, he might just survive this.

Yet that chance seemed to be fading. The men were being overwhelmed. More and more he was seeing revenants about to overcome a man and it was a matter of time before he would be too late to save him with a well-placed arrow. So, it was to his utter astonishment when all the revenants simultaneously began withdrawing with the Kadus knights following their lead.

"What's going on?" Creetan called to his father.

"Not sure," his father answered and addressing all the men, "Keep alert!"

After a few moments someone called out, "Look! Smoke!"

Scanning high above the trees Creetan saw a plume of smoke rising out beyond the undead's lines.

"Could it be Lord Teanas?" Creetan called over.

Gidon studied the smoke for a moment before nodding and stating, "It's possible that Almas and Cady found him. You and your mother said they fled that way."

Addressing all his men he continued, "See to the wounded. Archers keep a lookout.

Gidon began moving up and down the line healing and repositioning men as needed. Creetan watched the forest, knowing their enemy would return.

LORD TEANAS HAD HOPED to find the portal or possibly some lich lords before he was spotted but it was not to be. The undead must have feared he would appear for there were many undead scouts watching the border of the forest. Once he was spotted, he fell upon the army of undead with a fury as deep as his anguish.

Within moments he was the center of a growing firestorm. He plunged himself into first the scouts and then both the regular revenants and the Kadus knights that came to face him. At first none could even approach him without being consumed in flames, but eventually the flames died down and he had to contend with his foes one on one.

Even as the enemy surrounded him, he fought without thought of his own welfare. His son was dying, and he intended the undead to pay dearly for all they had done. They would learn that while Lord Teanas was slow to anger, woe unto those that finally kindled the fires of his rage.

ALMAS WATCHED ULEC as he rested. His shoulder was hurting more but he pushed the pain away. He studied the magic as it flowed around and from Ulec; he even saw the moment when his friend awakened.

He watched as his friend cast a spell over himself when he woke up and at first seemed to heal himself. It took him a moment to realize he didn't actually heal himself but changed himself. He changed his form from his injured self to his uninjured self like his mother and sister changed forms from their normal elvish selves to animals.

Ulec did this before he even showed any sign that he had awoken.

"How are you feeling?" Almas asked.

Ulec's eyes snapped open and he looked at Almas with a curious look, before answering, "Better; what...happened?"

Cady answered excitedly before Almas could say anything, "You stopped breathing, but Almas removed the curse, and I healed you.

Ulec got up on his elbows and asked confused, "Removed? How did you remove it?"

Almas answered honestly, "I'm not completely sure. I was watching Cady trying to heal you and suddenly I could feel all the magic around me; it was almost like I could see it.

"I could see the curse on your arm blocking Cady's healing power. Without thinking I tried grabbing the curse with magic and pulled it away from you. It worked–I removed the curse and Cady healed you as much as she could."

Ulec stared a moment at his best friend. "You can see, or feel magic and curses? How well?"

I can feel any kind of magic, I think. Along with the curse I seem to be able to sense magic abilities like Cady's paladin abilities and the one you are using now to hide how hurt you still are.

"I think I can see all the different types of magic, including the one you're using that you never told us about. You have Kaynarian blood in you–don't you?"

Now Ulec stared open mouthed at Almas. He sat there several moments before saying, "That cannot be known."

"Why didn't you tell us? Why can't anyone know?" Almas asked feeling a little bit hurt.

"The Kaynarian blood came from my real father, and it was his blood that was used to make the blood seal that imprisoned Destruction. If anyone knew who my real father was then my blood could be used to release the seal."

"That would mean your real father was Mundial!" Cady exclaimed.

"I can't believe I didn't see this before. You talk to plants and animals...the creations of Mundial," Almas murmured.

"Lord Teanas is the only father I've ever known. Wait...where is my father," Ulec perked up suddenly concerned.

Almas felt Ulec's ability to communicate with animals come alive and he could feel Ulec spreading his awareness throughout the forest.

"We were attacked outside the forest. Cady and I were forced to come back here, and Lord Teanas left to go help the rest of the refugees," Almas explained.

Ulec said nothing; he was focused on what he was doing with his magic. Suddenly Almas could feel Ulec's magic use seem to focus and Ulec's expression of staring at seemingly nothing narrow.

After a moment Ulec said, "They're in trouble. They found a defendable hilltop, but the undead army is huge."

"So, what do we do?" Cady asked tears coming to her eyes.

Ulec seemed to start scanning the area with magic again. Almas was amazed by what his newfound ability seemed to tell him. He was even more amazed he had never noticed any sign before that he even had it.

"We will send some help," Ulec answered Cady with a smile.

Chapter 12

FOCUS ON LORD TEANAS, if killing him can generate as much death magic as we just felt, killing him could win this battle."

TEANAS KNEW HE WAS out of time. He had used up all the magic in the area that he could use. Now he only had enough to change the form of Mimic, his magic ring, to whatever weapon he needed.

He had burned and cut his way to within sight of where Lord Gidon and the other refugees had fortified themselves.

The undead army seemed to have halted their attack on the humans and were focusing the whole might of their army on him.

He was striking down multiple enemies with each swing and evading blows with each step. Exhaustion would cause him to make the mistake that would end his life at any moment; which came when he moved just an instant too slow and took a deep cut to his leg.

He fell to his knees and with Mimic taking the form of a halberd he swung it in a circle around him cutting all enemies within its range in half. Teanas knew that would be his last action. He would be overwhelmed in an instant and soon be with his son in the next world.

"I failed you and your son my Lord Mundial," would be his last words

Yet the killing blow never came. It was replaced by an enormous crash all around him. Three trees had fallen practically on top of him crushing all enemies near him and creating a wall of tangled branches around him. For a short moment he was safe.

"Ulec?" Teanas whispered.

In answer a songbird landed on a branch in front of him and chirped Ulec's signal that he was alright. A sob of relief erupted from Teanas as he stood hardly noticing the pain from the gash in his leg.

He didn't know how but his son was alive; not just alive but he was okay now. The forest was coming alive all around him as large wolves, bears, and elk charged from the forest. Big cats sprang from trees and birds of every sort dived from the sky.

Teanas, feeling a surge of energy, sprang over the wall of branches and began cutting through the undead ranks again.

With the help of Mundial's creations, the plants and animals heeding the call of Mundial's heir, Teanas made quick progress towards the hill where Gidon's people were taking refuge.

Suddenly a large group of revenants preparing to meet him disappeared in a flash of golden light. He looked ahead and saw

Lord Gidon riding his dragon mount towards him, swinging a halberd at any enemy that dared come too close.

"Get on!" Lord Gidon called as he rode up to him.

Teanas grasped the arm being extend to him and swung himself behind his human friend.

Gidon told Teanas to hold on as he turned his mount back towards the hill, the dragon's tail swinging out and smashing a group of revenants to the ground as it turned. The undead were forming a line to block them but with a swing of his weapon a golden arc of light flew from the paladin's halberd destroying them at contact. They rode past the remains of the enemy and quickly made it to friendly lines.

Both Teanas and Lord Gidon leapt from the dragon mount and Gidon issued several orders to his men to ready them for an attack before turning his attention to Teanas.

"Almas and Cady?" Gidon said with a hopeful questioning tone.

"Both made it to me safely. I left them inside the borders of the forest with Ulec," Teanas answered as he knelt down from exhaustion and pain.

Lord Gidon knelt beside and placed a hand over the wound on Teanas' thigh; his hand emitting a gold light as he began to heal him.

"I wouldn't have thought Ulec still had the strength to do all this," Lord Gidon stated.

"Something must have happened. Ulec was unconscious and minutes if not moments from death when I left them. He sent a message that he's fine. I don't know what to make of it."

"What I make out," Lord Gidon said with a smile, "Is we just might make it out of this now."

IZYBEL TRIED TO WATCH through the dense trees with an ever-growing sense of foreboding as the undead army regrouped and prepared to attack once more.

She sat atop her husband's forest dragon mount, which had just been brought to her. With her were the few other mounted warriors, the dragons and horses not being very effective in the dense trees, along with those who were too injured for the front line.

They were to be the last line of defense for the non-combatants. She glanced back and took in once again the terrified group of children, elderly, and women tending the young; they had each been armed, everyone that could pick up and use a weapon.

Her own son, Giddy, sat on the ground with a group of children. He sat with his legs crossed holding the hilt of a short sword nervously on his lap. Izybel swore to herself he would never need to use it.

Her attention snapped back to the front line when she heard someone call out a warning that they were coming.

She couldn't see much through the trees, but she saw the archers in sight begin pulling arrows back on their bows and releasing them. Also, she saw flashes through the trees that could only be her husband attacking with his paladin magic.

Soon the sound of metal striking metal filled her ears; as did the sound of branches falling and various animals locked in combat. "Keep alert," she ordered to all those around her.

"With Lord Teanas here we might have a chance."

Izybel looked down and to the right and saw that Lemuem had approached her and had spoken. He continued, "The enemy is looking for weak points in the line. That elf is able to move quickly enough to reinforce any points they find before they can take advantage."

From what she could see it seemed to be true. The line was holding.

"I assume your tracking everything out there?" Izybel asked Lemuem.

The ranger smiled a mischievous grin at her and answered, "Only those on our side. I can't track anything I haven't been close enough to..."

Lemuem's voice trailed off as his attention returned to the battle.

"We might have a problem. We have a gap appearing on both the left and right sides of the line. The elf is moving to reinforce the right side. I think they might breach on the left."

Izybel signaled to the other defenders to be ready. Lemuem pulled out two daggers and said, "Here they come!"

Revenants began to pour out of the trees on the left side of the tree line. Izybel pulled her blacksmith hammer and hatchet and pushing a button on their thick handles, extended them into an elegant war hammer and war axe.

"Mounted warriors with me. The rest hold the line here," she ordered before commanding her mount to charge at the growing group of undead rushing towards them.

Her forest dragon ran into the enemy at full gallop, smashing revenants under its feet and picking up and crushing others in its jaws. Meanwhile Izybel's hammer and axe took out more on either side of the charging beast.

Eventually her mount slowed to a stop and the other mounted warriors formed up on either side of her to protect her flank. Now the battle became a flurry of snapping jaws, slashing claws, and flashing weapons.

Soon the flow of enemies emerging from the trees slowed and stopped as the warriors on the front line managed to close the hole in their line. As the number of enemies shrank, Izybel risked a glance behind her, where she saw the few revenants that had made it past the mounted warriors were being cut down by the few guards on foot charged with protecting the refugees.

"Form up and get ready for the next wave," she ordered.

Chapter 13

"THIS LAST WAVE SHOULD do it. They are tired, hurt, and running out of arrows."

"Hurry, I won't be satisfied till Lord Aguerius is dead at my feet. And we've nearly exhausted our supply of death magic. Between that cursed elf and that paladin we aren't getting enough kills to replace what we are using."

"I'M TELLING YOU I HEARD battle horns. They were faint but I know what I heard."

If the scout giving the report hadn't been one of his most reliable, Lord Mason would have dismissed the report out of hand. The thought of Aguerius soldiers fighting nearby was disturbing.

Word of the undead invasion had only just made it around the south leg of Aguerius forest and up to Debigroc the day before. How could any fighting have reached them so soon?

Lord Mason was lord of the city of Debigroc and tasked with guarding the north pass into the Forjad Province. Last he had heard, the undead were moving southwest across the Aguerius Province and he had assumed they would enter Forjad through the south pass. He also thought he had at least a few weeks before they made it this far.

If the scout was right, then the war had already arrived; and from the east of all places, appearing out of nowhere as if from the forest itself. Was it possible?

Lord Mason wasted no time sending messengers to Debigroc to alert the city and began organizing scouts to go find out what was going on. He had been out with a group of his men on a training exercise, but it looked like they might get some real action.

He was about to dismiss his scouts when he heard the howl. All activity in the camp suddenly stopped. It had been a dire wolf howl, but the loudest and deepest he had ever heard.

"Weapons ready," he ordered, drawing his own sword.

Watching the tree line at the edge of the field where they were camped, in the direction the howl had come, he was shocked to see the largest dire wolf he had ever seen come bounding from the trees. The beast was larger than even the largest bear he had ever seen.

Before he could give any orders, the wolf slowed its pace to a trot and stopped just out of the range of the archers who were already notching arrows and taking aim.

It was when the wolf laid down and lowered its head that Lord Mason realized the wolf wasn't alone–it had passengers. Three children had been riding on the wolf's back–on the back of a huge dire wolf! It was unthinkable!

Two of the children, a boy and a girl, slid off the beast's back and began running towards him and his men. Lord Mason ordered his men to hold their fire and watched in fascinated awe as they approached him.

The pair stepped up to him and the boy held up the crest that hung around his neck. He spoke in a voice of authority beyond his apparent years.

"I'm Almas Aguerius and this is my sister, Cady. We are children of High Lord Gidon Aguerius and Lady Izybel Forjad. Our family along with refugees from the Aguerius Province are under attack by forces of the Lich Lords and we request your aid on behalf of our parents."

Lord Mason stared in stunned silence at the siblings. The crests and the obvious family resemblance supported their claim. He could do nothing but accept that these two children were High Lord Forjad's grandchildren and accept that the enemy had already made it to the borders of his land.

He looked back to the third child still sitting astride the huge wolf. There was something about the boy that didn't seem quite...human. Something about the way he held himself and something about those ears.

"Who is he," Lord Mason asked indicating to the third child.

"A friend and ally to the House Aguerius," Lord Forjad's grandson answered simply.

Lord Mason didn't need to think long on it. Only one thing mattered. His Lord's daughter and remaining grandchildren were in danger and there was only one thing he could do.

"I verify the children's crests are true. Lady Izybel and her children need us! Ready the mounts and war wagons! We leave immediately!"

GIDON'S MEN WERE GETTING tired, and the enemy's numbers only seemed to increase with each wave. In the last wave he had lost two men, and had it not been for Lord Teanas' quick arrival the enemy would have completely broken and overwhelmed the line. As it was, he hoped that Izybel and the rear guard could manage the enemies that had slipped past them.

He didn't even want to think about the number of forest animals that had been slain in coming to their aid.

With a swing of his sword, he sent an arc of holy magic into the latest wave of undead turning several rows of revenants into dust. But more were coming. As a sword thrust came at him from the side, he stepped back putting a tree between himself and the undead creature attacking him. Twirling around the tree he cut down his attacker from behind.

Seeing one of his men get knocked down he extended his hand and a golden glowing bubble appeared around the guard protecting him as he quickly picked up his dropped weapon and regained his footing. The bubble disappeared as Gidon was forced to contend with the next line of revenants attacking him.

As he fought, he realized this could be the wave that broke them. There seemed to be no end to them. He bashed with his shield, kicked with his feet, and his sword glowed with holy power as it cut through enemies and sent deadly bolts of magic into the endless lines of undead.

He was about to lose all hope when he heard the horns. Not the ones that had been sounding from his own ranks calling for aid whenever a moment could be spared from combat to sound them but answering horns. Aid was coming!

Both he and those who heard and understood the meaning of the approaching horns began to fight with a renewed vigor! They just had to hold on a little longer!

The enemy also heard the horns, and they now knew they were quickly running out of time. They now surged forward to end it before the new threat to them arrived.

As the fighting intensified, he heard another answering call coming from the same direction as the horns. The deepest loudest howl he had ever heard sounded from the depths of the forest. It was joined by howls from all the wolves that had been fighting with them and by many more packs from all over the forest.

Even the forces of the lich lords seemed to hesitate a moment.

From the forest on the enemy's left flank came a pack of the largest wolves Gidon had ever seen. And standing impossibly on the back of the largest stood Ulec, armed with a bow.

The pack plowed into the undead army's flank with a flurry of snapping jaws. Ulec, somehow maintaining a standing position on top of the leaping wolf, fired arrow after arrow into the undead army.

Gidon saw Ulec leap to a low branch as the monstrous wolf he was riding stopped to bite a revenant cleanly in half. Ulec ran down the branch shooting arrows down into revenants before dropping to the ground to stand back-to-back with his father.

"Look out!"

Gidon heard the warning as he caught movement in the corner of his eye. A revenant was striking down at him but before he could react the blow was deflected by a short sword.

He used his own sword to cut down the creature and glanced just long enough to recognize his oldest son standing next to him. He didn't even have time to thank him as the undead army was now attacking with renewed effort. Following the example of the two elves he turned his back to that of his son's and they settled into the task of staying alive till help arrived.

The horns sounded again after several long minutes of intense fighting followed by the sound of falling trees. Gidon swung his sword unleashing an arc of magic clearing out all nearby enemies; giving Gidon a moment to see what was, in that moment, a truly beautiful sight.

Smashing through the trees were several huge beasts. They were huge creatures with thick brown fur and long tusks coming from the sides of their mouths underneath a very long nose. However, these weren't beasts of the forest for these animals wore armor over much of their body and carried baskets on their backs, which in each sat a man holding reigns and three archers. Being pulled by each beast was a long war wagon that was basically a long box on wheels with archer slits in the side.

"Mammoth Riders," Gidon exclaimed in awe as a line of mammoths began stomping through the undead army, crushing them under tree trunk sized legs and raining arrows down on the enemy from both the baskets and the war wagons.

Gidon turned his attention back to the work of destruction on all enemies that approached him. He fought with a renewed vigor as several mammoths broke off from the others that were plowing long lines of destruction through the enemy masses and created a line of mammoths and war wagons right in front of Gidon's defensive line.

Once they had made a wall between the main mass of undead and Gidon's men, the back of the wagons dropped, and armed soldiers poured out and created a new defensive line.

It was as the soldiers first started pouring out, that Gidon noticed the harp music coming from one of the baskets and smiled as he recognized the music being played and the strengthening effect it was having. He was now pretty sure he knew who to thank for bringing the reinforcements.

He couldn't see his second born son for he was sitting low in the basket, but he was relieved to know Almas was there and unharmed enough to be using his bard skills.

As he and his men finished the few remaining enemies trapped between the two human lines, he gave orders up and down his lines for those not wounded to go retrieve the refugees and get them and the wounded into the war wagons.

A man wearing the uniform of a Forjad officer approached Gidon and asked brusquely, "Where is Lady Izybel?"

"Helping to defend the refugees. She will be down with them shortly."

"I'm here now," came a voice from behind. Gidon looked behind him to see his wife riding up on Kitty, his war mount, with Giddy seated also on the mount in front of her.

The man bowed and said, "My lady, I am Lord Mason of Debigroc. We must leave. I do not believe my men will be able to hold off an onslaught like this for long."

"You will hold it until we have gotten all refugees safely in the wagons," Izybel responded.

Gidon stood silent. Now that they were in the Forjad Province, his wife was the highest authority present, and he admired how easily she slipped into that role.

"Is Cady with you also?" Izybel asked, allowing only a trace of the worry he knew she felt enter her voice. Almas could still be heard playing music from the top of the mammoth lending strength and alertness to those holding the line.

"Yes, both of your children insisted on coming and using their talents to aid in your rescue. Your daughter is in this wagon here."

Lord Mason motioned them to follow him into the back of the nearest war wagon which was filling quickly with refugees. He stopped short in utter shock when he caught sight of his daughter kneeling next to an injured soldier, holding glowing hands to the man's chest. She was using holy magic to help heal the man. When had she started doing that and how did he miss the fact she had learned to use paladin skills? Izybel had also stopped abruptly in surprise.

"That's the last of the refugees my lord!" A soldier called from outside.

"Signal the war mammoths to cover us as we retrieve our men and get out of here," Lord Mason called back.

THE OTHER SOLDIERS in the basket made sure Almas kept his head down low in the basket, so he didn't get to see the fighting; which was okay with him. His focus was on using his music to send as much power to those fighting as he could with his Bard skills and now with his newfound ability to feel magic, he could see it flowing from him to his instrument and from there to all the soldiers from Debigroc. He also focused on trying to ignore the pain from his shoulder where the curse that had jumped to him from Ulec had taken hold. It was beginning to sting.

Suddenly one of the men in the basket called to the others, "That's the signal! The refugees are in the wagons. Flame barrier now!"

The archers put down their bows and picked up jars that had been stacked at their feet and began to throw them over the side. With everyone's attention away from him, Almas snuck a quick glance over the side of the basket. The jars the men were throwing were breaking and bursting into flames creating a wall of flame between the undead army and the line of soldiers who were beginning to scurry into the war wagons. Meanwhile the war mammoths were stomping through the ranks of Kadus knights and revenants near the fires aiding further to the recovery of the last of the foot soldiers.

He was suddenly pushed back down by the nearest archer who told him stay down using words that men rarely used around children of high lords.

He heard someone yell, "That's it! Go!"

The mammoth lurched forward as the men continued to rain down arrows and those fire jars on the enemy as they dashed away.

After what felt like a long time but was probably only a minute or two one of the soldiers called on the other men to hold their fire. Another said in an awed voice, "Look at that..."

Almas peeked again and looked behind them. At the rear of the last war wagon trees were falling to the ground creating a tangle of branches, many in flames, keeping the undead from pursuing them.

It had to be Ulec. It was clear the soldiers had never seen anything like it. They had made it. They were safe for the moment.

Suddenly he felt someone grab his arm.

"You're hurt!"

It was the soldier that had been in charge. He was pointing to a wet red spot on the sleeve of his shirt right over where the curse was.

"I... I cut it in the forest earlier," Almas lied.

"We need to get a bandage on that," the man said.

"I'll take care of it."

Everyone whirled around to find Ulec standing in the basket folding a strip of cloth.

"How...when did you get up here?" The man asked.

Almas laughed, "I've been asking him that for years, I wouldn't expect much of an answer. He can help me with my arm."

The man shrugged and releasing Almas went to his spot in the basket and began scanning the land around them for threats along with the rest of the men in the basket.

Ulec knelt beside Almas and pulled up his sleeve. A cut was forming on his arm. Ulec looked at it a moment before beginning to bandage it. As he worked, he leaned close to Almas and said in a low voice that only Almas could hear, "That is my wound on your arm. How did you move my curse to you?"

"I'm not sure," Almas whispered back, "I just couldn't let you die."

"Better me than you," Ulcc murmured.

"Not in my opinion. We have more time to figure this out now. Neither of us are dead yet."

Epilogue

"THIS MAN IS AS SLIPPERY as an eel."

"So, after all of that you will use Lord Lich-El's plan after all?"

"Yes, provided they haven't discovered our spy."

"If they have it's your fault for acting outside of Lord Lich-El's orders.

"Remember your place human, just because you're favored by our leader, don't think you are beyond my reach."

GIDON WAS RIDING IN a basket atop a mammoth when they came into view of Debigroc. First there was the cliff rising high above the ground marking the beginning of the Barrier Mountains. It was a wall of stone that ran as far as could be seen to the north and the south.

They were riding towards a crack in the cliff with a manmade wall stretching the length of the crack. Gidon knew the wall was large but in comparison with the immense cliff on either side it looked tiny.

"How could such a thing come to be?" Gidon asked in awe to no one in particular.

"Mundial told me when he first found this world it was frozen. He told me this cliff was made by a mountain of ice much larger than these mountains. It carved the cliffs by sliding slowly south from the Dividing Mountains," Lord Teanas said from next to Gidon.

The high lord turned to his elvish companion, "If memory serves me Debigroc was once an elvish city?"

"It was one of our royal cities. I used to play alongside this very river with my siblings as a child."

Lord Teanas had a wistful faraway look in his eyes as he looked at the city.

"You elves built it well," Lord Mason said from behind them, "The Crafters Guild have a very high standard for their buildings and cities. We kept all the original buildings and have only added onto what was already here."

"The walls are enchanted also," Lord Teanas added," Even Lich-El could not break through them."

"That is well," Gidon said, "Our people can get some rest here and maybe we can see if we can't stop reacting in this war and start acting. By now the Aguerius Province should be completely evacuated and the first phase of our plan completed. Now it's time to start the second phase and show our enemies we can do more than run."

The Necromancer

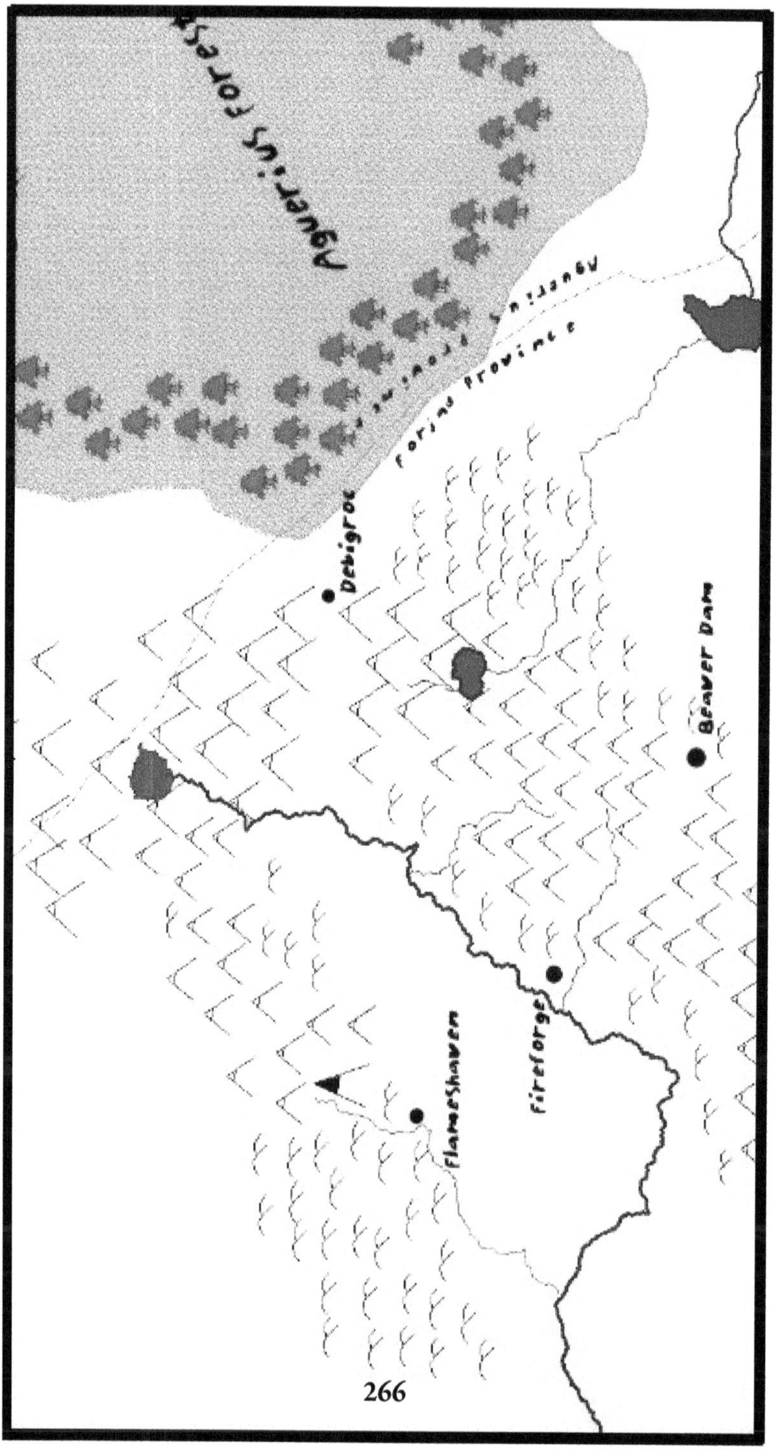
Aguerius Forest
Aguerius Province
Forind Province
Debigroc
Beaver Dam
Fireforge
Flameshaven

Chapter 1

"YOU WANT TO MOVE ALL of our people to the Forjad Province?"

"Yes, we must strike before they have a chance to prepare themselves. We can't let the people here escape us like those in the Aguerius Province did."

"No matter how isolated the spot you have found for our camp, you are asking my Kadus Knights to bring their families to the front lines of a war zone. The extra guards we would need to post to protect them while we are away to battle–"

There will be no guards posted. We will need all our men for the battles. Aren't your people a warrior culture? Do you not train your young to defend themselves?"

"Lord Lich-El would never –"

"Lord Lich-El is still away, which means I'm still in command. You will do as you are ordered. Now let's hurry and bring your people here and set up our camp. We have a battle tonight."

THE LINE OF WAR WAGONS pulled by huge mammoths proceeded towards the city that was protected inside a huge crack found inside an immense cliff face that stretched as far as one could see to the north and south. Inside the wagons, refugees from the Aguerius Province huddled together. In the basket of one of the lead mammoths, High Lord Gidon Aguerius looked over the caravan as it approached the city.

"Lord Mason!" A call rose up from the war wagon in front of the lumbering animal.

"Speak!" The lesser lord standing behind the high lord responded.

"Lady Izybel wishes to join you!"

Lord Mason stopped the caravan just long enough for Gidon's wife to exit the war wagon and climb up the rope ladder to the basket. As soon as she was in the basket, she spoke to Lord Mason.

"Stop the caravan outside the city wall. We will unload the refugees there."

"As you wish, your Ladyship. May I ask why? We can't be sure how far back the undead army is."

"Giddy told me he found a strange rock in our campground this morning. He said when we left the border of Aguerius Forest the stone became hot, and when he dropped it, the magic gate appeared right next to where it landed."

"A marked stone?" The elvish Lord Teanas asked, "In the Sacred Forest?"

"Someone in our group must have brought it with us! That is how they kept finding us!" Gidon exclaimed.

Izybel nodded, "We will need to do a complete search of everyone and everything we bring into the city."

"You think one of the refugees might be a Kadus Knight?" Lord Mason asked.

"There could've been one among the people from any of the other towns. Not to mention 30 people my son rescued from an undead dungeon. There could've been a knight among them," Gidon answered.

"So, as I said, we search everything, and everyone entering the city," Izybel said.

"As you say," Gidon responded. All things aside, it was good to see his wife this way, in command. She was always so careful not to overstep her authority in the Aguerius Province, but now she was once more in her own lands where only her father had more authority, and she wore it well. It was one of the things that had attracted him to her. If he had to be in the predicament they were in, he was glad to be in it with this woman.

ALMAS WAS SITTING ON the ground looking at the walls of Debigroc as the soldiers conducted their search. He sat with Ulec, Cady, and Giddy who were talking to each other, but he wasn't paying attention.

His arm was hurting more and more by the moment, and he was trying to push the pain to the back of his mind. He wondered how Ulec had been able to stand it for so many days.

When Ulec was dying of an infection from a cursed wound on his shoulder, Almas had somehow been able to not only see the curse but remove it to his own shoulder. They had been able to save Ulec but now the cursed wound was appearing on his own shoulder. Almas wondered how long before infection brought him down.

"Help me!"

Almas looked up, being pulled suddenly from his thoughts by the sound of his younger brother calling for help. He hadn't noticed Giddy wander away from the group, and now Almas saw that he had gone over to one of the nearby mammoths. He must have grabbed hold of the animal's trunk and then failed to let go when the large beast raised its long nose up into the air. Now the young boy was hanging from the trunk high above the ground. Too high to drop comfortably, but not so high to put him in danger of being hurt.

Cady was the first to respond to the situation, "Serves you right. I told you to leave them alone."

"Ulec, tell him to let me down!"

Almas glanced at his elvish best friend. Ulec could speak to animals but by the mischievous expression on the young elf's face, he was likely the cause of Giddy's predicament.

Ulec called up, "He likes you. I think he wants to give you a nice big kiss."

"No!" Giddy cried as the mammoth began to lower the hanging boy down towards its mouth. Almas could see however that Giddy was laughing. The mammoth gave the boy a lick which made the boy laugh even more.

"Stop, that tickles," Giddy begged after receiving a second lick. After a third time the mammoth put the boy down, the hair on his head on the side he was licked standing straight up.

"That felt really gross," Giddy said, a huge smile betraying how he really felt.

The smile made Almas feel better, Giddy had been quiet and pensive the whole trip to the city. It was a marked stone that he had found that let Tornal create a magic gate to the refugees, which allowed the undead army to attack that morning and Giddy had nearly become the first victim of that attack. The close call had really scared the boy. It was good to see him returning to his normal self again.

Suddenly his thoughts were interrupted once again by a much older voice.

"Almas. Ulec. May I speak with you?

It was Lord Teanas. Almas stood, as did Ulec.

"Of course, Lord Teanas," Almas replied politely.

They walked off with the elf lord far enough from others that no one would hear them.

Finally, Lord Teanas spoke, "Almas, tell me, what do you think of these city walls?"

A little surprised by the question, Almas hesitated a moment before answering, "They...um...look strong."

"Yes, they are, try looking deeper."

So Ulec must have mentioned his newfound ability to see, or more accurately sense magic. Well that really didn't matter, he trusted Ulec's father. He tried to look deeper and after a moment he saw what Lord Teanas wanted him to see.

"The walls are infused with magic," Almas said in awe.

"Yes, they are enchanted, Lich-El himself couldn't even break up these walls. Now look at your crest."

Almas pulled his crest out from under his shirt and studied it. It also was enchanted and every few seconds a small pulse of magic shot out of it. Following the pulse of magic with his eyes he saw it went right to his father who was standing a bit away overseeing the search.

Other pulses were converging on his father, and he realized they were coming from his siblings and mother.

"There is some kind of connection to my father," Almas stated with a questioning voice.

"Yes, your father has your crest magically connected to a compass so he can find you in an emergency. It was how we found where you were so quickly. Such an item as the stone your brother found would behave the same way. That is what you need to keep an eye out for. Those pulses of magic going out towards the undead army."

Almas scanned around him but seeing the world through magical eyes was still so confusing. Turning back to Lord Teanas he started, "I'll keep an eye...out."

He hesitated part way through his response because he noticed for the first time Lord Teanas held enchanted items.

"Your ring is enchanted?"

Lord Teanas glanced down at the ring on his hand. "Yes, this ring is a fieles—Mimic."

"Mimic?"

Ulec answered for his father, "It has the power to change form to any weapon it has had contact with before. If it has come in contact with a fieles then it can also mimic the powers of that fieles when it takes its form."

With a flash of light, a sword appeared in Lord Teanas' hand.

"Wow," Almas exclaimed and then asked, "What about the thing in your pocket?"

Lord Teanas smiled as the sword vanished and answered, "That is why I want both you and Ulec. I have a gift for each of you."

The elvish lord brought out what looked like two bundles of beads and strips of leather.

"This is called a rusica," he said spreading out one of the bundles.

It was a web of leather threads with colored wooden beads making a design that looked like a wolf's face with a brown background.

On one side of it, the leather strings were connected to a bracelet, while on the opposite side had four strings attached to four rings.

Lord Teanas slipped the bracelet around Almas' wrist and then slid the four rings on his fingers leaving out the thumb. The result was the web covered the back of his hand.

The elvish lord then put the other one on Ulec's hand which had a design of a tree rather than a wolf on it.

"They are both enchanted," Almas stated.

"Yes, they are both connected. If you press the center bead with the intention to make the magic active–"

Lord Teanas pressed the center bead and Almas saw a small burst of magic shoot out to Ulec's rusica and a bead on it started glowing.

"–it will cause the other one to point and lead the one wearing it to you."

"So Ulec can find me if I want him to and the other way around?"

"Precisely, as both of you seem to have a habit of getting into trouble, I thought having a way to call and find each other would be prudent."

Lord Teanas handed Ulec his rusica who wordlessly studied it a moment before putting it on, then the elvish lord motioned for the two boys to follow him.

"Now I believe it is about time for us to enter the city, let us go."

The city was amazing, it was so different than other cities that Almas had seen of the Forjad Province during trips to visit his grandfather. After passing through the wall's gate, he came to a large plaza lined on either side by stables and barracks with sheer cliffs rising high above on either side. In the center of it was a huge boulder the size of a large building.

Beyond the boulder, the plaza ended with a wall of buildings with only a single road passing though the center into the city beyond. The road only went a few hundred feet before splitting into two roads that angled towards either side of the passage through the mountain, the city filling up what amounted to a crack through the cliff just wide enough for two or three city blocks.

It was the architecture of the buildings more than anything that made the city so different. Most were so much more rounded and curvier than ones found in other cities in the province. Almas realized these were original elvish buildings.

"What's in those jars?"

Ulec's sudden question brought Almas back from all the sights of Debigroc. Ulec was looking at a stack of jars next to a ballista on top of a barrack.

"The jars?" Almas asked somewhat surprised, "Those are Forjad Firebombs. The same things that the mammoth riders were using against the undead army this morning."

"What is it made from?"

"I don't know, it is a closely guarded secret. I figured you would have found it out a long time ago."

Ulec shook his head and said," This city is too far from Aguerius Forest for me to easily see it."

They were silent the rest of the way. Most of the refugees were being sheltered in the city offices while the Aguerius family were given rooms in Lord Mason's home along with Ulec and his father.

The grownups went directly to war councils while servants saw to feeding the children and showing them to their rooms.

Exhaustion from days of fleeing the lich lords' armies caught up to them, and they were all asleep before sun had even set.

Chapter 2

“OUR SPY SHOULD BE OPENING the gates soon. We must be ready to attack."

"I want to know why I won't be with my men.

"Lich-El was clear when he left that you were to take charge of our spy when he returns to us."

"Do you really think he will open the gates? We are betting a lot on him succeeding."

"He has no choice, and no one will ever suspect him."

TEANAS WALKED ALONG the side of the immense boulder in the courtyard between the city and the city gates with Lord

Aguerius. Night had fallen and they walked in the shadow of the huge rock. They walked unseen by the sentries on the wall.

When they reached a depression in the side of the boulder Teanas put his hand on the side of the rock face and spoke an elvish word. An opening appeared in what a moment before had been flawless stone, revealing a staircase leading under the boulder.

As they began to descend the stairs Gidon commented as much as asked, "And I suppose no one in this city is aware of this little secret passage?"

Teanas smiled as he responded, "No one ever asked for a list of secret passages or chambers when I gave up this land, but I'm sure they will find it someday. Humans always seem to start tunneling underneath their cities eventually."

Before Gidon could give any response, the stairs ended at the entrance to a large room with floor to ceiling shelves on each wall. The shelves were filled with books and manuscripts covered with Elvish characters. There were also rows of bookshelves throughout the room.

"Nice library; now, why are we here?" Gidon asked after taking a long look around the room.

"I needed to look something up", Lord Teanas responded and then asked, "Almas still remembers nothing about how he was healed of his wounds?"

"No, he only remembers waking up in a room with Lich-El."

Teanas began looking through old tomes and manuscripts as he continued, "The hole in his shirt from the blast of magic was over his chest and his crest was badly melted. How serious would you say his injuries should have been?"

"They should have been fatal. The heat needed to damage his crest as it was should have burned deep into his chest."

"Could you have healed him if you had been present?"

Gidon hesitated a moment before answering, "No, my magic can only speed up natural healing, his lungs and heart should have been damaged beyond the ability to heal."

"So, to heal him the lich lords would have had to create new flesh?" Teanas asked as he found several old bound pages and removed them from a shelf and sat down at a table with them.

Gidon answered, "Correct."

Teanas continued, "To my knowledge, all healing magic used by mortals follow the same principle. They can't heal what the body itself couldn't do if given the time. But unless the lich lords have an immortal Kaynarian God that didn't die in the War of Destruction, they found a way to do it."

"Let me guess, the book you found tells how to do such a thing?"

Teanas smiled and responded, "This contains a desert elf's research. It speaks of what he calls Creation Magic. The magic to change something's nature. While mortals are limited to using magic to manipulate the world around them. The gods could create new things. That is how they made this world and the life on it."

"Wait," Gidon put one hand up to interrupt Teanas as he clutched the bow hanging on his shoulder.

Teanas realized he was speaking with the fieles known as Sacred Knight. Suddenly Gidon continued, "If that is a power that only gods can use then how did my ancestor Lord Morin do what he did?"

"*Read the last page,*" came a voice to his own head. It was his own fieles, Mimic. The one in his ring.

Teanas turned to the last page and began reading. After a few moments he found what he was looking for.

"It says here that Creation Magic requires huge amounts of magic. Mortals simply don't have access to the magic pools needed. Even in the rain forests where there are the greatest stores of Natela magic, there wouldn't be enough magic to do such a thing. A human would exhaust themselves before creating enough Trabar Magic. Lord Morin had Snipies' blood; that must have given him enough power to do what he did."

"So, you think they used Kaynarian blood to heal my son?"

"*Let me speak to him,*" Mimic spoke out.

Teanas extended his right hand to Gidon, "Take my hand, Mimic wishes to speak to us."

The human did as he was instructed and listened.

"You are missing some important points. While what that snot-nosed lunatic of an ancestor of yours created was impressive, the important point is what he did to himself. He healed his mind and gave himself magic abilities.

"Now another human has been subject to the same kind of magic and what are the odds that after having been healed by this power that your seemingly generous enemies stopped there?

"Do you really think that after being under the influence of this magic, it's a coincidence that he suddenly developed a new magic ability? How they got the magic to do what they did is irrelevant. What is important is this; what other alterations did they make in your son?"

Gidon let go and stumbled back in surprise.

"No, that can't be," he stammered.

Teanas' mind was also racing. Tornal had wanted Seacra for some sort of experiment. Almas had taken the blast meant for her. It was very possible that he had become the subject of Tornal's experiment in her place as well.

"Lord Gidon, I hope Mimic is wrong, but we need Almas to be watched at all times till we know for sure."

Teanas returned the pages to the shelf and was about to suggest they go find Almas when the muffled sound of horns started sounding from somewhere outside the rock.

"Are those...?" Teanas started to ask but was cut off by Gidon's answer.

"It's a call to arms...the city is under attack!"

ALMAS WAS HAVING THE nightmare again. The same one he had every time he fell asleep; the one he could never remember when he woke up.

He was back in Demon Mountain; in the same room he had woken up in right before he had met Lich-El. There was, however, something different, Lord Teanas was standing next to him.

"What are you doing here?" Almas asked.

Lord Teanas without looking at him answered, "I'm not. This is, after all, a dream. Perhaps we should see how it plays out."

Almas wasn't sure what he meant, but when he followed the gaze of the dream Teanas, he saw Lich-El and Tornal standing above a bed in which he saw himself lying in, asleep with his arms and legs bound.

The two Lich Lords were talking to each other.

"I gave one order, and you couldn't even do that right?" Lich-El said angrily.

"I was able to save him!" Tornal defended.

Lich-El shook his head and accused, "He wasn't supposed to be injured to begin with, Tornal!"

"How was I supposed to know he'd jump into my attack?"

"The boy is an Aguerius; self-sacrificing for others is bred into the Paladin line. Why do you think after over a hundred years, Gidon and his children are all that's left of the line?" Lich-El explained.

"I think you're forgetting about your 'pet'," Tornal countered.

"He abandoned that line years ago and the line has abandoned him. But he isn't what we're discussing. I'll be taking the boy into my personal custody from this point. I expect that is fine with you?"

"Yes...yes Lord Lich-El," Tornal agreed subdued.

"Is your experiment complete?" Lich-El asked.

"It is my lord, but I wish you had let me use the remaining prisoners; I would have liked to have altered his mind better, I think I could've bound his will more," Tornal complained.

"I have my own purpose for the remaining prisoners," Lich-El responded. "Now wake him."

Almas watched Tornal command his sleeping form to wake. He saw his own eyes open with a start and looked around with an expression of terror.

"Where am I? What happened?"

"You were fatally injured defending your friends. Tornal was forced to conduct his experiment on you in order to revive you."

Dream Almas looked at the two lich lords standing above him in horror, "What did you do to me?"

Tornal answered, "I trapped you in the doorway between life and death. I altered you and have given you the ability to lean either way; lean out towards life and you are in your human form as you are now, lean out towards death and you can take the form of a lich lord with all the powers of one of us. Remember however, no matter how far you lean towards one you will always have one foot in the other so that you will never be completely human or undead."

Lich-El continued, "Tornal made a few other adjustments. You have the ability to see magic and steal magical traits you may find in others. Also, Tornal has enslaved your mind in that you must obey his commands."

"So that is what happened," Dream Teanas muttered.

Almas was too horrified to pay attention. This was simply a nightmare, it had to be. He would have remembered this.

Lich-El continued, "Now take your lich form."

Dream Almas continued to just stare in shocked silence and after a moment Lich-El turned his head to give Tornal a stern glare.

Tornal quickly said, "I order you to obey Lord Lich-El's command."

When Lich-El continued to glare expectantly Tornal quickly added, "All of his commands!"

Dream Almas suddenly gasped as his skin started to turn pale and his eyes turned a yellowish color. Spikes of bone began growing up and down his arms. In just a moment Dream Almas had transformed into a lich lord.

"Very good," Lich-El said, "this will be most helpful. Tornal, give me one of your marked stones, then you will leave us."

"But my lord, he is my experiment -"

"And I told you he is now in my custody! Leave us!"

Tornal backed out of the room cowering all the way out. Once he was gone Lich-El turned his attention back to Dream Almas.

"Time is short, your father is on his way here to rescue you. Here are your orders. I will soon order you back to sleep, you will wake up after two minutes and remember nothing of what you have seen and heard since we woke you up. After you are rescued, you will be trapped by a force of undead before you reach Jaspen. Make sure you are forced to flee west across Aguerius Forest to Debigroc in the Forjad Province. On the far western side of the forest, you will drop Tornal's marked stone. Then after you have reached Debigroc you will remember everything in a dream during your first night there. You will then unlock the city gates and rejoin my army. You will obey all orders of the leader of the Kadus Knights from then on. Now sleep and forget."

Almas snapped awake with the sound of Dream Teanas swearing in elvish ringing in his ears. It took him only a moment to realize for the first time in weeks he remembered his dream...it was a dream, it had to be!

Almas closed his eyes to try to will himself back to sleep only to realize his eyes were still open and he was getting out of bed! He had to go open the gates to the city.

He shook his head; he couldn't do that! Yet there he was creeping out the door! Realization hit him that it hadn't been a dream, they had done something to him! He was the traitor! He had brought the marked stone that had allowed the undead to follow them to the Forjad Province. He remembered now that the stone had been in his pocket all that time; *he* had dropped it in the place where Giddy had found it.

He quietly left the building and began to make his way towards the city gates. He needed to figure out how he was going to open the gates. Wait, no! He needed to find a way to stop himself, lives depended on it; his family's lives, and his friend's life depended on it!

Almas made it to the courtyard between the city and the city gates. He couldn't pass without being seen so he didn't even try.

"What are you doing out at this hour?" The sentry immediately asked.

Almas tried to warn the sentry to stop him but instead found himself saying, "I need to find my father."

He lifted his crest into the light to make sure it caught the light of a nearby torch.

"Oh. Your father passed by here a little while ago with the elf. I last saw them near Sentry Rock," the sentry said indicating the huge boulder in the center of the courtyard.

"Thank you," Almas said as he left the sentry and entered the courtyard. Being the grandson of the high lord of the province had its privilege.

He moved around Sentry Rock and from its shadow looked around. There was no sign of his father or Lord Teanas. The barracks and stables were quiet. Only the sentries on the wall and by the gate were visible. The gate doors were thick metal with a large metal bar keeping them safely closed. Breaking it down was out of the question.

Almas looked closely at the flows of magic around the courtyard. He could see the Natela magic coming off of the men and also from the animals in the stables. Looking near the barracks he saw a different kind of magic.

It was emanating from a refuse pile on the side of the building. Rotting leftover food; fruit, vegetables, meat, and bones. As it decayed it slowly released a dark kind of magic.

An idea hit him, a terrible idea. He tried to banish it immediately from his mind, but he was already moving towards the rubbish pile.

As he approached, he heard a familiar voice behind him.

"Almas?"

It was Ulec's voice. He stopped in his tracks. His orders from Lich-El were to save Ulec's life; he couldn't kill him if he tried to interfere. The moment of relief that thought brought was quickly replaced once again by horror. What if someone else tries to stop him? What if someone from his family tried? He had to get away from those he cared for!

First, he needed to figure out how to both get the gates opened and not kill Ulec when his friend tried to stop him.

"Almas, what's wrong? You activated your rusica."

Almas glanced at the bracelet, rings, and beads on his hand. Sure enough, there were small bursts of magic leaving it and going to Ulec's rusica behind him. When had that happened? He didn't remember even thinking about activating it and calling for Ulec. In fact, the curse controlling him should have stopped him. What was going on?

Ulec gave him no time to consider it as he continued, "There are a few undead outside the walls just out of view of the sentries. We need to warn the guards!"

Time to plan was over, it was time to act. He felt that weird dark feeling that had been with him since Demon Mountain increase as his body took its undead form. He still had his back to Ulec, and his cloak blocked him from seeing his transformation.

"They aren't just outside the wall. They are already inside." Was that a warning? Did he manage to act outside his orders? No, it was a distraction. Ulec's attention would be looking for threats nearby now, not on him.

Almas reached into his sleeve and broke off one of the bone spikes that had appeared up his arms when he had changed to his undead form. He threw the bone into the refuse pile and in a flash of darkness a horror appeared in the form of a mass of bones resembling the skeleton of a cow with long horns.

"Almas?" Ulec cried in alarm as Almas finally turned to face his friend. Ulec looked at him with a look of pure shock and terror.

Almas stared back with an undead face still stained with tears that had been falling freely a moment ago.

"Please stop me—kill me," he managed to say right before several fluttering masses of bones, resembling the skeletons of birds, jumped out from behind the larger bovine skeleton and pounced on Ulec.

The elvish boy immediately began thrashing about trying to throw off the pecking and scratching undead creatures. Meanwhile the bovine creature began charging at the city gate. It had made it more than halfway before a horn sounded an alarm.

It was too late, the only guard that was able to try to meet the charging monstrosity was knocked to the side a moment before it hit the large doors which didn't even budge. As the other guard by the gate approached to attack, the skeletal cow lifted its head and used its horns to lift the large metal bar that was locking the doors. With a turn of its head, it slammed the bar into the second guard.

Now many horns were sounding along the wall. The city was beginning to respond.

"Almas! What are you doing?"

Ulec had pulled his dagger out and Metal was out of its bag spraying down one of the undead birds with acid. Ulec was cutting down the remaining creatures.

"I'm sorry! They did something to me, I can't resist their orders," Almas sobbed.

The city gates burst open as revenants and Kadus knights burst into the plaza. Outside the doors a magic gate could be seen glowing and pouring out an army. He had one more order, he ran to meet the invading army he had just unleashed on his family, friends, and thousands of innocent people.

Chapter 3

"WHERE DID TORNAL GO?"

"He is by the magic gate. He must be near it to anchor this side of it in place. He is bringing in the remainder of our forces. They are already putting up a stiff resistance. "

"He should be helping to secure the gate to the city. If we allow them to form an organized defense, we risk losing a lot of forces in winning this battle."

"Let us worry about taking the city. Just make sure your knights follow our orders and see to your new charge. Here comes the boy now, he looks rather unhappy."

"He was just forced to betray his family, friends, and people. I'm sure he is not."

GIDON EXITED THE ROCK and stepped into utter chaos. The gates were open and completely overrun. The plaza was filling with combat as more attackers and defenders poured into it.

He was loading an arrow into his bow when a ballista on the roof launched a projectile at the city gates which erupted in an explosion of flames.

Gidon charged the arrow with magic and released it at a group of invaders! The arrow became a beam of light and all in its path disappeared! More explosions could be heard near the wall and Lord Mason's voice yelling above the noise of combat calling for a retreat.

The flames near the wall suddenly began spinning into several vortexes that suddenly began gathering into one huge flaming vortex in front of the gates, blocking more invaders from entering the plaza.

"Fall back from the walls!" Lord Mason's voice continued to call and Gidon caught sight of him on the front line of the fighting. He was cutting down any undead or knight that was preventing his men from retreating.

Lord Teanas walked past; his hands outstretched in front of him towards the flaming vortex. Fireballs began to shoot out of the vortex, each striking down a revenant or Kadus Knight freeing up more city guards to retreat as ordered.

"They've destroyed the doors; we have no way to seal the gates!"

Lord Mason came up beside Gidon and helped him cut down several more undead as he spoke.

"We will make a line of defense at the entrance to the streets and hold them there as we evacuate the city through the rear gates."

"Will you have time to prepare? Lord Teanas can't keep that up for long."

"He won't have too. We just needed enough time to get all my men off the wall," Lord Mason responded.

He then gave a hand signal in the direction of the barracks and shouted, "Flame up!"

A line of stone pillars rose quickly from the ground to about 9 feet tall. They began spinning and belching out fire, creating a wall of flames.

"That should give us time to get my men into position," Lord Mason said as he and Gidon began jogging back towards the entrance to the city streets.

"What happened?" Gidon asked.

"I'm not sure, I haven't received a report from the men on the wall yet."

The plaza was a bustle of activity. Mammoths were being moved from the stables into the city streets, ballistae were being set up on the rooftops. Soldiers were everywhere with more appearing every moment.

"What can my men and I do?" Gidon asked.

"You can help the evacuation and guard my people till they get to Flameshaven."

"We should assist you and then cover your retreat. You should stay with your people."

"I appreciate your offer but as a strategist you know my men are best suited to defending this city and yours for seeing to their safety on the road," Lord Mason said flatly and before Gidon could respond, he called out to one of his guards, "Hartman!"

The guard stepped over to his lord and saluted.

"What happened to the gates?"

The soldier hesitated and gave a fearful look in Gidon's direction. Finally, he looked back to Lord Mason and said, "I heard a disturbance in the plaza. I saw two boys near the barracks, one seemed to be struggling with several small creatures while the other one watched. There was also some sort of beast made of bones running to the gates. I heard Guardsmen Cooper call out that there were undead outside the gates and so I called the alarm. The beast charged through the guards at the gates and used its horns to open them. Undead began to pour in from outside.

"Did you see who the boys were," Gidon asked, turning pale as a sickening feeling began to overcome him.

Again, the guard hesitated before answering, "It was dark, but they appeared to be your second oldest son and his elvish friend."

Gidon felt his legs begin to become unsteady. Out of nowhere Lord Teanas was at his side steadying him.

"What happened to them?" The elvish lord asked.

Addressing Lord Teanas the guard answered, "Lord Aguerius' son left through the gates unopposed by the undead. I lost sight of the other."

If Lord Teanas hadn't been supporting him, he would have collapsed. They had his son...they had done something to HIS son.

Lord Mason grabbed and shook his shoulder, "Lord Aguerius! We have no time to deal with this now. They didn't harm him as he left, so right now your other children and wife are in more danger than he is. We have to get the people out of here!"

Lord Teanas added, "Wherever Almas is you can be sure Ulec will be near."

They were right. He had to somehow push everything to the side and focus on his job, he rescued Almas once and he would find a way to do so again but right now he had a job to do. He gave a shaky nod and found his own footing again.

"Hartman, take Lord Aguerius and Lord Teanas to oversee the evacuation."

Lord Teanas interposed, "If it is alright, I'd like to stay here and help for a while."

"Very well," Lord Mason said before turning and walking away.

"This way my lord," the guard said as he led Gidon away.

TEANAS WATCHED LORD Gidon walk away, his heart aching for the man. Lich-El had tricked them, they had done something to Almas and had given the boy back only to use him against them.

He was also plagued with worry about his own son. He was sure he had gone after Almas and while he had faith in his son's abilities, he hoped Ulec wouldn't underestimate Lich-El or Tornal.

Lord Mason was lining up his soldiers across the entrance to the city proper. They all had long tower shields with notches in the upper right-hand corner. The edges also had some strange grooves on them.

Once all the men were standing in ranks Lord Mason began speaking as he paced in front of his men.

"Look ahead of you!" The men looked; flames could be seen dancing in the sky high above and beyond the boulder.

"Death is before you; behind you is everyone you hold dear! You are the wall that separates them! Look at the men standing around you. If they fall, or you do, the wall will be broken, and your loved ones might pay the price of our failure."

Lord Mason stopped pacing and facing his men ordered, "Lock shields!"

The first row of men stepped forward and attached their shields into a small grove in the cobblestone running along the width of the road. Once the first row was down the second line of men attached their shields on top of them. Several men then removed some cobblestones a few feet from the new wall of shields revealing holes from which they pulled out long beams of wood.

They angled the beams down towards the wall and attached them. In a matter of moments, they had a ten-foot-tall wall reinforced with beams of wood.

The notches he realized provided small holes in the wall for archers to shoot arrows through or to push spears out.

Lastly several benches were brought out and attached to the bottom of the wall creating a rampart allowing the defenders to be able to attack the invaders from above.

"Lord Teanas, would you care?" Lord Mason asked as he gestured to one of the benches.

The elvish lord stepped up onto the bench and looked over the top of the wall. The glow of the flames had dimmed.

"Won't be long," Lord Mason said looking over the wall next to him.

"Would you have a quiver of arrows to spare?" Teanas asked.

"Would you like a bow to go with them?" Lord Mason asked, raising a questioning eyebrow.

Teanas extended his arm and a bow flashed into existence. "Just the arrows will be fine."

"That is a nice trick," the human lord commented. A gesture to his men and a quiver full of arrows was handed up to the elf.

The glow from the fires faded completely and shortly the sound of many feet on cobblestone could be heard. Then they appeared, marching rank after rank around either side of the boulder and then right towards the wall of shields.

"Ballista take aim!" Lord Mason called out. "Ready...Shoot!"

Small bottles shot out from along the roofs on either side of the defenders guarding the wall. Each struck among the ranks of undead and exploded into flames. Next it was the archers turn. At Lord Masons command, the archers open fired. Arrows poured out from the rooftops, from over the walls, and from the archer slits.

Lord Teanas fired arrow after arrow into the oncoming hordes with perfect aim. Line after line fell from the onslaught of projectiles. Then the first undead reached the wall. Spear points rushed from archer slits while arrows, stones, and exploding pots rained from above. Now those manning the top of the wall had to duck between shots staying clear from enemy arrows and bone spikes thrown from the revenants. As Teanas crouched behind the wall loading another arrow, Lord Mason asked, "Is it me or weren't they fighting much better this morning?"

Teanas stood and shot his arrow as Lord Mason threw an exploding pot before Teanas answered," They do seem more sluggish than normal. Perhaps we are facing a different Lich Lord controlling them."

"Whatever the case, it will still be a long night I fear."

ALMAS SAT WATCHING helplessly as more undead entered the city. His own body had betrayed him. He had left unopposed by the undead hordes to find Deleta outside the city with a lich lord. The Kadus Knight ordered him to sit down and returned to overseeing the battle with the lich, pointedly ignoring him.

He couldn't see the battle past the walls, but he did see the whirlwind of fire blocking the gates. The sight kindled some feeling of hope. If anyone could save the city from being destroyed it was Lord Teanas. But the elvish lord could only block the entrance for so long. Soon the way would be opened again and everyone in the city would be killed.

He had to obey orders. Right now, the only one present that he had no choice but to obey was the leader of the Kadus Knights—Deleta. The only order he had to follow right now was to sit. So as long as he sat, he could do other actions he assumed, but what could he do? He didn't have any instruments, so no bardic skills. All he had was the necromancy abilities Tornal had given him. The thought of using that turned his stomach but what else did he have; everyone he cared about was in danger because of him, he had to try to do something.

There were a couple of problems however, the first being that there were no animal remains nearby to animate, the other being that using death magic for a lich was the same as an elf using Natela Magic; that when one used magic, others nearby could feel the drain the use of magic caused. He certainly could feel the Lich Lord using up a lot of death magic; so as soon as he tried using it the undead creature would know it. He needed to plan this out carefully.

The flaming whirlwind was starting to die down when Almas finally settled on a plan. First, he hoped that his necromancy skills applied to all dead remains, not just animal. He took his undead form and broke off one of the bone spikes on his arm. He then poked the spike into a stick lying on the ground. In a flash of darkness, the spike and stick disappeared and in their place was a long flute with its own bone-like spikes coming out the side.

"Hey!"

The Lich Lord had turned abruptly to face Almas. "That magic is mine. Your only orders are to sit."

"Sorry," Almas said cowering a little. "I just needed to make a flute so I could help you with the battle."

Luckily Deleta seemed to be ignoring him and he had no orders to obey the lich who now was looking at Almas with a somewhat confused look and seemed to be about to ask a question when Almas quickly put the flute to his lips and started playing.

If he directly used magic to work against the undead, then they would see it, resist it, and stop him. So, he had decided to try a more subtle approach. He started sending feelings of strength and power to those who could hear; making sure it was only the feeling and not the real thing.

The Lich's question was cut off before he had a chance to begin it. After a moment of being mesmerized by the music he spoke, "Lich-El was correct about you being an asset to us, just do not use my Mortai magic," and then he turned his attention back to the battle.

"I don't care what he can do. I should be fighting with my knights, not babysitting," Deleta growled not even glancing back to Almas.

"Had you led your forces into the city you would now be nothing but ash and smoke. Your babysitting task saved your life," the Lich Lord responded. Deleta didn't answer.

With no one watching him Almas continued to hold and play his flute with one hand while he used his other hand to remove another bone spike and stuck it into the ground in front of him. This was the moment of truth, did his magical abilities only work with certain kinds of magic or could he use different sources?

The ground he had put his bone spike in was full of dead leaves, twigs, dead insects and other formally living things too small to see. Almas tried using some of the magic he was creating with his flute, and in a small flash, his bone spike disappeared, and a strange looking form appeared in its place.

It was a hand sized creature that looked to be made of assorted leaves and twigs. Like every undead thing Almas had ever seen, it had small boney spikes on its limbs.

Almas glanced at the Lich Lord, but he didn't seem to have noticed or sensed anything. It had worked! He had used necromancy using bardic magic! With a thought he sent the little undead creature scurrying into the bushes where he had it put one of its own little bone spikes into the ground and with another flash a second little undead creature came into being. He had made this one slightly different. He had it spread out its leafy wings and it flew up and over the wall. He could now see the battle through the eyes of his creation. The flaming whirlwind was now gone, and the undead army was assaulting a wall that Lord Mason's people seemed to have made from shields. Lord Teanas was there but he couldn't see his father or any of his other family members.

Almas continued flooding the area with feelings of power, but he made it a feeling of drunk power and added a bit of recklessness into it. Hopefully no one would notice, and it would help the defenders.

Almas almost stopped playing when a bird suddenly landed on his shoulders and startled him, but he managed to hit his notes and keep his spells going. At the same time another bird landed on the city wall next to his flying undead creature. Ulec was watching him and saw what he was doing. The bird on the wall flapped its wing in a signal asking him what he was doing. Turning his head to the bird on his shoulder, Almas whispered, "This is me. Please trust me."

Both birds fluttered off. Ulec would be watching, but thankfully didn't seem to be planning on interfering for now. Almas sent his own creature down to the garbage pile he had used to make the undead bull—he was going to need more help.

Chapter 4

"WE NEED TO BREAK THROUGH their shield wall!"

"Bring in our cavalry, our mounts should be able to break through that wall without any problems."

"Are you alright? You seem to be a little bit slow. Maybe I should tell the boy to stop."

"I have never felt better, leave the boy be. With his bard powers I feel more powerful than I have ever felt before."

"I don't think we should be trusting him to–"

"I said leave him be. Take care of getting the cavalry ready for their attack!"

"I CAN'T FIND ALMAS!"

Izybel was frantic when she found Gidon amiss the turmoil of the evacuation. Creetan, Cady and Giddy were all right behind her. All around them people were moving; soldiers loading the old, young and infirm into war wagons as mammoths were hitched to them. Others were searching for missing loved ones in the crowd while others headed to the rear city exit. Gidon took a deep breath, facing an army of undead would be easier than this.

"He was with Ulec when the battle began. I'm not sure where they are now but Lord Teanas says Ulec is still with him, and they are safe for now."

"We need to find him!"

"The gates are breached; Lord Mason is holding them at the plaza, but he could be overrun at any moment. We need to move these people out now!"

Izybel's face was a mask of confliction; her duty to her people at odds with her need to have her children safe. Just as with Gidon, what she could do, won over what she wanted to do.

"You see to the rear of the evacuation, I'll take point."

"Just be careful," Gidon admonished.

"You find our son. Take Cree with you," Izybel responded and then herded Giddy and Cady away.

"Now what?" Creetan asked his father.

"We make sure no one is left behind. Come on."

THE UNDEAD WERE PULLING back. Teanas wondered what they were up to. So far, their makeshift wall was holding, but they were pulling back far too soon for them to be giving up. That's when their mounted troops arrived.

"What in Mundial's name are those?" Lord Mason exclaimed.

A line of Kadus Knights had appeared riding on top of massive bears.

"Bear Lords," Teanas muttered.

"I think we're about to get run over as if we aren't even here," Lord Mason said as he gave a hand signal to the rear. Instantly the men began removing the supports for their wall and took positions to take down the wall.

The mounted knights began to charge, and Lord Mason motioned Teanas to step down from the benches which were taken away. Ballista from the roofs opened fired.

"What are you planning?" Teanas asked.

"Their animal lords are big. Ours are bigger." With another hand signal a line of Lord Mason's war mammoths came into view behind them. The beasts walked side by side with only just enough room for a man to stand with his back pressed against the wall of the buildings on either side of the line of mammoths. Men scurried to get out of the way and just moments before the two mounted forces met at the shield wall Lord Mason shouted an order and the men manning the wall disconnected their shields and moved out of the way just as the mammoths reached them. A moment later the two opposing forces met.

The first Mammoth lowered its head and scooped up the first mounted bear with its tusks and tossed it to the side to be trampled by another mammoth. As they entered the plaza the men in the baskets began shooting arrows from their bows and explosive jars from their slings.

As soon as the mammoths were past, the soldiers formed ranks in a defensive position. There would be no time to reform their wall.

"What about your mammoths?" Teanas asked as he took a forward position with Lord Mason and watched the mammoths disappear behind the boulder.

"Either they will break through and escape or they won't. The men knew the risks."

There was no time for more discussion as the undead slammed into their lines yet again.

CREETAN'S WORLD WAS confusion. He had been awakened suddenly by the horns sounding the alarm only to immediately find both Almas and Ulec were gone. Where the two could have wandered off too after the day they had had was beyond him. Then having to convince his frantic mother that he had no idea where they had gone. Then his father had told them the pair had gotten themselves stuck on the other side of the enemy force. What was going on?

He was now with his father helping people flee towards the rear of the city, helping some onto war wagons, ordering others to abandon bulky objects that would do nothing but slow down their escape. Meanwhile the sound of clanging swords could now be heard coming from the front of the city.

His father heard it also.

"Come on, we need to see how bad off things are."

Creetan followed his father, his Uncle Jarad, and a few other of his father's men to the front of the city. The narrow entrance to the city proper from the outer plaza had been turned into a kill zone by Lord Mason and his men. Arrows and exploding jars rained down from the rooftops of the buildings while the guards cut down anything that made it pass the deadly hail.

As they approached the rear ranks, they passed a row of pillars that seemed to have risen from beneath cobblestones. A man was on the ground with his head in a hole where one of the pillars seemed to have failed to rise and was tinkering with something.

Meanwhile Creetan's father drew his sword and also raised his hand and Creetan saw a glowing golden shield appear between a guard on the ground and a revenant that was about to overcome him. The guard regained his footing immediately and rejoined the fight. Lord Mason and Lord Teanas appeared from the front ranks covered in the sweat of battle and Lord Mason addressed his father.

"We will have to fall back; we were going to create another firewall but one of our fire screws is jammed. If we can't fix it there will be a gap in the flames, they will be able to pass through."

As Creetan's father gave Lord Mason a brief update on the evacuation a bird landed on Teanas' shoulder and started chirping in his ear. After his father had given his update Lord Teanas spoke as the bird flew away.

"Ulec says he thinks that Almas may have found a way to keep the undead army from pursuing us past the rear city gates."

"Did your bird friend happen to tell you how he was planning to do that?" Jarad asked.

"No, but I wouldn't underestimate either of those boys. If they think they found a way then I would consider their success a good possibility," Lord Teanas responded. There was something in his voice Creetan hadn't seen before. He almost seemed to be trying to convince himself.

"If they did succeed then the undead would have to march south to Fireforge's Pass," Lord Mason murmured.

"How many settlements would be in their path?" Gidon asked.

"Several small towns and villages before getting to Fireforge itself."

"Is Beaver Dam along the way?" Gidon asked.

"Yes, why?" Lord Mason asked.

"The people of Jaspen evacuated there before the city fell."

Lord Mason gave Creetan's father an incredulous look and asked, "How did you get them there? Even if you could pass through the forest that would take several days."

"I won't speak of how it was done on a battlefield, but Ulec assured me they made it there. They will have to be warned."

Creetan couldn't keep quiet any longer, he had to speak up, "What about Almas?"

All the men looked to him, so he continued, "He and Ulec are out there; what are you going to do about them?"

"Creetan," his father began," Things are complicated. Don't think for a moment that every fiber of my being isn't screaming at me to go out and fight my way to your brother, but I not only can't fight my way through an army, but I have thousands of lives depending on me. I will do everything I can but for the moment we have to trust Ulec to watch over him."

"That's it? He's trying to save us but all we do for him is hope an elvish boy can protect him from an army?" Creetan couldn't believe what he was hearing, his brother was out there and not even his own father was going to do anything!

"Creetan, there is more going on here than you know about," his father started, " and we don't have time to discuss it, there is a battle going on!"

At that moment someone called from the ranks of defenders," My Lords, the enemy is regrouping! "

"I must go," Lord Mason said and turned to Lord Teanas and said, "Thank you for your assistance but I believe you will be of more benefit to my people if you go with Lord Aguerius." Then without another word he was back into the fight.

"We have to go too, son," Creetan's father spoke with a gentler tone.

Creetan thought back to just that morning when Almas had brought Lord Mason and his men to save them, he also thought about the battle a few days earlier when Almas had used his bardic abilities to steady his shaking hand and focus his panicked mind. His brother had saved him twice; he couldn't walk away.

"I'm going after him."

His father who had already turned to leave stopped cold and faced his oldest son.

"What was that?"

"If you're not going to do anything then I will. I'm going after him."

Lord Teanas quickly spoke before Creetan's father had the chance to respond, "That won't be necessary, I will go after the boys."

"You have a way out of the city past them?" Gidon asked with raised eyebrows.

"There is a tunnel I can use."

"I'm going with him," Creetan quickly spoke, "He shouldn't go alone. I can help."

His father didn't say anything for a moment, he just stared at his son, then, to Creetan's shock, he reached out and snapped his family crests from around his neck, the crests that identified him as his parent's son, and said, "If you go, then you will not be needing this."

Then before Creetan could react his father removed his own crest and placed it over Creetan's head.

"This one will serve you much better. With this I recognize you as my heir. With this crest you will have all my titles, authority and responsibilities; your words will be my words, your acts will be my acts."

Creetan didn't speak, he could only stare in complete shock while his father continued, "Go with Lord Teanas to Beaver Dam and see to our people's safety there. Your authority will help you both in finding and helping Almas and in assisting the people down there that will find themselves in the Lich Lords path."

Looking at Teanas he addressed the Elf Lord, "Will you take him with you?"

"Yes, his authority will be of great assistance in working with your people."

"Then it is time to go, take this," Gidon removed his bow from his shoulder and handed it to Creetan, "This is a special bow, it can protect you, Lord Teanas will explain. Now go before I realize what I'm doing and change my mind."

His father then held him by his shoulders for just a moment before turning around and walked briskly away followed by his men; his Uncle Jarad gave him a grin and said, "Good luck *Lord* Aguerius," before turning and following the others.

"Come, we must be off," Lord Teanas spoke motioning for him to follow.

Creetan followed, wondering just what he was getting himself into.

GREYSEN CURSED HIMSELF; he had designed these flame screws and it was now of all times he found a flaw in those designs. When he had tried to raise the screw to get it ready to use, it had failed to rise. One of the metal pegs had come loose and had wedged itself just right in the machinery so that it couldn't deploy. He had removed a panel to try to remove it, but he couldn't quite reach it. He tried dislodging it by hitting it with whatever tool he could reach it with, but so far it would not budge. He didn't have time to disassemble the whole thing to reach it, so he kept trying to pound it out with the top of his hammer.

Around him he could hear guards begin to retreat past him; he was running out of time. He heard Lord Mason's voice above him, "Greysen! We have to go now!"

"I just need one more minute!"

"One minute!" Lord Mason promised. The sounds of fighting were right behind him, he didn't dare look up to see what was happening, he just kept pounding. It was at that moment something crawled past him into the hole. It was...well, he wasn't sure what it was, it looked like some small creature that had been put together from small bones, tree, and plant clippings. But the small spikes coming out of what the thing was using for legs clearly marked it as undead.

He was about to smash it when the thing put one of its spikes into a wooden panel; there was a flash of darkness and a section of the panel had disappeared. He noticed two things at that moment, the first was that the sound of fighting behind him had ceased; he was out of time. The second thing was with part of the panel missing he now had a much better angle to hit the wedged piece of metal from. He gave the hammer one last swing with all he had left and with a snap the fire screw shot up out of the ground. He had done it!

A shadow appeared on the screw taking the form of a revenant raising a sword above him. Greysen smiled, his life for the life of hundreds wasn't a bad trade. He extended his hand toward the switch to start the screw. It was out of reach, but he had built this device, he could feel his connection to it; with a little push from magic the switch moved and all the screws in the row began to spin. Then there was a brief flash of heat followed by nothing as flames consumed everything.

THE FLAMES FROM THE row of spinning screws ignited the buildings on either side creating a massive wall of flames that burned solid for an hour giving the defenders time to clear the city.

Gidon watched as guards helped the last of the people out of the gates and into the narrow road passing between two solid rock faces.

"Are there any people left in there?" Gidon asked.

"None we can find my lord."

"And Lord Mason?"

"He was last seen guarding Graysen as he worked on the fire screws. That was moments before they turned on; he hasn't been seen since," the guard responded sadly.

Gidon cursed himself. He should have been there.

"Alright let's go," he ordered his men. He mounted his forest dragon as the others mounted their own dragons and horses. They then rode to a spot as far from the gates as they could and still be able to see them.

He watched as more and more plumes of smoke appeared closer and closer over the city. Then he heard pounding at the gates they had closed and barred as they left. Soon the gates were broken down and the undead army began passing through.

Gidon sighed in disappointment. He didn't know what the Lich Lords had done to his son, but when Ulec had sent the message that Almas was trying to stop the undead from pursuing them, he couldn't help but hope; but here they were, still coming. Now he would need to set up ambushes all along the way to slow the enemy down.

His thoughts were interrupted by what sounded like an extremely loud clash of thunder, only the rumbling wasn't fading, in fact it seemed to be growing louder.

"Look up there!" Someone shouted.

Gidon saw it. A huge rockslide coming down both cliffs right above the undead army. He caught a glimpse of the army retreating back to the city before falling dust and debris blocked his view.

It seemed to take forever for the dust to clear enough to reveal the massive pile of large boulders and rocks blocking the passage. It would take months to clear the passage enough to pass an army through now.

Gidon took in a breath and fought back a sob of relief. Maybe there was hope after all. For them, and for his missing son.

ALMAS DROPPED HIS BONE flute and collapsed onto his back as the lich near him cried out in dismay. Even from the front gates of the city the landslide was visible.

Deleta was the first to speak, "They rigged the cliffs to collapse and block pursuit!"

"He will not escape us that easily, I swear every last one of them will suffer," the undead monster swore as he stomped off.

Almas was only vaguely aware of this. He couldn't believe it had worked. He had sent some of his undead creeps, as he had started calling his little creations in his head, up to the top of the cliff and began building up as much magic as he could. Once the undead army began moving into the passage, he used these creeps to turn all the trees and plants along the edge of the cliff into undead minions and used their root systems to break up the rocks and soil and start the rockslide. It had taken everything he had but it had worked! For now, at least, his family was safe.

He didn't get much time to bask in his victory as he suddenly felt hands grab him by his shirt and lift him off the ground. In an instant his feet were dangling over a foot off the ground, and he was face to face with a very angry Deleta.

"Don't think you fooled me for a moment with that spell you cast with that song. The only reason you're still alive is Lord Lich-El's orders, but if you ever try to deceive me like that again you will be sorry."

Almas took his full undead form and looking Deleta in the eye said, "You think you can do more to me than has already been done? If you want to kill me then trust me when I say I would welcome it!"

Deleta dropped Almas in surprise. Almas collapsed back down to a sitting position but never broke eye contact with the Kadus Knight. Deleta's expression stayed surprised for a few moments before softening for just an instant to a look of pity. But after that instant it was replaced once again by cold hate.

"Well, I'm afraid you're going to have to get used to your new life, apparently there are plans for you. Welcome to the service of Lich-El.

Chapter 5

"THEY BLOCKED THE PASS with a landslide?"

"Yes, we will have to bring our army back to camp for now. Unless you can create a gate to the other side of the landslide?"

"By the time I get a revenant over the slide, it won't matter. We can start raiding nearby villages and towns to build up our strength."

"Very well, send out your runners and I will see to getting the army ready to pass through your gate back to camp."

THE LICH LORD IN CHARGE was angry. Almas saw that as a good thing. Especially when he learned that he was angry at the small number of prisoners and dead from the battle. Most of the few prisoners taken were surviving guards, and the dead didn't nearly come close to the number of revenants lost invading the city.

Deleta was also angry, but Almas could tell he was also a bit disturbed at seeing his father's 12-year-old namesake in the form of an undead lich. Almas made it a point to stay in that form and let him see exactly what the creatures he was serving did to those with the last name Aguerius.

"Come with me boy!" The Lich Lord in charge commanded him after returning from organizing the removal of the undead army back to their new base camp.

Almas responded by making a rather rude face at the creature. He had no order to obey this particular monster.

"Get up and do as Trumion says!" Deleta ordered.

Okay, now he did have to listen to that particular monster. He got up and followed the even angrier lich.

"By Lich-El's command you are to help us come up with optional battle plans. Why he thinks a child has any valuable insight on war is beyond me."

"I wouldn't expect too much, I have a cursed wound on my shoulder and should be dying of infection in a few days."

"I wouldn't be so sure about that," Trumion said with a wicked grin, "In your undead form your regeneration powers will wipe out any infection. You also have no blood flowing so as long as we make sure you don't spend too long in your human form; I think you will be just fine."

Almas realized the lich was probably right. He couldn't feel the pain he had had in his shoulder since taking Ulec's curse on himself. So much for that hope.

Almas was led with Deleta into a tent with a table covered in maps. The lich, Trumion continued, "With the pass blocked we will have to attack towns and cities to the north and south. We will give you what information we have on the towns and cities that will be in our path. You will make the best plans you can in taking these cities and we will see if you are worth the trouble Lord Lich-El thinks you are."

"North *and* south. You won't be attacking in just one direction?" Almas asked.

"No, we will send out scouts to all the cities and use gate travel to focus our forces in the attack."

Almas looked at the map and the names of villages, towns, and cities in the path of the undead horde. How could he make plans for attacking them? There were thousands of people in towns and cities that would soon come in range of an undead attack. To his absolute horror he realized part of his mind was already working out attack plans.

He was relieved for the distraction when another Lich-Lord came in and said, "Lord Trumion, forgive me but one of our prisoners says he has information that he will only give to you."

"Who is this prisoner?"

"It is the Lord of this city."

"Let him in but make sure he is unarmed."

After a moment Lord Mason was brought in, although it took a moment for Almas to recognize him. His clothes were shredded, and he looked to be a bloody mess. Almas stared at him in horror as Lord Mason looked around the room, his eyes landing on Almas who realized he was in his undead form. Without even thinking he switched back to his human form, looking away in shame. Lord Mason's city was a wrecked ghost town now because of him.

Aside from being beaten, Lord Mason looked oddly ill and was looking at Almas with a sorrowful look.

"So, it is true, they did do something to you."

Almas tried to explain, "I'm so sorry, I couldn't stop myself. I tried... "

Lord Mason said, "No, I'm sorry. I had three exploding jars with me and had a long drink before being captured. I'm afraid I can't put this off any longer. Have to do this where it will do the most good."

Trumion and Deleta both looked confused, but Almas understood immediately. He grabbed Deleta by the wrist and shouted "Lookout" as he, without thinking, stepped in front of the Kadus Knight. He felt himself thrown into Deleta as the tent suddenly turned into an expanding fireball and the world went dark.

"Thank goodness I'm finally dead," was the first thing Almas thought to himself.

A familiar voice answered, "Not yet I'm afraid. You're in another dream."

Almas sat up and looked around. In this dream he was in Aguerius Forest and sitting on a log near him was Lord Teanas.

"You were in my last dream. You aren't the real Lord Teanas but you aren't just a dream, are you?"

"No, I'm not just a dream, I'm a fieles."

"What about Lord Mason?"

The fieles shook his head, "He used magic to ignite the explosives he drank. I'm afraid he sacrificed himself to take down a high-ranking Lich Lord. He knew he would have been made a revenant and he didn't want that. He also wanted to hurt the undead army as best as he could."

"How am I still alive? Wait, I think I have this. You're a fieles, one that must have been made from a piece of Lord Teanas' soul, and one of his powers is being fireproof. Let me guess, I have you to blame for my continued existence?"

The fieles nodded, "I was made because Teanas wanted you to be protected. My name is Fireweaver. He decided not to tell you about me when he gave you the rusica because he suspected the undead had done more to you than we had been told. He wanted me to try to find out what."

"Well, he was a little late. Any bright ideas how I can get out of this situation?"

The fieles Fireweaver shook his head sadly and said, "I'm sorry I don't. But remember, *you* are not responsible for what *they* choose to do."

Almas responded, "What they can do, is use me how they want to hurt whoever they want me to; and now they have your abilities to add to that once they find out about you."

Suddenly Almas began to feel the dream collapse. He opened his eyes, the first thing he saw was Deleta crouched over him.

"Well, my head really hurts, what hit me...besides a wall of flame?" Almas groaned.

Deleta looked a little conflicted, but he answered, "The blast threw you into me and you hit your head really hard on my armor. You wouldn't wake up till I ordered you into your undead form."

Almas could feel a tingling in his head as the bad bump he got quickly healed. This undead regeneration had its good points, he was already thinking of ways to use that.

"How did you protect us from the fire like that," Deleta demanded.

Almas sighed and answered, "Apparently, my friends snuck a fieles on me. When we touched after the explosion pushed me into you, the protection I had must have extended to you."

"Why did you try to shield me?"

"Besides the fact you're my cousin? I guess you can call it a bad habit. That is how I ended up with a hole in my chest to start off with, a bad habit of trying to protect people."

By now Kadus Knights and a few revenants from other lich lords could be seen approaching. Deleta seemed to think for a moment and said, "They will take your fieles if they know about it. Tell them we were on the edge of the blast, you shielded me and regenerated already from the burns."

Almas' eyes widened in surprise. "You're helping me?"

"Lich-El demands I pay all debts of honor. Besides, a fieles like that might come in handy, but not if it is in the hands of Tornal or any of the other lich lords besides Lord Lich-El.

"I won't argue with that." Almas surveyed the destruction around them and tried not to think about Lord Mason. By now Kadus Knights were arriving. Deleta waved them off when they asked him if he was alright.

Deleta led Almas away from the devastation. Almas asked as he followed, "So.....who do we need to let know that they just got a promotion; now that Trumion is a pile of ash?"

"That would be me," came a familiar voice, one that Almas had hoped he would never hear again. Looking up ahead he saw Tornal grinning at him.

Almas didn't even hesitate, not wanting to give anyone a chance to order him to stop. He just pointed his right hand straight at Tornal, the one who had made him into the monster he now was.

Tornal must have felt Almas draw in all the surrounding death energy because his sinister grin vanished, and he started to move aside.

Almas' right arm vanished in a dark flash, being replaced by a long bone spear that caught the moving Tornal in his shoulder, right at the base of the arm. Before Almas could do anything else, Deleta called out, "Almas! Stop!"

The bone spear, that had been Almas' arm, crumbled into dust as did Tornal's arm from the point the bone spear had struck him.

Almas was the first to speak, "Well, I really thought that would hurt a lot. It didn't hurt at all. That will be good to know once my arm regenerates."

Tornal, his face a mask of fury, sputtered, "How dare you...I am your master."

Almas smiled, "You kinda forgot to order me not to try to kill you, so you know I had to try. Guess I need to work on my aim."

"You are as of now forbidden to attack or hurt any lich lord," Tornal ordered, glaring at Almas.

"Knew that order would come eventually," Almas said sadly.

"What did you do? And how?" asked Deleta.

Almas responded matter-of-factly, "The bone spikes on our arms converts dead things to undead things. Undead things are technically still dead, so I converted my undead arm into an undead bone spear. You guys never put a whole lot of thought into what is possible with your powers have you? Seriously, couldn't Lich-El find anyone with half a brain to join up?

Then without waiting for an answer, Almas changed the subject, "By the way, out of curiosity, Lich-El told my father you were being punished for what you did to me. What was the punishment?"

Tornal answered, "He said you would be my punishment and I was forbidden to get rid of you. Now we have wasted enough time. You are to come with me and put that supposed brilliance of yours to work on battle plans."

The idea of making planes against his family, friends, and people made Almas feel sick, but he had no choice but to obey. He began to follow the Lich Lord along with Deleta but couldn't resist one more jab; after all, he was supposed to be Tornal's punishment. "Bet you I can grow my arm back before you can."

Tornal glared at him while a glance at Deleta showed the Kadus Knight struggling not to laugh.

Chapter 6

"SO, THE BOY IS A STRATEGIC genius after all."

"Just as Lich-El said. Imagine the plans he could come up with if he was doing it willingly."

"I hope you are not becoming fond of him. Just remember he belongs to me, and don't think I will tolerate that annoying brat for one moment past the second he stops being useful to me."

"You might have turned him into what he is now but don't forget he belongs to Lich-El. Besides, he is only an annoying

brat to you. He has taken his role of being your punishment very seriously."

"And just where is our beloved Lord Lich-El? No one has seen him since the battle of Jaspen."

"I don't care where he is, so long as he is keeping Lady Alixia there, and not here."

CREETAN FOLLOWED LORD Teanas through yet another destroyed village. The undead army so far was moving rapidly south and Creetan was unsure if they would make it to Beaver Dam before them. In fact, he was increasingly certain that they wouldn't.

With every wrecked village came survivors. Mostly children that had fled and hidden in woods and fields. Others that had been hidden by parents and not discovered. They had found one of the war mammoths along with two men from its basket that had fought their way through the undead army and had escaped pursuit. They had found a usable war wagon near one of the ruined villages and were using it to move survivors.

Where to take them was the problem. He couldn't keep following the undead army with them. He would only be delivering these people to the very doom they had just escaped. Yet he had to get to Beaver Dam as he promised his father, and he needed to find Almas.

"If you head south-east from here you might be able to get the refugees out of undead controlled lands and then send them on to the Yucaipa Province. If you then hurry to the south-west, you might be able to get past the undead army and beat them to Beaver Dam."

It was the fieles, Sacred Knight, which had spoken directly to his mind. It would seem that during the War of Destruction, Lord Morin Aguerius had allowed a fieles to be created from a piece of his soul. The fieles had then been passed down the Paladin's line. His advice had so far been greatly helpful.

"They are moving so quickly. Do you really think we can overtake them by going so far around them?" Creetan asked.

"You will never overtake them with these people with you, nor could you protect them if you did."

"Creetan!"

Creetan looked to the source of the voice that had called his name. It was Teanas. The elf moved ahead of him as he had been deep in thought and now approached him quickly.

"We have six more survivors," Teanas said.

Six more people that Creetan was responsible for. How did his father do it? How could he take responsibility for an entire province without his insides twisting up or going crazy?

"Sacred Knight thinks we should head towards the Yucaipa Province and send all the survivors there once we are clear of the undead. Then try for Beaver Dam," Creetan said.

"We would get there too late," another voice stated.

Creetan whirled around to see another familiar face, "Ulec! Where have you been?"

"Making friends with the local animals and trying to keep track of Almas."

"You know where he is?" Creetan asked hopefully.

"It took a little while, but yes, they have him at a hidden base up in the mountains. Most of their army stays there. They only leave when one of Tornal's scouts reaches a village or town, he just opens a gate, and the Lich's armies attack."

"So that is how they are moving so fast," Teanas said.

"Yes, it is," confirmed Ulec, "That's the bad news. The good news is that there are only a few scouts between here and Beaver Dam. If we hurry, we might be able to get there first."

"Why do you look like you have more bad news?" Creetan asked.

"Because I do. The Lich Lords have been having Almas make the battle plans."

"What? He's twelve!" Creetan exclaimed.

"Yes," Teanas said gravely, "but he is also brilliant in strategy, even more so than your father. Even with his lack of experience, he would be the undead's greatest asset."

"But he would never help them. He would find ways to sabotage their plans," Creetan argued.

"And he has been trying," Ulec answered, "But when he is ordered to give his best plan, he has no choice but to give them his best plan. The curse he is under doesn't allow him to do differently."

"So, if you know where he is, why haven't you rescued him? Get him out of there so they can't use him!"

"I would if I could. He is under orders. I'd have to fight him to get him out of there, how would he feel about that? And even if I did get him out, he would still be under their control. Remember what happened to Debigroc? He feels every death in that city is his fault. Any place we take him we risk having the same thing happen," Ulec said defending himself.

Creetan sighed in frustration. He needed to do something for his brother. But even if he knew what to do, how could he do it when he had to take care of so many people.

"Do you really think we can get these people safely to Beaver Dam?"

Ulec nodded.

"Let's hurry than."

"There is something else," Ulec said turning to look at his father, Almas knows about the fieles you snuck on him. The one made from a piece of your soul. When were you going to tell me my rusica is a fieles too?"

To make his point he extended his hand and, in a flash of light, his rusica turned into a sword. "With a piece of Mother's soul, it works just like your ring, Mimic."

Lord Teanas winced and said, "Not telling you was your mother's condition in having them made. She was hoping to learn more about what happened to Almas while he was with the undead. I only wanted extra protection for both of you."

"Well, you will be happy to know it has already saved his life as well as Deleta's. Let's just hope the Lich Lords don't find out he has an item that makes the wearer fireproof and able to control fire."

THE UNDEAD ARMY WAS just about how Almas had always pictured it. They were...well...dead. Even the Lich Lords lacked just about any kind of personality.

It was the Kadus Knights that surprised him. He was expecting the living servants of the undead to be the worst people humanity had to offer. Men filled with everlasting hate for the rest of mankind. It was true that a few of the Kadus Knights were like that, but he was shocked, not to mention a little unsettled, to find that most of them seemed to be friendly.

What surprised him the most was the fact that there weren't just warriors in the camp...there were families. When Almas had first been to the human part of the war camp, he had been horrified at seeing children of all ages present. What kind of monsters took children with them on a campaign of murder?

After so many days being forced to tag along with the leader of the Kadus Knights, something was starting to tell him that these humans weren't anything like he had assumed them to be. At the moment, that something was Kade.

Kade was a boy about the same age as Almas, who seemed to have an endless supply of questions. His father was second in command of the Kadus Knights despite being over a decade older than Deleta.

"So, is it true that the Guardian Spirit of Aguerius Forest is an elf kid?" The boy asked him as he was writing out another battle plan for Tornal. The boy had slipped into the tent and had been hurling questions at him. Almas had considered telling him to go away but he hoped that maybe the boy would distract him and lower the quality of his work. He could tell that it wasn't working even as he responded to Kade's question.

"You mean Ulec? You know about him?"

"Of course, all the survivors from the battle against High Lord Aguerius speak about the two elves, one that controls fire and another that controls the very forest itself, oh and they talk about the elvish lady that can kick blasts of energy at people; I hear she is almost as strong as Lich-El."

Kicks blasts of energy? He must have heard about when Lady Alixia killed the lich that almost had taken them all prisoner at Demon Mountain. Lady Alixia had taken the form of some other elf and had tapped her toe on the ground. A small crack had shot out to the lich, and he had disappeared in a pillar of energy that had erupted from the ground.

"That was Lady Alixia, she is strong, but I think Ulec might be even more powerful, at least he will be if he isn't already," Almas said.

"We had always heard that there was a great power that protected the Sacred Forest of Mundial, but we never guessed it was an elvish boy. My father says he watched the boy take out the entire force that tried to follow your people into Aguerius Forest with ants. He was sure he was a dead man before Deleta thought of a way to escape the trap."

Almas was feeling extremely awkward. He hadn't thought much about the Kadus Knights that had fallen in the battles he had seen, after all, they were the evil servants of the Lich Lords, weren't they? Now he was starting to wonder; how many children had lost parents during these battles? And what kind of parents were they?

He had seen Kade training with his father. It reminded him of watching his own father training with Creetan. Kade's father seemed to be a really good one. It was really hard to keep hating your enemy when you find out so many of them are people just like you. And here Almas was making battle plans that would result in so many deaths of these people and in the deaths of so many of his own.

"So, what is he like?" Kade asked, pulling Almas from his thoughts.

"Who? Ulec? He's well...Ulec. He's really smart and really fast and is the best weapons master I know except maybe his father. He's kinda quiet around people he doesn't know well. He's been my best friend for over four years now."

"Do you think I could meet him sometime? Everyone says I have the quickest knife fighting skills of all the apprentices. Maybe we could dual?"

"You do realize you are on opposite sides of a war, don't you? I'm afraid a dual against Ulec would leave you not only defeated but likely dead."

"Being killed by the best would be a glorious death. Defeating the best would be glorious beyond compare."

Okay, while Kadus Knights were admittedly human, they were also weird. With the current battle plan finished it was his turn to ask some questions.

"So, where did the Kadus Knights come from? We all thought that they were made up of fugitives from the Yucaipan Kingdom, but I get the feeling that isn't true."

Kade answered, "Many of our people are ones that have fled from the oppression of the Lords of your people. But many of us are descended from Chaos Knights. They were Snipies' Honor Guard. In the early days of the War of Destruction Snipies tried to end the war by attacking Destruction's Sacred Forest far to the east of here. It was the final battle between Kaynarian Sky Chariots, they all destroyed each other and crashed to the ground. Those that survived continued the fight on the ground. In the end we won. With the Sky Chariots gone there was no way to rejoin the war or even let Snipies know there were survivors. He and the other gods were too busy with the war to look for any.

"After they found out that Snipies had been killed in the final battle they renamed themselves Kadus Knights after the man they appointed their leader."

"How did you end up working for the undead?" Almas asked.

"About 50 years ago the village we had made was attacked by demons. Lich-El came and saved them. We have had an honor debt to him ever since," Kade answered.

"And how did my cousin become your leader?"

Kade shrugged, "He's the best warrior. Lich-El brought him to us when his father died, and we adopted him as one of us. When he became our greatest warrior, he earned the right to lead. Hey, do you want to have dinner with my family?"

"You do realize I'm here against my will and if I ever get free of this curse, we'll be enemies trying to kill each other, don't you?" Almas asked.

"If you get free of your curse then we can always fight to the death. Till then, you should come have dinner with us. My parents will be going with the troops attacking Beaver Dam tomorrow, I want you to meet them before they go."

"As much as fun as having dinner with some of my captors sounds, I need to get these plans to Deleta." Almas answered dryly.

"Okay," Kade responded cheerfully, "Maybe when they get back."

Almas watched Kade leave, the boy's enthusiasm not suffering any apparent loss. These Kadus Knights were really weird.

"I am sure they find you equally weird. Do not forget they have been taught since their earliest childhood different values than you. If they are descended from survivors of Snipies' honor guard, then they will reflect his values, not all of which are bad." The voice of the fieles on his hand said, after obviously reading his thoughts.

Almas responded with a question, *"So you think that story is true?"*

The answer came after a moment of waiting, *"I believe it is very possible. Most of Snipies forces were lost in the battle Kade mentioned, and the Knights do seem to reflect Snipies' influence. Their focus on bravery, honor, and glory and their putting a lesser importance on the value of life whether it is their own or that of others, being the best evidence. The war gave us little time to search for survivors after any of the battles."*

"Just keep reminding me that they are trying to kill my family if I start liking them too much".

Almas took the battle plans he finished to Deleta. Tornal preferred not to deal with Almas since he made sure to take his role as Tornal's punishment to the full extent he knew how. So, he spent most of his time with Deleta, who wasn't so bad ever since Almas saved his life.

Almas arrived at Deleta's tent and went in. "More battle plans his Royal pain in-"

Tornal was in the tent so Almas had to stop speaking abruptly. Not that he cared if Tornal heard him, but because Tornal had ordered him to never speak in his presence. So, once he saw Tornal, the curse effectively gagged him. As if Almas needed to speak to find ways to pester a Lich Lord.

Almas handed the battle plans to Deleta and then stretched his arms out with a big yawn making sure to exaggerate wiggling all his fingers, especially the ones that had already grown back. Tornal was still working on regenerating his own fingers. Almas smirked at the lich.

Tornal glared at him a moment before speaking. "You will come with me. You will be going with us on our attack on Beaver Dam and we have things to discuss."

Almas didn't say anything...he couldn't if he had wanted to, but he was sure his surprise showed on his face. He hadn't participated in any battle since he had been forced to open the gate at Debigroc.

Tornal left the tent and Almas followed. Was that a pitying look Deleta gave him right before he left the tent?

They walked through the tents of the Kadus Knights and stopped at the grounds they had been using for training. Kade was there practicing combat skills with his father.

Both he and his father were practicing with the same odd looking knifes he had seen them practice with before. The blades didn't come straight out of the handles but at an angle. The handles were also shaped strangely, being in a similar shape as the blades, just not sharpened.

As before when he had watched them practice, Almas couldn't help but be a little nervous. When his father had taught sword fighting to Creetan they had used dull practice weapons; Kade and his father were using real weapons and at the speed they were sparring, Almas was sure someone was going to lose a hand.

At one point, Kade took a step back and threw one of his knives. Almas always found this part interesting because he didn't throw it at his father but to the side and as he attacked his father with his other knife, the spinning odd-looking knife, rather than keep going the direction it was thrown, it moved in an arc around to the back of his father till it was about to strike him from behind. At the same time Kade lunged at his father forcing him to deal with an attack from both in front and behind him both together.

His father blocked Kade's thrust with the knife in one hand and deflected the thrown knife with the knife in his other hand.

The deflected knife shot upward and then suddenly arced downward right back to Kade's empty hand.

"Did you see what happened there?" Tornal asked and then quickly added, "You may answer the questions."

"The weird knife moved in an arc by itself but after it was deflected Kade used magic to change its direction to bring it back to his hand," Almas responded.

"Can you see his magic ability?"

"Yes."

"Describe it," Tornal ordered.

"It seems to grow a little each time he uses it."

"How does it compare to the abilities your elf friends have or like your father's paladin abilities?"

"It is a lot weaker and doesn't seem as stable. It becomes stronger as it is used and weakens when it isn't. My father's paladin abilities are always the same, only the magic put into it changes," Almas answered.

Tornal nodded, "I have found there are two types of magic abilities; talents and gifts. Talents are abilities that come by study and practice. They grow as you build them, but they can also be lost if neglected. Gifts are abilities that one is born with or given, such as your father's paladin abilities or Lady Alixia's ability to take the form of those she comes in contact with. Those abilities are always there regardless of practice or effort."

Tornal stopped watching the father and son as they practiced and faced Almas as he said, "When I gave you the powers of undeath I also gave you the ability to take these gifts and talents from others and also the ability to give what you take to others, just as you took that curse from your friend and took it on yourself."

Tornal smiled and patted Almas' shoulder where the cursed wound that had once been on Ulec's shoulder was now slowly bleeding underneath his own bandages. The contact really hurt but Almas didn't even flinch; he was becoming used to the pain.

Lucky for him it only affected him while in his human form. While undead the wound stopped bleeding and his regenerative abilities wiped out any growing infection before it became a problem. In other words, there was little threat of this curse killing him like it had nearly done to Ulec unless he spent too long in his human form.

Almas wanted to ask Tornal where he was going with all this, but he couldn't and was also a little afraid he knew the answer. Tornal didn't make him wait.

"Tomorrow during the battle, you will help me by taking abilities from our enemies and then give them to me."

Almas wanted to ask why Tornal didn't give himself the power to steal abilities and let him go home, but he couldn't due to the gag order. His fieles answered his question for him.

"He said you were an experiment. He would need to make sure everything turns out as he wants before doing it to himself."

"So why keep me around, if he knows it works, he could give himself the abilities and get rid of me."

"I'm not sure. It might be Lich-El has ordered him to keep you around or he hasn't finished his experiment or perhaps for some reason he cannot repeat it."

"I'll add that to my list of things to find out."

Meanwhile Kade's practice session had ended and while his father left, the curly haired boy came up to his audience.

"Hi Almas, are you still under the gag order with Tornal around?"

Silence from Almas was his answer. Tornal answered him instead, "Go home boy, we have no time for you, we have a battle to prepare for."

Kade ignored the lich lord and continued speaking to Almas, "Since you can't speak, would you like me to pester Stubby for you?"

Was this kid crazy? Almas vigorously shook his head no, but Kade—being Kade—ignored it and directed his next words to Tornal, "Almas says he hates you and hopes you get turned to ash really soon."

Yes...Kade was most definitely crazy. Tornal glared as he spoke, "I would recommend you go home now boy, or I can guarantee you will never go home again."

Kade smiled, "That would violate the terms of our alliance."

"Only if it can be proven it was me. Trust me, I would make sure your disappearance would forever be a mystery. I'm very good at such things."

The boy and the lich stared at each other for, what felt to Almas, an extremely long and tense moment, which was probably in reality just a few moments before Tornal said, "I haven't the time to deal with nuisances like you. I have a battle to prepare for. But I wouldn't expect to grow much older if I were you." And with that he stormed away.

Once Tornal was gone Almas got his voice back. "Are you completely crazy? Tornal is going to kill you and he will probably use me to do it!"

Kade shrugged, "Everyone hates him. Most of us wish he would hurry up and betray Lich-El like we all know he is planning to; that way we could be done with him. But he won't any time soon. He would lose the Kadus Knights as allies if he did, and he still needs us. Their revenants aren't powerful enough; by themselves they lose far more revenants than they create. Without us they would need to enter the battle themselves, and most of them, Tornal included, are too cowardly for that."

"What if they find out there is a better way to create an undead army than making revenants from dead humans? How much will you and the rest of your people be worth then?"

"Better than revenants?" Kade asked with a hint of confusion on his face and then suddenly breaking out in a huge grin, "You already figured something out! You've been the Necromancer for how long? And you have already figured out something they haven't in the hundred years they've been doing this? You have to tell me about it."

"Necromancer?" Almas asked confused.

Kade explained, "Well, you aren't really a lich, but not human anymore either. Some of the knights have started referring to you as the Necromancer. Anyway, what did you figure out?

Almas wasn't sure about this new title of his and was about to tell Kade to go away when he heard a voice in his head say, *"Go ahead and show him."*

"If the Lich Lords hear about the creeps I learned to make, they will win this war and kill everyone in no time," Almas argued with the Fieles. So far Almas had found enough leeway in his orders in making battle plans to have not revealed what he had done and created at Debigroc.

"It is only a matter of time before they will give you an order that forces you to reveal them. We both know the Lich Lords will betray the Kadus Knights eventually, wouldn't it be nice if we could somehow use them against the undead when that happens?"

There could be something to that. The more he learned about the Kadus Knights the more he began to believe that, as a people, they weren't evil. They were certainly strange, but not evil.

Almas took his undead form and broke off one of his bone spikes and told Kade to watch. He pushed some dead leaves and twigs together into a pile with his foot and put the bone spike into the ground. In a flash of darkness, the bone spike and pile vanished, and a small undead creature took its place. It looked like some kind of huge bug that could pass itself off as part of a plant. It had a leafy body and legs like twigs. It also had two crab-like pincers.

Kade looked at it in wonder and exclaimed, "That is amazing. How sharp are those claws?"

"Cut your finger right off, go ahead and stick one of yours in and see, then we can call you stubby like you called Tornal."

"No thanks, I don't have a grow-back option on mine like you do...are those small little bone spikes on it? They aren't also poisonous, are they? "Kade asked.

"Yes, they are, just not as poisonous as these are," Almas answered indicating to the bone spikes going up his arms, "but they will pretty much make a man unable to fight or defend himself. I can also use this one to make more like it, with different weapons and different abilities. I call them creeps"

Kade looked around and said, "There are plants, bugs and other animals all around us. You could make an army of these in minutes. You could turn a battle just like that."

"And I could do it without any help from the Kadus Knights," Almas added, "Which is my whole point. If the other Lich Lords learn they can do this, how long do you think it would take for them to decide they don't need your people anymore?"

That thought finally seemed to sober Kade who after thinking a moment shook his head, "Tornal and the other Lich Lords would try to betray us, but Lich-El wouldn't; and even with this new ability they couldn't stand up to him."

"He can't protect you if he isn't here, how long has it been since anyone has seen him?"

"Not since our attack on Jaspen," Kade admitted.

"You can't rely on him to save you if he isn't here. Ally or not, when you are dealing with the likes of Tornal, I think your people may be in as much danger as my own. You might want to think about that. Especially if you insist on pestering him into a fury, which is my job by the way, not yours," Almas said.

Kade seemed to think about that bcforc finally saying, "I'm latc for dinner. I'd best be going." He began to step away but stopped suddenly and added, "Be careful tomorrow, it would get real boring around here without you." The boy then headed off towards his family's tent at a jog.

Chapter 7

"LORD LICH-EL! YOU'RE back!"

"Hello Kade, training by yourself?"

"Everyone is leaving right now to attack Beaver Dam. Where have you been?"

"Delaying a very angry and powerful force from descending upon us in her wrath."

"Lady Alixia?"

"Her too."

DAWN WAS BREAKING AS Creetan and his band of refugees came in sight of Beaver Dam. He was in the basket of the mammoth with Lord Teanas and Ulec.

"It looks like we made it before the undead armies," Creetan observed with relief.

"We should be to the city gates in about 10 minutes, my lord," The driver said.

Creetan glanced at Ulec, who was sitting down in the back of the basket and appeared to be meditating. "Have you found any undead scouts nearby?"

Ulec shook his head as he answered, "Not yet. The animals around here are very uncooperative. They have never had their minds touched by anyone before. Nearly all the animals push me out of their heads in fear."

"Sounds like you need to start getting out of that forest more," Creetan said teasingly.

"Well, now that my existence isn't really a secret anymore, I might do that," Ulec responded with a faint smile but otherwise not moving from his position of concentration.

Then suddenly he jerked up, his eyes flying open! "I found them!"

"The scouts?" Creetan asked.

"Not just scouts. Their army is coming through a magic gate. They are getting ready to attack the city."

Creetan hesitated a moment before remembering he was the one in charge now. Speaking first to the mammoth's driver he said, "Get us to the city now!" Then turning to one of the guards from Debigroc he ordered, "Signal the city that we are coming, and to be on alert for an attack."

The guard immediately put his horn to his lips and began sounding a loud series of trumpeting calls.

Now it was a matter of getting to the city before the attack began. "How much time do you think we have before the attack starts?" Creetan asked Ulec.

"They heard our warning. They are trying to form an attack quickly now, but I think we should make the city before them," Ulec answered.

As they approached the city Creetan noted that the walls and gate weren't nearly as big or strong as those of Debigroc.

Lord Teanas also noticed. "It won't take the undead long to breach those walls. We will need to be prepared for close combat in the streets."

Creetan could see soldiers taking positions on the wall as they approached. The doors, however, remained closed. Once they were in calling distance Creetan called out. "Open the gates! We have refugees in the war wagon!"

A voice answered from the walls, "They will need to exit the war wagon and enter the city on foot."

"The undead army is about to attack! We don't have time for this!" Creetan answered. Creetan kicked himself. He should have expected such mistrust in a time of war; of course, those protecting the city would need to verify that they were who they claimed.

Luckily, another voice on the wall shouted, "Open the gate, that is Lord Forjad's grandson!"

Immediately the gates began to open, and the mammoth and the war wagon quickly entered the city.

Inside the gates, they were quickly surrounded by soldiers. Creetan hurried down from the basket.

"Creetan!" Called the same voice that had ordered the doors opened.

Creetan looked to the voice and smiled as he called back, "Uncle Marpel!"

A man with graying hair and a strange looking staff stepped forward and embraced the young lord. Creetan was surprised to see his uncle. He was High Lord Marpel Vatan, ruler of the now empty Vatan Province. Since the undead had invaded and destroyed the Vatan Province 4 years earlier he had only been around a few times to continue Almas' bard training.

"Uncle Marpel, what are you doing here?" Creetan asked.

"We will talk later my boy," Lord Vatan started then stopped when he caught sight of Creetan's crest. After a moment's hesitation he continued, "I'm sorry...we will talk later Lord Aguerius, you signaled us that we are about to fall under attack. This is Lord Cordwainer, he is the lord of Beaver Dam. Can you tell us what is going on?"

It was Ulec that spoke startling both men who hadn't noticed the elvish boy approach. "They are gathering to the south. I think they are going to send in Revenants first to try to catch you before you are fully ready to defend the city."

Uncle Marpel stretched out his hand to Ulec, "You must be the famous Ulec, and your father, Lord Teanas. I'm glad to finally meet you both."

First Ulec and then Lord Teanas took his hand in greeting as Lord Cordwainer quickly motioned his soldiers to prepare for the battle.

"I am glad to finally meet you also," Teanas responded. If I might, I believe I could help most on the wall."

"Yes, if you and Creetan will join me, the guards will see your refugees to safety. Ulec, if you would like to go with...where did he go?"

Ulec was nowhere to be seen. Creetan answered his uncle, "You eventually get used to that. He comes and goes as he pleases and always ends up where he is needed most."

"I see—come with me."

Uncle Marpel led them up to the top of the city walls where they took positions on the center of the south walls. Now it was a matter of waiting, although from what Ulec said it wouldn't be much of a wait.

"Is your father alright?" Creetan's uncle asked, indicating the new crest that was around his neck.

"Last I saw him he was fine. He was taking refugees from Debigroc and the northern end of our province to Flameshaven."

"And my sister and your siblings?"

"Mother is with him along with Cady and Giddy," Creetan said and then hesitated a moment before finishing, "Almas was taken again by the Lich Lords, I'm with Ulec and Lord Teanas to try to find and rescue him."

Uncle Marpel muttered something under his breath before saying out loud, "I'll help you when this battle is over. All the people brought from Jaspen have been moved back towards Forjad."

"They are coming," a voice said in his head before he could question his uncle about how the people from Jaspen had arrived there.

Sacred Knight had spoken and sure enough he could see numerous figures leaving the tree line and charging the wall.

Uncle Marpel held up his staff in front of him and put a piece of wood protruding from the staff to his lips. A deep sound resonated from his staff and Creetan realized his uncle's staff was an instrument.

A feeling of calmness and focus washed over him like it had in his first battle when Almas had used his bard skills to help him. He pulled an arrow from his quiver and notched it onto the string of his bow.

Sacred Knight spoke again, *"Channel magic through me into the arrow."*

Creetan did as he was told, putting all the magic into the arrow that he could. Sacred Knight continued, *"When the command to fire comes aim for the largest group of revenants."*

The mindless undead creatures came into archer range, and he heard Lord Cordwainer command the archers to release their arrows. Creetan released his and was nearly blinded as a beam of light shot out from his bow and created a cloud of undead dust in the ranks of the oncoming undead attack. Another such beam came from Lord Teanas' position with the same result. Creetan couldn't help wondering how Lord Teanas had used what he thought was a Paladin spell.

"Mimic can copy the magical abilities of any weapon it comes in contact with. Your father let Mimic touch me so that Teanas would have one more powerful weapon in his arsenal."

"Cover!" Lord Cordwainer called out at the same time Sacredknight's answered His unspoken question.

Hearing Lord Cordwainer's command, Creetan saw many of the revenants break off bone spikes from their arms. Creetan ducked behind the parapet and heard several objects strike the wall near him and felt the stir of air as objects flew over right above his head.

"Move to another part of the wall and reload your bow. We will be a primary target for them," Creetan's fieles advised him.

"Thanks," Creetan thought back sarcastically, *"I always wanted to be a primary target."*

Creetan moved several paces down the wall keeping his head down as he prepared another arrow. He rose just long enough to unleash another blast of magical destruction on the undead before ducking back under cover. This became his pattern for what seemed to be forever; at least it was until a blast of magic blew the wall apart where he had been standing just a few moments before.

The force of the blast sent him flying forward where he landed hard and rolled a few feet. He got into his hands and knees dazed and heard someone yelling something about the wall being breached.

Creetan looked behind him to see a portion of the wall was missing. Revenants and Kadus Knights were entering into the gap of the wall while city defenders were attempting to push them back. He saw both Lord Teanas and Ulec fighting together at the front. His uncle was also there with his staff, each swing and strike creating sounds that somehow his uncle was able to manipulate into music. Creetan could feel magic from the music still helping to give him strength and focus.

His uncle's bardic abilities did more than that, however. Creetan saw him put the mouthpiece to his mouth and blow a long staticky note that seemed to fit perfectly with the music his fighting made, and when he blew that note it looked like lightning erupted from his staff the jumped from enemy to enemy, bringing down a dozen or so all around the bard.

"You don't have time to watch, you need to rejoin the fight!"

Creetan scrambled to pick up arrows that had been thrown from his quiver and scattered around him when he was struck by the blast. After stuffing as many arrows as he could into his quiver that he could quickly grab, He notched an arrow and began scanning the growing battle for a target, but the fighting was too close; the chances of hitting an ally was too great.

"Look for those in danger and use me to shield them," Sacred Knight told him.

"How?"

"Picture a shield to protect them and channel that thought and magic into me!"

Creetan saw a soldier who was in trouble and did as Sacred Knight instructed. He extended his arm toward the struggling soldier and a golden glow surrounded him. The revenant attacking him crumbled to dust when it came in contact with the glowing shield. Creetan dropped the shield once allied soldiers came to assist him.

Suddenly there was another deafening blast down the wall as another magic explosion opened up another breach.

"How are they doing that to the wall?" Creetan wondered.

"The Kadus Knights have mages."

"Mages can do that?"

Creetan fought as he talked with Sacred Knight. Now the lich lord's forces were pouring through both breaches.

"Mages focus their magical abilities through their knowledge. Several mages combining their knowledge and magic can exploit weakness in the wall. Draw a light shield around yourself, mages are very deadly if they focus all their magic at once."

Creetan noticed a Kadus Knight approaching his Uncle Marpel who was engaged with two revenants. Calling out a warning to his uncle, Creetan quickly sent an arrow at the knight who was able to step out of the way with barely a glance at Creetan.

He was about to send another arrow at the knight when he felt a strange sensation coming over him.

"More magic to your shield, now!" Sacred Knight warned.

Creetan poured more magic into the Holy Shield protecting him. He could feel something attacking the shield, draining it of power, draining him. Around him just outside his magic shield he could see mushrooms springing from the ground and saw the hilt of a dagger on the ground start to crumble as rust covered the metal.

"A mage is attacking you with some kind of decay spell. Keep the shield up!"

Suddenly the attack cut off. Creetan collapsed to his knees, utterly exhausted. Looking up he noticed the Kadus Knight who had been about to attack his uncle was now retreating helping a female knight who looked as wiped out as he felt. She must have been the mage. She must have put as much energy into the attack as Creetan had put into blocking it.

"Look out!" Sacred Knight warned.

Creetan saw a shadow come over him; a Kadus Knight was about to strike him with a sword. Creetan tried to put up another magic shield but knew he didn't have enough power left to stop the strike.

Suddenly a small form scooted in between him and the knight.

"Stop!" The form yelled, putting both his hands up in front of him. Creetan recognized immediately who it was.

The knight angrily began to order, "Almas, Get ou–"

"Please! It's my brother," Almas pleaded.

The knight gave Creetan a strange look and asked in an unbelieving voice, "Cree?"

Creetan suddenly recognized who the knight was. It was Deleta, his older cousin that he had always followed around and idolized back when Creetan had been 3 or 4 years old. He hadn't seen him since right before Almas had been born.

The surprise soon faded from Deleta's face and was replaced by a colder look. Addressing Almas, he said, "You shouldn't be this far into the battle, come with me now!"

Deleta turned and started towards the rear lines of the attackers.

Almas turned to look at Creetan even as he started to follow the Kadus Knight down the stairs and off the section of wall he was still standing on.

"Almas?" Creetan said softly.

"Sorry," Almas said tears sliding down his cheeks.

Creetan dragged himself back to feet in order to follow his brother when he heard a signal horn blow.

"Fall back to the secondary wall!" Lord Cordwainer called out as he ran up to where Creetan was standing. His order was followed up by him addressing Creetan, "Please Lord Cree, come with me."

"That was my brother, I have to go after him."

"You can't help him if you're dead, we must withdraw!"

Creetan looked for his brother again, but he had already disappeared in the press of men and revenants. He didn't like it, but he had no other choice.

Lord Cordwainer led him downstairs where his personal guards directed them to the rear lines where defenders were already moving past those soldiers assigned to cover the retreat. Creetan looked at the breach in the wall. He couldn't see his uncle, Ulec, or Lord Teanas anymore.

"What about Uncle Marpel?"

"He was injured, and Lord Teanas took him to the rear lines already. He should be fine but right now we need to get you out of here," the lesser lord answered as he tried to hurry Creetan along.

The city's guards were now executing a slow retreat, holding the front lines of the attackers back as the defenders retreated.

Again, Lord Cordwainer urged Creetan to hurry, and they ran with the other retreating soldiers several blocks through the city to a second wall. They passed through the gate and upstairs to the wall's battlements where he found his uncle sitting

"Uncle Marpel, are you okay?" Creetan asked.

"I'm...not sure. I saw you under attack by a mage, I was moving to help you when I felt someone touch my arm. It felt like something pulled out of me...I'm not sure what. Now, when I try to play any music it's like my fingers have forgotten what to do." Uncle Marpel stuttered a bit in shock as he tried to explain.

"We will have to figure it out later. We need to get into defensive positions. Lord Vatan, just rest for a few minutes here," Lord Cordwainer instructed.

Creetan took up a position next to a large ballista that looked like it could fire two long rows of large bolts. It was positioned so that it could be pushed forward and fire down the street approaching the gate. Right now, that street was full of retreating soldiers.

The soldiers came through the gate and formed up on the training grounds that were between the walls and the keep, which was where the people of the city who hadn't already fled the city in the days before, were taking shelter.

Soon the soldiers covering the retreat came in view still engaged in their own fighting retreat. He saw that Lord Teanas was with them now.

As they began to near archer range of the wall Creetan heard Lord Cordwainer command, "Gates ready! Archers ready!"

As Creetan readied an arrow, the men on the front line suddenly in unison threw jars on the ground in front of them which erupted into large balls of fire. Jars thrown, the men turned and ran for the gate. Lord Teanas was the only exception; he slowly walked backwards with his arms outstretched as he shaped the flames into a wall holding the undead army at bay as the rest of the last of the men passed through the gate. After a moment he too turned and ran the rest of the way as the flames began to die.

Creetan joined the other archers in shooting down the first few pursuing undead to come near the walls as Teanas passed through the gates which were already closing. The ballista was pushed forward, and the large bolts cut down several ranks of enemies as the gate was secured. Creetan strung another arrow as the battle continued, he was starting to recover from the effects of the mage's attack.

After sending a couple of bolts of holy magic through the ranks of the attackers, Creetan heard a voice behind him call, "You boy, firing magic from your bow. Come here!"

It was one of the soldiers who were operating the ballista. This soldier surprised him in two ways. First the soldier was about his age. Secondly, from the sound of the voice, the soldier turned out to be a girl.

The young lady and her crew were getting the ballista ready to shoot again. She looked up and motioned for him to come over again. Creetan approached her and she said, "You're down to your last few arrows; any chance you can work your magic on these?"

She indicated the bolts ready to be fired from the ballista. Creetan gave the only response he could give. "I have no idea."

"Could we?" Creetan asked Sacred Knight.

"I don't know either...I never thought to try."

Creetan spoke out loud, "I guess now is a good time to find out."

The young lady nodded. "You give it a try. When you're ready we'll push it forward and aim; then you will pull the trigger."

Creetan put one hand near the trigger and the other held onto the fieles. He pictured magic flowing from the fieles into all the bolts and pushed all the magic he had left into making it happen. All the bolts lined up and ready to fire began to glow. Creetan gave the girl a quick nod and she pushed the ballista forward with the help of her crew.

"Okay! Shoot!"

Creetan pulled the trigger and a couple dozen beams of light shot from the ballista and through rank after rank of enemies clearing out most of the street. The remaining revenants and knights quickly retreated away from the wall and out of sight.

Cheers rang out from the top of the wall as they pulled the ballista back and began reloading.

"Well done, Creetan," Uncle Marpel said stepping over to him, he seemed to be recovering quickly. "That will give us a moment to regroup while they figure out what to do about that. Are you okay?"

Creetan suddenly felt like he was about to pass out and must have looked it the way his uncle suddenly took him by the arm to hold him up.

"I'm fine, it just took a lot out of me."

"Here, sit down here," the girl said indicating a spot where he could sit up against the ballista that was out of the sun.

"Thanks," Creetan said as he sat down. His Uncle stayed just long enough to make sure he really was okay and then left to get the defense ready for the next assault.

"Here, take a drink of water," the girl said offering Creetan a water skin. As Creetan greedily drank she continued, "Are you a paladin?"

"I'm not. My bow is Sacred Knight, a fieles made from the soul of a paladin. I'm Cree Tanis Aguerius, do you have a name?"

"Kara Bolt. So, you're Lord Forjad's grandson?"

"I am," Creetan answered before stating, "You are really good with that ballista."

"None better. I'm the best siege weapon operator in the town," Kara answered matter-of-factly.

Creetan nodded his agreement, and then after a moment he asked, "So do you know why my uncle is here? I haven't had the chance to ask him."

"He was the one who brought the people from Jaspen," Kara answered.

"How *did* he do that?" Creetan asked.

"It was brilliant, in the basement of the keep in Jaspen they painted the wall to look like a door into the basement of the keep here in Beaver Dam. Meanwhile here they painted a doorway into the one in Jaspen. They made a magical connection between the two that created an actual doorway."

"And the people from Jaspen evacuated here," Creetan finished.

"Then they destroyed the paintings and destroyed the spell," Kara concluded.

They sat a moment in silence before the call rose, "They're attacking again, to the wall!"

The alarm went down the wall and Kara and Creetan jumped back to their position. The battle was on again.

ULEC HAD FOUND A SPOT to hide between a tree trunk and a building. He had a clear view of Almas and Tornal. With so many revenants nearby, he couldn't get close enough to the lich to strike, and since he didn't know how that would affect the curse Almas was under, he didn't even know if killing Tornal would help Almas or hurt him.

Almas was being sent out to prisoners with Deleta while Tornal stayed back near an open magic gate, the coward was ready to flee to safety should any danger to his person appear.

He wasn't sure what Almas was doing to some of the prisoners but occasionally Almas would touch a prisoner which caused some kind of pain to them. Ulec could tell that whatever his best friend was doing, it horrified him.

Whatever he was doing must have been planned before the battle because there was no communication between them. In fact, Ulec had never seen Almas so quiet.

Ulec watched as his best friend went over and placed his hand on Tornal. Almas had a look of pure disgust as he did.

"He's stealing magic from them, and giving it to Tornal," came the voice from the fieles in his rusica.

Ulec had found out that his rusica was a fieles made from a piece of his mother's soul and had the same powers that his father's ring had. He had named it Changing Hand. The power to take the form of any weapon could come in very handy, but right now it didn't give him power to break the curse that held Almas to Tornal.

"The same way he took my curse from my arm I bet," Ulec responded.

"I should've had you hold Sacred Knight before the battle started. I could have taken its form and one shot of a holy arrow could've ended him," Changing Hand lamented.

"I'm not so sure, it would be a long shot, and he has a lot of revenants in front of him. He wants to make sure no one can do to him that Lord Mason did to that other lich," Ulec observed.

The elvish boy continued to watch the Lich Lord with intense hatred for a moment longer when Changing Hand spoke again, *"Look down!"*

Ulec looked down and took a moment to recognize the small creature crawling up the tree towards him. It was one of those small undead things that Almas had used at Debigroc!

The creature stopped and looked at Ulec for a moment. Looking back up he saw Almas look right at Ulec for just a moment, just long enough to lock eyes with him. Almas then quickly looked back to the group of prisoners. As normal, the undead were only keeping prisoners alive that they didn't think would be useful as revenants, meaning they were mostly children. They were moving one group through a magic gate, destined to be sacrificed before a future battle or one of Tornal's future experiments.

Ulec looked again to Almas, who gave him a brief glance again but a look full of pleading. He wanted Ulec to save the prisoners.

It was clear what he was being forced to do to these people was destroying him. Ulec knew his friend wouldn't be able to stand much more of the pain he was causing. The next glance between them Ulec nodded his agreement.

Almas moved his hand down to his side and opened his hand and then one by one began to close his fingers into a fist. It was a countdown. Ulec let Metal out of his bag and gave him a mental command. Then he moved.

Once Almas' silent countdown reached zero, a building that was somewhat near Tornal suddenly erupted into flames. For just a few moments all the revenants that weren't searching for threats from the flaming building were putting themselves around Tornal. None, not even the prisoners, noticed that the last group of prisoners had gained one extra member, the hood of his cloak pulled tight to hide his elvish ears. They also didn't notice the slime that had moved through the magic gate.

Once the undead were certain that there was no danger, they started to prepare to send the last of the prisoners through the gate when two other figures stepped out from the gate. It was an older lich and a living boy.

"Lord Lich-El," Tornal exclaimed, "You've returned."

"Tornal, how is the battle progressing?" Lich-El asked.

"Very well, we smashed through their first wall. Soon we will do the same at the wall around their keep."

"So glad to hear that, since you will be doing it without the Kadus Knights. I will be taking them to begin preparation for an attack on Flameshaven." Lich-El stated flatly.

"What? We are in the middle of a battle. How can you just take them?"

"I did not bring them into this alliance for you to use as a shield, as you have been. I will be taking personal command of them."

“What of Fireforge? Do you intend to just bypass them so we can be attacked from behind?” Tornal asked.

“Fireforge has already been emptied. Lord Gidon has evacuated the entire valley to Flameshaven

Ulec noticed Almas was staring at Lich-El with a surprised look. Something about the old lich had gotten his attention. Meanwhile the boy with Lich-El had excitedly waved to Almas when he saw him, and his enthusiasm didn't seem to dip even for a moment when Almas didn't show that he even noticed the boy.

"I expect you to join us at Flameshaven as soon as you are done here," Lich-El said finishing his conversation with Tornal. He then addressed the boy that was with him, "I will be going straight to our staging ground near Flameshaven. Kade, please see these last prisoners to our main camp and put them with the rest of the prisoners. Tornal will bring them to Flameshaven when he is done here."

"What about the elf, do I take him too?" the boy casually asked as he gestured toward Ulec.

All heads turned to the group of prisoners at once. Almas looked on with a horrified expression. The boy, referred to as Kade, continued to look expectantly at Lich-El. Ulec never even saw the boy look in his direction. How had he noticed Ulec? No one ever noticed him when he didn't want to be noticed! Lich-El was the only lich that didn't seem to be surprised, he just smiled and said, "Ulec, my boy. How good to see you again. I don't believe I've seen you since you were a baby. You certainly have grown."

I took a moment for Tornal to find his words...well, word anyway. He just glared at Ulec and said, "You!"

Ulec's mind was racing. Being spotted wasn't something that ever happened to him.

Tornal looked like he was about to speak again and possibly act, as he was pulling out his staff, but Lich-El spoke first, "Yes Kade, you can take him back with the rest of the prisoners."

Tornal looked at Lich-El in astonishment. "Do you think this elvish child is just going to go quietly with him?"

Lich-El responded, "I do believe that was his intent all along."

"Of course it was! He is up to something. He probably intended to assassinate you or me!"

"No, I think he is more likely looking to rescue the prisoners. I suppose we will have to do something about that," Lich-El mused before coming to a decision, "Tornal, you will continue your attack on Beaver Dam. I will make sure Ulec is suitably restrained."

"Can I fight him?" Kade asked excitedly.

Almas was silently trying to get Kade's attention and was vigorously shaking his head. Lich-El meanwhile seemed to consider the request a moment before saying, "I suppose that would be fine, you may go ahead and be the one to restrain him."

There was something strange about this boy, he reacted to Lich-El's permission like he just got the birthday present he always wanted rather than just permitted to get in a fight that could easily end with him being killed. Ulec was still sitting among the prisoners still unsure how to get out of this. There were so many revenants around him.

"Are you seriously going to let this boy–" Tornal started to say but was cut off by Lich-El.

"Yes, I am, but this isn't your concern. Take Almas and return to your battle. Once these prisoners are secured, I will be taking the Kadus Knights as I have already said. You may leave us now."

Lich-El spoke with finality. Tornal stared in pure hate at the leader of the lich lords, and ordering Almas to follow him; he then turned and left, the magic gate vanishing as he went. Almas, looking twice as horrified as before, silently followed.

"Ulec," Lich-El called, "You may want to step away from those prisoners. We wouldn't want any of them harmed, unless you were planning on letting us restrain you without a fight."

Ulec stood up and stepped away from the prisoners. There was no way he was going to put them at risk. Kadus Knights replaced the revenants in forming a very large circle around Ulec, ensuring there was no way for him to escape. Kade stood now across from him, shaking with excitement. Ulec didn't like the idea of fighting a young boy who obviously mistook Ulec's own youthful appearance and underestimated his chances of victory.

Kade spoke, "I'm glad to meet you; Almas told me all about you. You don't have any weapons on you, do you? Here take two of my daggers."

The boy spoke in a rush and gently tossed two of his own daggers at Ulec's feet. Ulec picked up the strangely shaped daggers, he didn't want to reveal he had a fieles quite yet.

Ulec had a question of his own and asked, "How did Almas tell you so much, seeing how little talking I've seen him do?"

Kade continued speaking, now with a hint of sarcasm in his voice, as he took up a fighting position, "Tornal kept getting annoyed with him and ordered him not to speak in his glorious presence. Almas still finds ways to annoy him though. He is a genius. Are you ready to start?"

"If you think so highly of Almas, why are you trying to kill his best friend?" Ulec asked, now with Kade's daggers in either hand.

Kade shrugged, still beaming with excitement, "Just to see if I can win. How's this? If you win you can go free."

"And the prisoners?" Ulec asked.

"Sorry, I can't do anything about them, they aren't my prisoners. So, are you ready to start or what?" There was a hint of impatience in Kade's voice now.

Ulec nodded and to his surprise watched Kade throw both of his daggers to either side, crossing his arms in front of him. Ulec saw the daggers arc in their flight and soon both were coming at him from either side. Ulec took a step back and the incoming daggers changed direction slightly still coming at him. So, the boy was using magic to manipulate the flight of the daggers. This fight might be harder than Ulec thought.

Ulec raised his own daggers to deflect the two spinning blades when a voice entered his head, *"Look out!"*

Ulec deflected to daggers on either side of him and at the same time jumped and kicked out to knock away the two daggers being thrust at him by Kade who had pulled out two more daggers and rushed at him while Ulec's attention was on the attacks coming from either side. This boy was very good.

In one motion Kade threw the daggers in his hands and almost simultaneously caught the other two which had arced right back to him. Ulec soon found himself fending off four daggers that relentlessly attacked him from all sides. Kade amazingly juggled the daggers, catching them as they returned and holding onto them just long enough to either strike out at Ulec or deflect one of Ulec's own attacks before throwing it in order to catch another returning dagger.

He was so focused on the fight, that Ulec almost made a fatal mistake when he stumbled in surprise when Kade started speaking to him with an almost casual tone as he fought. "Maybe later I can teach you how to throw the boomerang daggers. They are pretty awesome weapons when used right. Don't you think?"

"Duck!" Changing Hand warned

Ulec ducked and felt a breeze as a shining dagger passed right over his head.

"Careful," Kade said, "That almost had you."

Ulec said nothing, he just struck out to try to slash Kade's chest. To Ulec's astonishment something underneath deflected his blow. The boy must have had some kind of armor underneath his shirt, but Ulec couldn't see any outlines of armor.

Kade smiled and said, as he tried attacking Ulec from four directions at once, "That's my Chaos Breastplate. They are very rare, only families descended from officers of the original Chaos Guard have any. When you put them on, they mold themselves right to the skin so they always fit and can't be seen. My father gave me mine."

This boy was unbelievably good for a human child. Ulec decided he needed to finish this fight. When he had an opening, he threw one of the daggers he was using at the boy.

Kade deflected the attack and saw the boy's eyebrows raise in surprise as a sword appeared in Ulec's hand swinging down at him. Before the sword could make contact, a spinning dagger struck it allowing Kade to dodge the blow.

"So, you do have a weapon of your own!" Kade exclaimed, seemingly unfazed by his close call, "Is that a fieles?"

Again, Ulec didn't answer them. He continued to fight, only now the weapon in his right hand would change forms from time to time, but the boy was expecting it now and Ulec still couldn't seem to get through his defense. On the positive side he wasn't taking the offense anymore.

Ulec was starting to get a feel for the boy's fighting technique and was starting to develop a plan when Kade switched subjects. "Hey, by the way, Almas told me about how your mother killed the lich Rynos back at Demon Mountain. How she tapped her foot, and a pillar of energy came out of the ground. After talking about it with my mother—she's a scholar and a mage—I finally figured out how she cast that spell."

At the moment three of Kade's daggers were closing in on him, two from the sides and once from behind. His first attempt at an attack since Ulec revealed Changing Hand. Meanwhile Kade was in front of him. This was the fourth time that Kade had tried this four-pronged attack on him and Ulec was ready to turn it around on him. But instead of rushing forward to strike at him, Kade casually tossed the dagger so that it landed blade first into the ground. At the same time the other three daggers suddenly dropped to the ground so that he had a dagger sticking in the ground on each side of him. Ulec's fieles shouted a warning to his mind but he was only able to pull some magic around him in a poor imitation of a paladin's shield when the ground erupted beneath him. The blast wasn't nearly as powerful as the one his mother had done to Rynos but Ulec still felt himself lifted from the ground and thrown back. He landed on his back, hitting his head hard, and everything went black.

Chapter 8

"WELL DONE, KADE. YOU truly do have remarkable skill. How were you able to reproduce one of Lady Alixia's spells like that?"

"My mother said the ground is full of stored energy, like dead plants and bugs, oils and fats left behind by living things. All I had to do was learn all I could about them and develop a magical connection to them so I could use magic to release that energy. So, I didn't kill him like you asked. What do you want me to do with him now?"

"I will take you and the prisoners back to the main camp with a few knights to help guard the camp. You will place Ulec

with the other prisoners. Make sure he is restrained and have a couple of guards keeping an eye on him at all times."

"You know that probably won't be enough once he wakes up."

"I would suggest making it enough, unless you want to make Tornal very, very angry."

"HERE THEY COME AGAIN!"

Three times now Creetan had worked with Kara and her team to help stop the undead's relentless attacks. This 4th wave looked to be the largest so far, although he noticed there were no Kadus Knights this time.

The exhausting battle was taking its toll. Not only were they starting to run low on the darts that were fired by the ballista, but its crew was taking longer to prepare it for each shot and Cree just couldn't put the magical power into the shots that he could do at the first. He just couldn't build up enough magical power between shots.

The crew of the ballista pushed the enormous crossbow forward and Creetan charged the bolts with magic and once again several beams of light shot out and ranks of revenants vanished leaving nothing but dust.

The crew pulled the crossbow back again to reload and Creetan saw a bird land on the crossbow. Thinking Ulec must be trying to tell him something, Creetan looked closer. It took a moment to realize the creature busily scratching on the ballista wasn't a bird, it wasn't even alive. It was some sort of undead creature. He was about to draw his short sword to destroy the thing when he noticed it had scratched two words on the ballista. "Cree jump!"

Remembering what had happened to the first wall, Creetan didn't hesitate. He yelled to everyone else to jump and grabbed

Kara, who had stepped next to Creetan to see what he was looking at. She gave a Yelp of surprise as he pulled her with him as he jumped from the wall.

They hit the ground and rolled to help soften their impact on the ground and Creetan obeyed Sacredknight's order to shield himself with magic just in time as the wall they had just been standing on erupted in an explosion.

Once the rocks stopped falling Creetan looked up. There was a gaping hole in the wall and revenants began to pour out. Kara immediately stood up and went towards the keep. There were several small catapults lined up by the wall of the keep.

"Aim for the breach!" She ordered as she began to adjust the aim of the catapult that she took command of. In just a moment there was a series of twangs, and several small barrels flew into the gap in the wall which erupted in explosive fire.

Creetan notched an arrow and looked over the battlefield. The catapults had stopped the flow of the undead for the moment and the guards and soldiers were handling the ones that had gotten through.

Lords Teanas and Cordwainer were in the forefront of the battle having come down from the wall which was emptying of defenders who were getting ready to make their last stand in front of the keep.

Suddenly the wall exploded in two more places on either side of the hole. Several of the catapults turned to fire upon the new breaches but something strange happened. A strange wind started blowing through the gaps in the walls.

"It's Tornal. He's using the fieles Cyclone, to control the wind." Sacred Knight said, *"Take cover!"*

The wind picked up and soon large pieces of the broken-up wall began flying through the gap. The large rocks began to smash into the catapults.

"Look out!" Creetan called as he pulled Kara away from her catapult just before it was smashed to pieces.

"I think we are in trouble," Kara declared looking at the remains of her catapult.

Revenants were now pouring out of the gaps. Creetan felt despair overcoming him. The defenders wouldn't last long against such numbers. He had failed to save Beaver Dam and he had failed to save his brother; the two main things his father had assigned him to do.

"Don't give up yet! As long as you are still breathing there is hope," Sacred Knight urged.

Creetan began firing his remaining arrows. If this was the end, then he would do as much damage as he could. He continued to fight as the defenders were slowly forced back.

After several minutes of intense fighting Sacred Knight spoke again, *"Something new is coming. Look above."*

Creetan looked up and saw two creatures flying in circles above the city. At first, he thought they were large bats but soon realized they had arms and legs. They were some sort of demons.

Kara followed Creetan's gaze and asked, "Are those imps?"

"I think they are, but what are they doing here?" Creetan answered.

As if in answer to two small demons swooped down towards the ranks of undead. As they flew over the ranks of revenants, the imps fired dozens of blasts of magic turning dozens more of the Lich Lord's army to dust.

The revenants backed off; the Lich Lords not sure what to make of the unexpected attack. Creetan and Kara moved over to where Lord Teanas was standing as one of the imps swooped down to land right in front of the elvish lord and transformed into a small elvish girl, the second imp landed and perched itself on her shoulder.

"Seacra!" Creetan exclaimed. It was Ulec's younger sister, who like her mother could take the form of other creatures. She had gone north with her mother just before the undead had started their invasion.

Seacra didn't respond to him. She just looked at her father with fury in her eyes and asked, "Where is Ulec?"

"He was going to see if he could help Almas. I think something happened to him as he hasn't checked in with me for a while," Lord Teanas answered in a worried tone and then asked his daughter, "Where is your mother?"

"There isn't time to explain right now. Please excuse me, I have a score to settle with Tornal. Just cover me so I can end this battle and deal with him," Seacra answered with enough venom in her voice to kill the most venomous snake.

Seacra turned to face the undead and began marching towards them as the imp on her shoulder took off into the air. As she stalked away towards the Lich Lord's army she turned into the biggest and most frightening creature Creetan had ever seen. It stood at least 20 feet tall and resembled the imp except it was much, much bigger.

"That is an Elder Demon, a lord of demons," Sacred Knight said in awe.

"I thought she could only take the form of things she has touched," Creetan thought back.

"She does. Somewhere she had to have had come across an Elder Demon and survived the meeting."

The revenants reacted by attacking, but Seacra took out the first row of revenants with one swipe of her clawed hand and began ripping through the mass of undead as the imp flew above her raining down blasts of magical energy.

"Are we sure this isn't Lady Alixia pretending to be Seacra?" Creetan asked Lord Teanas.

"It is certainly my daughter; I will be very much interested to know what has happened up north these last several weeks." Lord Teanas responded.

"Everyone forward and attack!" Lord Cordwainer called. The rest of the defenders charged forward cutting through the revenants that Seacra missed. Soon the revenants were in full retreat. They pursued the revenants through the streets of the city.

Soon Lord Cordwainer called a halt for fear of running into an ambush. Seacra didn't halt; she turned back into an imp and flew off.

Lord Teanas motioned for Creetan to follow him, and they approached Lord Cordwainer. Lord Teanas addressed him, "We will scout ahead and look for ambushes and see what is happening outside the city."

"I will go with them."

It was Uncle Marpel. He still looked pale, but he had a determined look on his face. Lord Teanas nodded his agreement and the three left. They moved quickly but cautiously to the broken up outer walls.

They hid behind some rubble and looked out. They saw the undead army retreating into a magic gate. He also saw Almas with a Lich Lord holding a staff which Creetan assumed was Tornal near the gate. He saw no sign of Seacra or the imp that was with her.

"Looks like Seacra really scared them, but I still can't believe she scared them enough to make them flee like this," Creetan commented.

"It isn't just me they are running from."

Creetan turned around to find Seacra had appeared right by them, the imp perched on her shoulder again.

Seacra continued, "I found Lord Gidon in Flameshaven, he asked me to take a message to King Yucaipa. He and his army should be here in less than an hour. Their scouts must have spotted them."

"Seacra!" Lord Teanas addressed his daughter, "What have you and your mother been up to since we parted?"

"I can explain better after we take care of Tornal. Short story is Mother, and I were at a village of shadow hunters when we found out it was about to be attacked by an army of demons. That's where I picked up Tricker here," Seacra said indicating to the imp on her shoulder. She continued, " I ended up getting separated from Mother, so I came looking for you guys. Like I said I found Lord Gidon at Flameshaven and he sent me to Yucaipa for reinforcements. Now, what more have you found out about Almas? I think I know how to help him."

They filled her in on what little they knew, which wasn't much. Seacra quickly told them her plan.

When most of the undead army had gone through the magic gate, Lord Teanas approached the fleeing undead, followed by Creetan and Uncle Marpel.

"Tornal!" He called out, "We will let you leave but it is time you let Almas return to his family!"

Tornal's response was to send a group of revenants at him as he continued to evacuate his army.

Lord Teanas cut his way towards Tornal, hardly being slowed down by the small group of revenants. Watching the determined elf approaching Tornal pointed his staff at him and a whirlwind formed around Lord Teanas. However, before it could lift him off his feet and throw him, the elvish lord snapped his fingers creating a spark that quickly turned the whirlwind into a flaming tornado, which expanded to consume the remaining revenants around Lord Teanas. For several seconds it looked to Creetan that the lich lord and the elvish lord struggled over control of the flaming whirlwind.

"Is there anything we can do?" Creetan asked.

His uncle shook his head and responded, "I can feel my abilities starting to return but not enough to help."

"You need to distract Tornal. Quickly!" Sacred Knight warned.

Creetan didn't even ask why, he just quickly notched an arrow and let it fly at Tornal. The lich lord waved his staff and the arrow changed course and flew harmlessly past, but the distraction worked, and the flaming whirlwind dispersed around Lord Teanas. That was when he saw the vines of some sort of plant snaking up and around the elf's legs. They were smoking from the heat of the flaming whirlwind.

Lord Teanas started to cough and fell to his knees. He had breathed in the smoke of whatever those things were.

Tornal laughed and spoke, "Who would have thought such a weak magical ability from a farmer would be so useful."

Lord Teanas was in danger. Creetan didn't hesitate, he rushed forward to Lord Teanas and put a magic shield around them both just as Tornal shot a blast of magic at them. His shield took the blast and held and Creetan started putting as much healing magic into Lord Teanas as he could.

Tornal continued laughing, caught up in his victory over the elvish lord that he almost didn't notice that Almas had stepped close to him with a look of desperation as he watched the battle.

"Well, boy," Tornal said, "If they want you so badly...go over there and you finish them off. Take their magic and kill them.

Almas responded by grabbing Tornal's arm and Tornal sank to his knees in pain. After just a moment Tornal gave Almas a hard shove away. It was only then that he noticed a second Almas standing nearby with a surprised look on his face. It only took him a moment to figure out what was going on and opened his mouth to say something, but before he could speak, the fake Almas had turned into a fake Tornal and spoke first.

"Almas, I order you to be free and to make all your own choices from now and forever!"

Then the fake Tornal turned back into Seacra.

"Kill them all now!" Tornal bellowed.

The real Almas, still with a stunned look, faced Tornal and spoke one simple word, "No," then he smiled and said it again, "No!"

Then Almas' smile turned into a glare, and Tornal's turned into an expression of fear. Realizing the danger, he was suddenly in, Tornal leapt into his magic gate which immediately vanished. Leaving a couple dozen revenants behind.

The revenants started to withdraw but suddenly hundreds of those small undead creatures like the one Creetan had seen on the wall just appeared from bushes and other hiding places and swarmed the revenants turning them into dust in a matter of seconds. Then it was quiet.

Creetan quickly looked down to check on Lord Teanas who nodded and signaled that he would be fine, the healing magic having done its job. He then turned his attention back to his brother.

Seacra was the first to speak.

"Almas?"

She took a step forward as Creetan and the others approached.

"Stay back," Almas said the fury on his face changing to a blank, lost look.

"Almas, you're free now," Creetan said

Almas shook his head and said, "You don't understand, you don't know what they made me do. How many people are dead or hurt because of me? I was killed weeks ago; I shouldn't be here. "

Creetan walked towards his little brother cautiously and spoke carefully, "You didn't hurt anyone. Tornal did. You found so many ways to save lives in spite of Tornal. That includes me, a few times I think."

Almas continued, "All those villages and towns, those were my battle plans they used!"

"And now your plans can help us stop the Lich Lords and save lives."

Creetan now stood right in front of his brother and dropped to one knee to be eye level with him. Almas' face had lost its undead features and tears were flowing freely.

Creetan put his hands on Almas' shoulders and said, "Welcome back little brother," and pulled him into a hug while Almas broke down and began sobbing.

After a couple of minutes Almas suddenly pushed Creetan away.

“Lich-El is leading a huge attack against Flameshaven! They also took Ulec! We have to go get him!"

"We will," Uncle Marpel said, "Just as soon as King Yucaipa arrives, we will figure something out. For now, we rest...and it’s good to have you back.

Epilogue

KADE RECOGNIZED THE two Kadus Knights being brought into the hospital tent as being the two men left to guard the prisoners. He had been helping to tend those who had been too wounded to go to Flameshaven.

"What happened?" He asked.

One of the youths helping the men into the tent answered, "We found them outside the prisoners' cage, unconscious."

"Let me guess," Kade asked, "The prisoners are all gone?"

"Yes," the young man confirmed.

They got the unconscious men onto a couple of sleeping mats and Kade asked, "Did you find their tracks and see which way they went. They shouldn't have been able to get too far away."

The young man hesitated a moment and then said, "They didn't leave on foot. I think they rode away."

"Rode?" Kade asked, his eyebrows rising.

"All we found were what looked like prints from very large wolves."

"You're saying all the prisoners escaped riding on large dire wolves?" Kade asked and then said, "That...is...brilliant! Almas wasn't kidding about him, he is brilliant!"

"So, what do we do now? Almost all the grownups have gone to Flameshaven."

"I don't know," Kade laughed, "but Tornal is going to be very, very angry. I think things are about to get interesting around here real soon."

He held up his hand and admired the rusica he now wore that he had taken from Ulec.

"This plan is insane; it will never work." The unspoken voice from the fieles said.

"Yes, it is. It is going to be glorious." Kade silently responded, "*Absolutely glorious.*"

Paladin's Rise

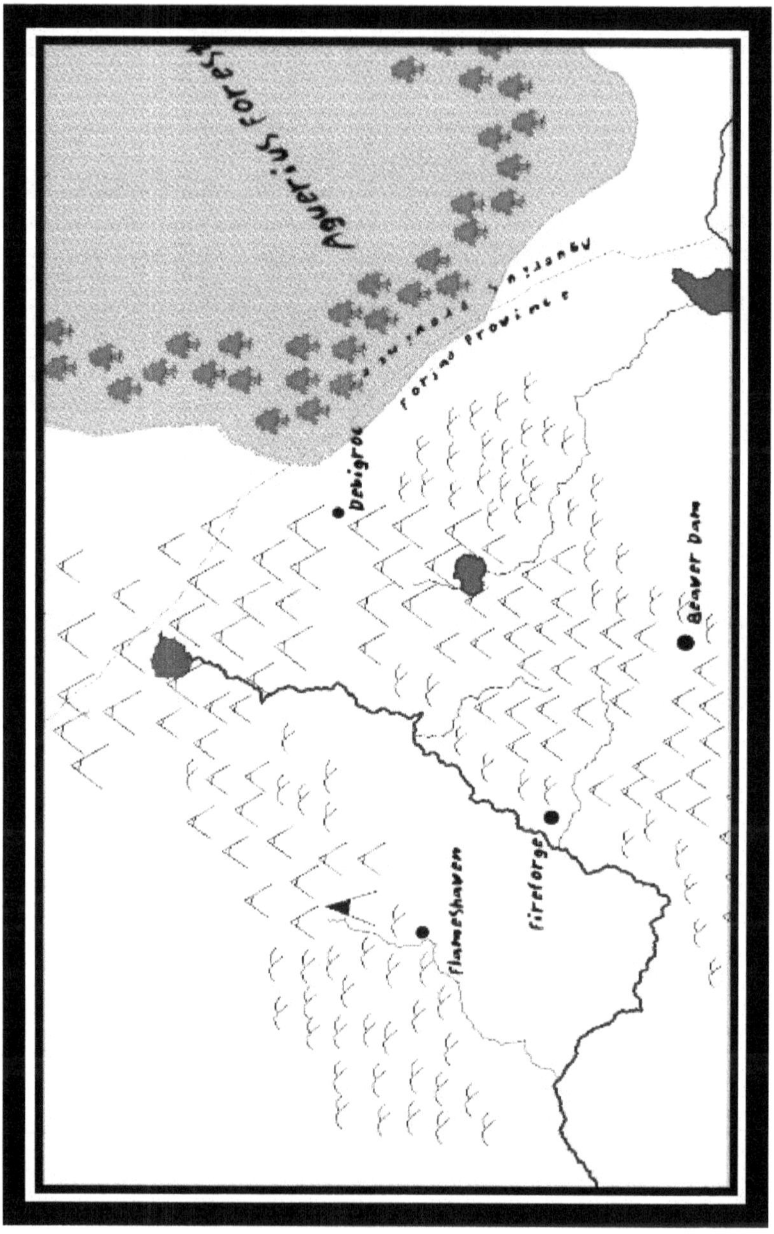
Aguerius forest
Debigroc
Beaver Dam
Fireforge
Flameshaven

Chapter 1

"WE WILL ATTACK TOMORROW morning."

"Why not tonight? I believe we can be ready by then. The longer we take to attack the longer they have to prepare.

"Tornal is still bringing the prisoners from previous battles for sacrifice. We will attack when we are strongest."

"Should you really be trusting Tornal with such a task. You know he is planning to betray us at his first opportunity."

"Tornal has already doomed himself. It is just a matter of time; you have no need to be concerned with him. Just make sure your people are ready by morning."

"As you will."

HIGH LORD GIDON AGUERIUS watched from the city wall of Flameshaven as the doom of all that was dear to him dug into fortifications around the city. The army of Kadus Knights and undead had seemingly come from nowhere and had begun a siege of the city.

He had tried to send for aid to the capital of the Forjad Province, but the Lich Lords' armies had moved too swiftly and blocked all paths from the Valley. He had led two counterattacks to try to break through, but both had been a disaster. It was as if the undead knew every plan and trick he would use. For the first time in all his years as Royal Strategist, he felt he was up against a mind far more brilliant than his.

As he gazed down upon the preparations of the enemy forces, his thoughts turned to his two older sons, Almas and Creetan. The thought of Almas being held captive and in the hands of the Lich Lords pained him deeply, and he wondered how his brave, determined son was faring in the clutches of such darkness. There was also the question of what the undead had done to him. With the reports from Debigroc it was clear that Almas had served at least some part of the gates to the city being opened to the army of revenants that had taken the city. He wondered if there was anything left of his son to save.

At least he had some comfort in knowing that Creetan was with Lord Teanas, an elvish prince, attempting to rescue his brother. They were both capable warriors, and Gidon prayed they would return safely.

Determined to focus on the present, Gidon turned his attention to the city below. The urgency of the situation weighed heavily on his heart, but he needed to ensure the safety of his wife and two younger children. With that in mind, he left the city wall and hurried towards the city keep where Izybel and the children were.

He found them in the main hall of the keep, Giddy and Izybel were hard at work. As heir to the lordship of the Forjad Province and leader of the crafter's Guild there was no better crafter in all the kingdom than his wife. At this moment they were making what she called a golem. She was crafting it to assist in the city's defense and it was a formidable creation, resembling a giant warrior made of stone and metal.

Giddy, with his eyes shining with excitement, exclaimed, "Dad! Mom and I are building a golem to protect Flameshaven! It's going to be awesome! I'm naming him Rocky!"

Izybel chuckled, wiping her forehead with her sleeve. "Yes, Rocky will be quite the defender if those invaders make it this far. But let's hope it won't come to that. Your father is a brilliant strategist, and he'll come up with a plan to drive them away."

Gidon smiled at his wife's confidence in him but couldn't help feeling the weight of the situation bearing down on him. "We'll do our best, Izybel. Every defender counts, including this formidable golem you and Giddy are crafting."

Giddy beamed with pride, puffing his chest out a little. "I'm going to make sure it's the best golem ever!"

"Of course, you will," Gidon said, ruffling Giddy's hair affectionately. "You have your mother's talent for crafting, and your determination will make it exceptional."

Gidon motioned for Izybel to move to the window so he could speak to his wife away from young ears. Izybel followed and said,

"If we hurry, I believe we can finish in time for this golem to be of help."

"Time is a luxury we don't have," Gidon muttered, watching the soldiers scurry about the courtyard. Their armor clanked as they gathered weapons and supplies, the scent of sweat and steel filling the air. A cacophony of shouts and hammer strikes echoed off the walls, drowning out the howling wind.

"Have faith, my love," Izybel whispered, placing a warm hand on his shoulder. "Our people are strong, and we have allies who will come to our aid. We will stand against this darkness, as we always have."

"Sometimes, I wonder whether we'll ever see an end to this strife," Gidon confessed, his voice heavy with the weight of his fears. "When will we be able to live in peace, without the constant threat of death lurking around every corner? When will our family be together and safe again?"

"Only when we have defeated the Lich Lords, once and for all," Izybel replied resolutely, her eyes blazing with determination. "And that day will come, Gidon. We must believe it will. You trusted Creetan enough to send him after Almas. All we can do is continue to trust that both of them will make it back to us."

Gidon sighed. "You're right, of course. Let us prepare for the storm that approaches, and pray that we can weather it together. Speaking of which let me go check on Cady and make sure she is ready."

He found Cady at the hospital wing of the keep, where she was putting her newfound paladin skills to work. The 10-year-old moved amongst the wounded soldiers with a serene grace, her hands aglow with the warm, golden light of her Paladin magic. She touched each man's brow, whispering words of comfort and healing.

"Rest now, it will be okay," she murmured to a soldier whose leg had been mangled beyond recognition. As the soothing energy of her magic flowed into him, he sighed in relief, his pain momentarily forgotten.

It filled him with pride to see his daughter, at such a young age, embracing her abilities to help and heal. "You're doing great work, Cady," he said with a warm smile. "The city is lucky to have you here."

Cady blushed, looking down at her feet. "Thanks, Father. I'm just doing what I can to help."

"I feel the battle will begin soon. I'm sorry to put this on you but we will need your healing powers," Gidon warned.

"I will do my best," Cady responded bravely.

"I know you will Sweetheart. I know you will do great."

IN THE DIMLY LIT COUNCIL chamber in Beaver Dam, Creetan, Almas, Uncle Marpel, Seacra, and Lord Teanas stood before King Yucaipa and High Lord Cree Forjad. The aging King's face bore the weight of many years of ruling, and he listened intently as Almas spoke of the Lich Lords' battle plans.

Almas, with a determined glint in his eyes, said, "I know the Lich Lords' strategies. I... I've seen their plans, and I know how they intend to attack Flameshaven."

Creetan exchanged a cautious glance with his younger brother, unsure of how much Almas should reveal. He knew that Almas had once been under the control of the Lich Lords, but with the help of Creetan and Seacra the younger boy had managed to break free from their influence, regaining control of his will.

King Yucaipa leaned forward, his expression earnest. "Tell us what you know, Almas. It might be the key to turning the tide in Flameshaven's favor."

Almas hesitated for a moment, deciding how much to divulge. "Lich-El will be there personally. He will be able to bring down the walls and then they will use their numbers to sweep in from the south, east and west."

Lord Teanas, ever composed and wise, nodded thoughtfully. "If we know their plans, we can prepare countermeasures and reinforcements to defend the city effectively."

Almas nodded, relieved that they understood the urgency of the situation. "Exactly. But I need to get to Flameshaven as quickly as possible to help implement the countermeasures. Time is of the essence."

High Lord Cree Forjad, who also happened to be Cree and Almas' grandfather, stroked his long beard, deep in thought. "We will move our army to aid Flameshaven as swiftly as we can, but it will take a few days to mobilize. Unfortunately, time is a luxury we might not have. Especially if what my grandson says is true about Tornal moving their forces with magical gates. For all we know the battle could already have started."

"Indeed," agreed Lord Teanas, his fiery gaze piercing through the gloom. "Our first priority is to reach Flameshaven as quickly as possible. Seacra, are you ready to bear us there?"

Seacra, her elvish features expressing determination beyond her apparent age, answered, "I can get them there in a few hours, Father." Tricker, Seacra's pet imp chirped an agreement as it perched on her shoulder.

Lord Teanas looked at his daughter with a mix of pride and concern. "Seacra, it's a dangerous journey. Are you sure you're up to it?"

Seacra's eyes burned with unwavering resolve. "I can do it, Father. I can use my mountain dragon form, and with Almas, Creetan, and Lord Vatan on my back, we'll fly faster than any other means."

The elvish lord nodded and said, "Then we will go."

Uncle Marpel, High Lord of the now destroyed Vatan Province grinned, his adventurous spirit evident. "Well, then I'm in! Flying on a dragon's back is not an opportunity one gets every day!"

Creetan nodded in agreement. "If Seacra is willing to take us, then we should leave immediately. Every minute counts."

King Yucaipa regarded the group with a mix of gratitude and concern. "Very well. If this is your choice, then go with our blessings. May the winds be swift and the skies clear on your journey."

Creetan's grandfather nodded at the group and added, "We will hurry to join you as soon as we can," then turning to address his son, Uncle Marpel, he continues, "I trust you to find your sister and see that the remainder of her family is safe. Uncle Marpel nodded to his father respectfully and left the building with the rest of the group.

Creetan followed the group and once outside, Seacra took a deep breath, channeling her elvish magic, and in an awe-inspiring flash of light, she shifted into a magnificent mountain dragon. With wings that spanned wide, she gracefully lowered herself to the ground, allowing Almas, Creetan, her father, and Uncle Marpel to climb aboard her back.

One by one, they climbed onto Seacra's broad back, finding handholds among her scales. As they settled into their positions, Almas felt both excitement and trepidation surging within him.

Seacra growled a questioning growl, asking if everyone was ready.

"Ready," Almas confirmed, taking a deep breath. "Let's go!"

She growled once more before launching herself skyward with a mighty beat of her wings, Tricker following right behind her flapping his wings hard to keep up.

As they soared toward Flameshaven, the wind whipping through their hair, Almas couldn't help but feel the weight of their mission pressing down upon them like the earth beneath Seacra's powerful wings. The fate of their loved ones, and perhaps even the realm itself, hung in the balance – a burden they would bear with every beat of their hearts and every step of their journey.

"Let's just hope," he whispered to himself, his voice lost to the winds, "that we're enough."

High above the clouds, Seacra's powerful wings beat a steady rhythm, carrying her passengers toward their uncertain future. Almas clung to a ridge of scales along her back, his heart pounding as he surveyed the land below them. The world seemed so small from this altitude, and yet the stakes had never felt higher.

"Father would be proud," Creetan murmured from his position at the front of the group, interrupting Almas' silent reverie. "We're riding a dragon into battle. It's like something out of a legend."

"Let's just hope we can live up to those legends," Almas replied, his voice tinged with worry. "I don't want to let anyone down. He already has a son cursed with undeath. How will he feel the first time he sees me in my undead form, or when they find out how I helped the Lich Lords?"

"He will be glad to have his son back and not a slave to the undead. We do not blame you for how the Lich Lords used you and neither will your parents," Lord Teanas answered.

As they continued their flight, Almas found himself reflecting on the task that lay before them. His thoughts drifted to his family – his father's stern but loving guidance, his mother's unwavering faith in their ability to overcome any obstacle, his sister's caring for everyone she meets and his younger brother Giddy, whose curiosity and determination served as a constant beacon of hope.

"Uncle Marpel," Almas ventured hesitantly, "you've faced impossible odds before. What's your secret?"

"Ah," Marpel replied, a wry smile playing at the corners of his lips. "The secret, my boy, is to never believe that the odds are truly impossible. There's always a way – you just have to find it."

"Even when it feels like we're walking into a trap?" Almas asked, his voice barely audible over the rush of wind around them.

"Especially then," Uncle Marpel confirmed, his eyes glinting with determination. "That's when we need to be our bravest."

The group fell silent, their thoughts filled with equal parts dread and resolve. They knew the battle ahead would test their limits and force them to confront their darkest fears, but they refused to back down. Instead, they focused on the task at hand, their hearts set on defending their loved ones.

As the sun dipped below the horizon, casting an eerie glow over the landscape below, Almas couldn't help but wonder what the future held for them all. But in that moment, surrounded by his friends and family, he felt a surge of determination.

"Whatever comes," he vowed under his breath, "we'll face it together."

And with that, they pressed on, the shadows of night swallowing them whole as they raced toward the dawn and the challenges that lay beyond.

Chapter 2

"IT IS JUST ABOUT TIME, prepare your knights. We move as soon as Tonal says the sacrifices have begun."

"I still don't trust Tornal, something is strange, the other lich lords won't let any of my men anywhere near where Tornal has taken the prisoners. He is up to something."

"If he is, I promise this battle will be his last. Whatever happens, I appreciate your loyalty, it has been nice working with an Aguerius again."

THE COLD WIND HOWLED through the barren landscape, stinging Kade's cheeks with its icy bite. He stood shivering among the other captured children, their hands bound behind their backs, awaiting their grim fate. The ragged line of young prisoners trembled under the gaze of the lich lord Tornal and his equally sinister ally, Vorath.

"You are here to pay for the insolence you showed when you let our prisoners escape," Tornal hissed, his voice like a thousand venomous snakes slithering through the air. His skeletal fingers traced the edge of Kade's chin, the touch colder than the harshest winter storm. "Your lives will be the price you pay for your failures. You will be sacrificed in the place of the prisoners you lost. It is an honor, really, to be chosen for such a vital role."

Kade's eyes blazed with defiance despite the chill settling into his bones. "Oh, I'm honored all right," he spat. "How about you untie me and let me show you how grateful I am?"

Tornal's pale yellow eyes flickered with anger. "You insolent brat! I've looked forward to the day I could silence that mouth."

"Should I take this as an end to the alliance between the Kadus Knights and the Lich Lords?" Kade asked, a wicked smile spreading across his face.

"Silence!" Tornal snarled. Turning to Vorath, he commanded, "Sacrifice this one first, and make it slow." With that, Tornal vanished in a swirl of darkness, leaving the children to the mercy of Vorath.

"Your death will serve a greater purpose," Vorath sneered, circling Kade like a vulture over carrion.

"Really?" Kade shot back, his voice dripping with sarcasm. "Because from where I'm standing, it looks like you're just a bunch of boneheads playing dress-up."

Vorath's bony jaw clenched in fury, his yellow eyes burning brighter than before. "You will rue your insolence when your soul is torn asunder!"

"Yawn," Kade replied, rolling his eyes. "You'd think after all this time, you undead creeps could come up with some new material."

Kade smirked as Vorath approached him pulling out a dagger to end him. Seeing Kade's grin he narrowed his eyes at the boy. "What do you have to smile about, child?" he hissed.

"Two reasons," Kade replied nonchalantly. "First, there's only one lich lord left for me to deal with. Second, these bindings? Not as secure as you thought." He raised his hands, revealing that they were no longer tied behind his back. In one hand, he gripped a boomerang-shaped dagger with a gleam in his eye.

Vorath's eyes widened, but before he could react, Kade hurled the dagger with all his might. Like a bolt of lightning, it sliced through the air, cutting deep into the lich lord's bony frame. Vorath crumbled to dust, his last gasp echoing across the battlefield. As he disintegrated, so too did the revenants under his command, their lifeless forms collapsing like marionettes with severed strings.

The dagger continued its deadly arc, slashing through two more revenants that must have belonged to other lich lords before being snatched out of the air by a figure that seemed to materialize from nowhere. Ulec, an elvish boy who appeared no older than twelve despite his true age of 126, caught the weapon effortlessly. In a flash of light, the boomerang dagger transformed into a short sword in his grasp.

"Nice timing, Ulec!" Kade exclaimed while scooping up a fallen dagger from one of the destroyed revenants. He began cutting the bindings on the other children, his fingers working deftly even as his mind raced with strategy. "I see there was no hard feelings about losing our dual the other day.

Ulec ignored Kade's quip and continued to fend off the undead. "Stay focused, Kade. We have to ensure the safety of these children."

"You got it, pointy ears," Kade replied, always ready with a nickname for his elvish friend.

"Kade, behind you!" one of the children shouted.

Kade smirked and casually sidestepped a lunging revenant. "Thanks for the heads up, but I got this!"

As the kids that Kade had cut loose continued freeing the others Kade turned to defend them from the attacking revenants.

"Let's finish these boneheads off!" Kade shouted, rallying the other children. Together, they made quick work of the remaining revenants, each one crumbling to dust as it met its end. Kade couldn't help be impressed at the skill Ulec showed as he fought and couldn't help but laugh as he noticed a couple of revenants fall to sudden spray of acid from something hiding in the tall grass.

"Is that your slime Metal? Almas mentioned him before."

"Yep, just don't get to close, he isn't sure he trusts you yet and he thinks your Chaos Breastplate smells delicious," Ulec answered.

"Umm, tell that slime it is off limits, the god Snipies isn't around anymore to make replacements."

As the last of their enemies fell, Kade turned to Ulec, his green eyes blazing with determination. "We did it," he breathed, a mixture of exhaustion and triumph etched on his young face.

"Indeed, we did," Ulec agreed, his own expression mirroring Kade's. He bent over to pick up Metal and put the slime in his shoulder bag as he continued, "But this is just the beginning."

Kade nodded, knowing that it wouldn't take long before the other lich lords sent an army to finish the job Vorath never even started.

With the battlefield now momentarily clear of revenants, Kade's attention shifted to Ulec. The elvish boy wiped the sweat from his brow, his eyes reflecting a quiet gratitude. "Thanks for returning Changing Hand," he said, referring to the fieles that had transformed into a short sword in his grip. "I hope she wasn't too hard on you for stealing her from me."

"Hey, no problem," Kade replied with a smirk, rubbing the back of his neck sheepishly. "Honestly, while it was handy in sneaking a weapon past their search, you're welcome to take it back. That woman's voice coming from it was kind of mean."

Ulec chuckled softly, his eyes flickering with amusement. "Yeah, Changing Hand can be quite... assertive. It was created by a piece of my mother's soul, so I guess you could say 'mean' would be an understatement."

"Your mother, huh?" Kade mused, his eyebrows knitting together in thought. He imagined what it must be like to have a piece of one's parent living on in such a way, a constant reminder of their presence and power.

"Anyway," Kade continued, attempting to steer the conversation towards more comfortable territory. "I'm glad we got to fight at Beaver Dam before ending up on the same side. Gave me a chance to see what you're really made of."

Ulec nodded, a wry smile playing at the corners of his lips. "That fight did have its benefits - getting captured and thrown in with the other prisoners allowed me to help them escape."

Kade smiled as he started to agree, but then he paused, a sudden suspicion creeping into his mind. "Wait a second... did you lose on purpose?" His tone was laced with indignation, the mere thought of winning due to his opponent's intentional loss leaving a bitter taste in his mouth.

"Whoa, whoa," Ulec held up his hands defensively. "I never said anything like that! I merely pointed out the silver lining in our situation."

"Uh-huh," Kade grumbled, unconvinced. He glared at Ulec, his eyes blazing with the intensity of a thousand suns. "Fine," he snapped, his voice dripping with sarcasm. "But I want a rematch as soon as this is all over. And no losing on purpose this time, got it?"

Ulec raised an eyebrow, the corners of his mouth twitching with amusement. "Kade, we have a battle starting, and the Lich Lords are preparing to send a horde of revenants to recapture us and the other children. Perhaps we should postpone any duels until after the war?"

The wind howled around them, whipping their hair and clothes like angry spirits seeking vengeance. Kade's heart thundered in his chest, a mix of fear and excitement coursing through his veins. He knew Ulec was right, but his pride still stung from the implication that his victory at Beaver Dam may not have been entirely earned.

"Fine," Kade muttered begrudgingly, forcing himself to focus on the task at hand. He turned to the other children, his green eyes flashing with determination. "We need to prepare our defenses. Gather anything you can find and start building fortifications."

As the others scrambled to follow his orders, Kade set off in search of his collection of boomerang daggers, which had been taken by the undead when they captured him. The ground beneath his feet was cold and unforgiving, each step a reminder of the dark forces that had brought them here.

The shadows seemed to reach for him, tendrils of darkness grasping at his limbs, eager to pull him into their depths. Kade shook off the unsettling feeling, refusing to let fear take hold.

"Those daggers better be around here somewhere," he mumbled under his breath, his inner thoughts bitter and resentful. He had worked hard to perfect his skills with those weapons, and their loss felt like a part of himself had been torn away.

After a few minutes he noticed a glimmer from polished metal in the dust of a fallen revenant.

"Found them!" Kade cried out triumphantly, locating his precious daggers hidden among the debris left by the fallen revenants. He gripped their familiar handles, feeling a surge of strength and determination course through him.

"Alright, Lich Lords," he whispered, a fierce grin spreading across his face, "you have no idea who you're messing with."

With his weapons in hand, Kade turned back towards his friends, ready to face whatever challenges lay ahead with unwavering courage and resolve. This was their chance to become legends, and he would not let fear or doubt stand in their way.

Chapter 3

"WELL, I SUPPOSE WE can't wait any longer for the sacrifices to begin."

"The way Vorath's revenants all just crumbled I'd say we have a prisoner revolt on our hands, maybe we should put off the attack until that is taken care of?"

"King Yucaipa and Lord Forjad are on their way now. This battle must end before they arrive. We will begin now. If Tornal can't handle a few prisoners than he deserves his fate."

HIGH LORD GIDON AGUERIUS stood on the city wall of Flameshaven, his eyes scanning the armies below. Something was amiss; he noticed some of the revenants veering away from the main group and moving towards the rear lines. His instincts screamed a warning, but before he could fully comprehend the situation, Lich-El approached the wall before him, wielding a massive war hammer.

"Well, well, well, Lord Gidon," Lich-El said with his usual confidence. "How is the defense of your precious city going?"

Gidon shot back with his quick wit, "Oh, you know, the usual-preparing a warm welcome for anyone trying to attack the city."

Lich-El grinned wickedly. "You could save yourself a lot of trouble by simply surrendering. It's not too late."

Gidon chuckled, refusing to be intimidated. "As much as I'd love to hand over the keys to Flameshaven, I'm rather fond of breathing, so I'll have to decline your generous offer."

Lich-El nodded, feigning understanding. "Fair enough, Lord Gidon. But I must say, your city walls, while fine and strong, lack the magical protections that our elven allies put on their walls."

The implication hit Gidon like a bolt of lightning. He realized that Lich-El was referring to the elvish walls' magic protection which protected them from magic attacks. Panic gripped him as he frantically ordered the defenders to clear the wall, urging them toward the stairs.

But it was too late. With a tap of his war hammer on the ground, Lich-El unleashed his devastating attack. Enormous stone spikes erupted from under the wall, causing it to explode section by section. The destruction spread rapidly, leaving a trail of devastation in its wake.

Gidon watched in horror as the wall crumbled before his eyes. He tried to escape the destruction, but as a stone spike erupted beneath him, he was knocked unconscious and buried under the rubble of what was once a formidable defense.

The wall fell, and the armies of the Lich Lords advanced towards the now exposed city. Flameshaven's defenders were stunned, their voices silenced without the guidance of their Royal Strategist. Fear gripped their hearts as they tried to reorganize and protect their home with only the rubble of their once-mighty walls as a barrier.

The battle for Flameshaven had taken a dark and desperate turn. The Lich Lords' calculated assault had left the city vulnerable, and Gidon's fate remained uncertain. As the undead horde closed in, the defenders rallied, drawing strength from their determination to protect their loved ones and their city.

The clash of steel against steel, the roar of the undead, and the screams of battle filled the air. Flameshaven's defenders fought valiantly, refusing to yield to the darkness that threatened to consume them. But with their leader seemingly lost, they faced an uphill battle, and the odds weighed heavily against them.

In the chaos and devastation, one thing remained clear: the war had reached a critical turning point, and the fate of Flameshaven hung in the balance. The city's survival rested on the bravery and resilience of its defenders and their unyielding spirit in the face of insurmountable odds.

AS SEACRA DESCENDED gracefully to the outskirts of the raging battle, Almas, Uncle Marpel, Creetan, and Lord Teanas clung tightly to her back. The city of Flameshaven lay before them, enveloped in chaos and the relentless onslaught of the undead.

Almas surveyed the battlefield with a sense of urgency, his mind already working out a plan. He sent out his little undead creatures, the creeps, to scout the area and gather vital information.

"They'll keep an eye out for any surprises or hidden threats," Almas explained to his companions.

Uncle Marpel patted Almas on the shoulder. "Good thinking, lad. Now, what's our move?"

Almas looked at the situation and made a quick decision. "Creetan, Lord Teanas, and Seacra, I think you should head to the city and bolster the defense there. I'll go with Uncle Marpel to assist Kade in protecting the Kadus Knight children," Almas smiled, "Ulec is already there."

Creetan nodded, understanding the importance of each task. "Alright, Almas, you take care of Ulec and Kade. We'll do our best to protect the city."

Seacra shifted back to her elvish form, and with a determined expression, she said, "We'll give them all we've got. Then I get to beat my brother for worrying me." Tricker on her shoulder chirped in agreement

Lord Teanas, the elvish lord and father of Ulec and Seacra, clasped Almas's shoulder in a show of support. "Stay safe, Almas. We'll meet you back at the city when our tasks are done."

Almas gave them a reassuring smile. "You too, Lord Teanas. And thank you for all your help."

With that, Creetan, Lord Teanas, and Seacra took to the skies again, heading towards the besieged city. Almas and Uncle Marpel moved swiftly towards where Ulec and Kade were holding their ground.

As they approached the area, Almas could see the intense battle taking place around a group of children-Kade and the other Kadus Knights' offspring. The young glory seeker was in his element, fighting with unyielding determination.

Uncle Marpel began playing his instrument which was a cross between a wind instrument and a battle staff. Almas immediately felt focused and energized, a result of the music spell his uncle was casting. Almas used his creeps to attack revenants in front of them clearing a path to were Kade and Ulec were engaged.

"Kade, Ulec!" Almas called out as they got closer.

Kade looked up, a grin breaking across his face at the sight of Almas. "Well, if it ain't the Necromancer! Took you long enough to get here! Heard you finally ditched Tornal."

Ulec, who had been locked in a fierce duel, managed a nod of acknowledgment as he continued to fight off the undead.

Uncle Marpel chuckled, joining the fray with his staff swinging, the noise of it cutting through the air and smashing into revenants creating a melody that Uncle Marpel used to continue his music spell. "You know Almas, he never could follow orders, Tornal learned that the hard way. Keeps us all on our toes."

"Who's the old guy. I could get used to fighting with a bard," Kade asked clearly liking the enhancing effects of Marpel's bard magic.

"Kade, meet my Uncle Marpel. And if you like one bard, let's see how you like two!"

Almas put his own ocarina to his mouth and joined his music to his uncle's. The results were the attacking revenants seemed to slow down as the defenders fought with enhanced skills.

As the battle raged around them, Almas and Uncle Marpel fought alongside Kade, Ulec, and many of the older children, forming a formidable team to protect the Kadus Knight children.

"We'll hold them back, but we need to make sure the children stay safe!" Almas called out, trying to be heard over the clash of weapons.

Kade smirked, parrying a revenant's attack with skillful precision as his boomerang daggers circled around him forming a protective barrier. "Don't you worry, Almas. We'll make sure everyone gets through this in one piece!"

With renewed determination, they fought side by side, a united front against the darkness threatening to engulf them. The children of the Kadus Knights looked up to their defenders with awe and gratitude, finding courage in their bravery.

In the midst of the battle, Almas couldn't help but be thankful for his allies-Uncle Marpel, Kade, and Ulec-and for the friends defending the city. They were a band of heroes, fighting for the safety and hope of Flameshaven.

As the battle raged on, Almas knew that they had to give it their all, for the fate of their city and their loved ones rested on their shoulders. They fought with the determination and resilience that only true heroes possessed, standing strong against the relentless tide of darkness.

As the last of the revenants retreated, the defenders took a moment to catch their breath and assess their fortifications. Kade led Almas and his uncle through the makeshift barriers and obstacles they had constructed, pointing out the strategic placements with a sense of pride.

"Check this out, Almas," Kade said, gesturing towards a small shack nearby. "That's our latrine. We built it right on top of Vorath's remains. Figured it was the perfect way to show the Lich Lords what we think of them."

Almas couldn't help but chuckle at Kade's audacity. "You really have a way with making a statement, Kade. I have to hand it to you."

Kade grinned mischievously. "Oh, I'm not done yet. I've got plans for Tornal too. Just you wait."

Curiosity got the better of Almas as he looked towards the spot Kade mentioned. "You're going to build another latrine on top of Tornal's remains? That's... quite a unique approach."

Kade nodded, his eyes gleaming with a glint of humor. "Yep, exactly. I want to make sure those undead know that we're not just going to let them trample all over us."

Almas agreed, knowing that such actions might help boost the morale of the defenders and make a clear statement of defiance to their foes.

But then Kade's tone turned serious as he mentioned the Kadus Knights. "We need to let them know about Tornal's betrayal. They can't keep fighting alongside the undead."

Almas nodded, understanding the importance of the Kadus Knights knowing the truth. "You're right. The undead will use them as a shield during the battle and then turn on them once they're no longer useful."

Kade sighed, understanding the gravity of the situation. "I'll have to be the one to go. The Knights won't believe it coming from an outsider, especially in the middle of a battle."

Almas offered to accompany him, but Kade shook his head. "No, you, Marpel, and Ulec will be needed to defend the little children until I bring the adult Knights back."

Almas gave Kade a reassuring pat on the back. "Alright, be careful out there, Kade. We'll hold the fort here until you return."

Kade nodded with determination. "Thanks, Almas. I'll be back as soon as I can. Just don't have all the fun without me! Save some for me when I get back!"

With that, Kade set off on his mission, leaving Almas to continue defending the children alongside Uncle Marpel and Ulec.

As Almas watched Kade disappear into the distance, he couldn't help but admire his friend's courage and resourcefulness. Despite the odds stacked against them, Kade faced the challenges head-on, with humor and a determination to protect his loved ones.

In the midst of battle, they all found strength in each other, and Almas knew that as long as they stood together, they had a chance to overcome the darkness threatening to consume them all.

Chapter 4

"ARE YOU OKAY LORD LICH-El, you don't look so well?"

"I will be fine. Once this ends, I will be fine. Go take your Bear Riders and attack from the south. And watch yourself. I feel treason in the air."

"Very well my lord, why don't you withdraw to the rear lines. My Knights can handle things for now."

FROM A CLOUD OF DUST and debris, Jerad emerged, his armor battered and his axe dusty from the remains of the undead. He surveyed the chaos around him: revenant soldiers clawed at the remnants of the city wall, their grotesque fingers grasping for purchase, while far-off shouts of the Kadus knights and their Bear Riders echoed through the air like thunder. Cold sweat beaded on his brow, making each breath feel like he was swallowing ice.

"Lord Gidon is missing, sir!" a young messenger stammered, almost tripping over his words as much as the rubble beneath his feet. "And the south and eastern sides are in danger of falling!"

"Missing?" Jerad's voice was tinged with disbelief, his heart clenching like a fist. The weight of responsibility settled heavily on his shoulders as he took charge of the defense, barking orders to the nearest soldiers. Their eyes flickered with doubt—a feeling that mirrored his own—but they obeyed nonetheless.

"Fall back! Brace for impact! We need a defensive line here, now!" Jerad shouted, his voice strained from exhaustion and fear. As he turned to face the oncoming wave of revenants, he couldn't help but wonder how things had become so dire. It felt like the world itself was conspiring against them, pushing them to the brink of disaster.

The ground shook and trembled, announcing the arrival of a monstrously large dragon that descended upon the battlefield. With a roar that rattled the very core of Jerad's being, the creature landed between his men and the revenants. A single swipe of its colossal tail sent the undead hurtling through the air like ragdolls, their bodies crumbling like old parchment under the force of the blow.

"Snipies..." Jerad breathed, unable to tear his gaze away from the awe-inspiring sight. But before he could fully process what had just happened, the dragon transformed into a familiar elvish woman—Lady Alixia.

"Where is my son?" she demanded, her voice laced with equal parts fury and concern. "Is Ulec alive? Has his curse been lifted?"

"Last I saw him, he was fine," Jerad assured her, raising his voice so it could be heard over the din of battle. "Almas and Cady found a way to lift the curse."

Around them, revenants attempted to regroup, but they were no match for Lady Alixia's wrath. With casual flicks of her wrist, she sent bolts of magical energy hurtling towards the undead, incinerating them in brilliant displays of arcane might. Yet her focus remained solely on Jerad, as if the fate of her son held more weight than the entire city.

"Ulec is strong, my lady," Jerad said, trying to reassure her. "He can handle himself."

"Take me to Ulec!" Lady Alixia demanded, her voice sharp and unwavering.

"Forgive me, my lady," Jerad replied, exasperated. "I don't know where he is right now. In case you haven't noticed, I'm a bit preoccupied with trying to save everyone's lives."

Lady Alixia huffed indignantly, her eyes flashing with irritation. "Fine. I need to teach these Lich Lords a lesson about not attacking my family anyway." She gestured for Jerad to move his forces to the south and east sides of the city while she dealt with the undead attackers on the western front. "Go. I'll handle things here."

With a fluid motion, Lady Alixia transformed into the largest elder dragon Jerad had ever seen. Her scales shimmered like moonlight on water, and the air around her crackled with power. Without wasting another moment, she unleashed a wall of flame that roared across the battlefield, immediately sending the Lich Lord forces on the west into a full retreat.

"Oh Snipies..." Jerad muttered under his breath as he watched the devastating display of arcane might before him. He couldn't help but marvel at how quickly the tide of battle had shifted in their favor. As the heat of the dragon fire washed over him, he felt a newfound sense of determination surge through his veins.

"Alright, you heard her!" he barked at his men, the bitter sarcasm replaced by resolute conviction. "We've been given a chance. Let's make the most of it! Split up and reinforce the south and east!"

As his forces divided and hurried off to back up the other two battlefronts, Jcrad couldn't shake the nagging feeling that this day was far from over. The darkness seemed to cling to the very air around them, suffocating hope and casting doubt upon even the bravest of hearts.

"Stay strong, my friends," he whispered to himself, the weight of responsibility heavy on his shoulders.

With a deep breath, Jerad charged forward into the fray.

CREETAN'S HEART POUNDED in his chest as Seacra's powerful wings beat the air, carrying him and Lord Teanas to the southern end of the city. The wind whipped through Creetan's hair, stinging his eyes and drowning out all other sounds. Below them, the undead and Kadus Knight Bear Riders surged against the battered remnants of the city wall, their twisted forms illuminated by the flickering flames of destruction.

"Ready?" Lord Teanas shouted over the roar of the wind, his stoic expression betraying no hint of fear or doubt.

"Ready," Creetan replied, his fingers tightening around the grip of Sacredknight, his father's magic bow. The fieles within the bow hummed with power, its ancient Paladin soul resonating with his own determination to protect his friends and home.

"Get us down there!" Lord Teanas commanded, and Seacra, her majestic Mountain Dragon form casting an imposing shadow on the battlefield below, angled her descent towards Jarad's position.

As they touched down amid the chaos, Seacra's fangs, tail, and teeth immediately leapt into action, tearing at the undead creatures with savage precision. The little imp Tricker flew circles above her raining bolts of energy down while dodging ranged attacks aimed to shoot the little demon down.

Creetan drew back the string of Sacredknight, feeling the pulse of sacred energy coursing through it as he released an arrow that transformed into a beam of light, slicing through the oncoming horde.

"Good shot," Sacredknight whispered in Creetan's mind, offering encouragement and advice as it guided his aim.

"Thanks," Creetan thought back, smirking despite the dire circumstances. *"Any other tricks up your sleeve?"*

"Focus, young one," the fieles chided gently. *"There will be time for humor when this battle is won."*

Nearby, Lord Teanas wielded his fire powers and Mimic, the shape-shifting weapon, with deadly grace. Flames danced around him, consuming the undead in their fiery embrace as he shifted effortlessly between forms – one moment a sword, the next a spear.

"Jarad!" Creetan called out, spotting the battered but determined retainer among the fray. "Where's my father?"

"Missing," Jarad replied tersely, his eyes never leaving the battlefield. "The wall fell, and we lost sight of him."

"Then who's in charge?" Creetan demanded, concern etching lines of worry across his face.

"Congratulations," Jarad shot back, a bitter smile twisting his lips. "You are. As Gidon's heir, you have all his authority so it is up to you."

"Great," Creetan muttered, feeling the weight of responsibility settle onto his shoulders like an ill-fitting cloak. "Just what I always wanted."

"Embrace your destiny, Creetan," Sacredknight urged, its voice filled with wisdom and assurance. *"You were born for this moment, and together, we shall lead these brave souls to victory."*

"Alright," Creetan said aloud, steeling himself as he surveyed the chaos around him. "Let's push them back! We have a city to save!"

With renewed vigor, Creetan, Seacra, Lord Teanas, and Jarad fought on, their combined efforts turning the tide against the relentless undead. And as they began to reclaim precious ground, the darkness that had threatened to swallow them whole seemed just a little less suffocating, replaced by a glimmer of hope that shone like the first light of dawn.

AS THE BATTLE RAGED on and the defenders began to push back the undead, Lord Teanas surveyed the destruction around him. The city lay in ruins, its once proud walls crumbling under the relentless assault of the Lich Lords' forces. Despair clawed at his heart like a ravenous beast, threatening to consume him entirely, but he refused to let it take hold. A fire burned deep within him, fueled by the knowledge that if he did not act now, all hope would be lost.

"Enough," Lord Teanas whispered, more to himself than anyone else. His voice was like the smoldering embers of a dying flame, barely audible above the cacophony of battle.

"Seacra!" he called out, raising his voice to be heard above the din. "Take me to the rear lines of the undead army! I must confront Lich-El personally. This madness has to end."

"Are you certain, Father?" Seacra's voice held a note of concern as she glanced toward him after changing back to her elvish form to speak, her eyes filled with worry.

"Never been more so," Lord Teanas replied, steeling himself for what lay ahead. "I cannot stand idly by while our world crumbles around us."

"Very well," Seacra acquiesced, changing back into a mountain dragon to allow her father to climb onto her back.

"Before we go," Lord Teanas addressed Mimic, the fieles ring on his finger, *"I need you now more than ever. Transform into the weapon most suited for this task."*

"You will need to move quickly to avoid his attacks, let's try copying the powers of Swift so you don't immediately die." Mimic replied in Teanas' mind, its tone tinged with sarcasm. In an instant, the ring shifted and morphed, becoming a gleaming silver sword with intricate runes etched along the blade.

"Let's hope this recommendation of yours is worth its weight in gold, Mimic," Lord Teanas muttered, gripping the hilt of the sword tightly.

"Trust me," Mimic responded dryly, *"I'm worth more than my weight in gold, but I don't think it will save you from Lich-El. He is beyond you. Yet I know you won't listen so let's go save the world or whatever it is we're doing."*

With a powerful leap, Seacra took to the sky, soaring above the battlefield as they made their way toward the rear lines of the undead army. The world seemed to shrink beneath them, the chaos engulfed in an eerie silence that sent shivers down Lord Teanas' spine.

Seacra landed with surprising grace for a creature her size, allowing Lord Teanas to dismount. As he prepared to face Lich-El, he looked back at his daughter one last time, offering her a reassuring smile.

"Go," he said, nodding toward the city. "Assist your mother and our people. I'll take care of Lich-El."

With a final, reluctant nod, Seacra spread her wings and took flight once more, her little demon pet always right behind her, leaving Lord Teanas alone to confront the darkness that threatened to swallow them all.

"Alright, Lich-El," Lord Teanas whispered, raising his sword as he faced the ominous presence looming before him. "Let's see what kind of monster you've become."

Chapter 5

"WE CAN'T LET THAT BOY reach the Kadus Knights or Lich-El. Send whatever revenants you can and kill him."

"He is already being surrounded. How you could have messed things up so badly is beyond me."

"What's done is done, just kill the boy and get ready. We will be able to create many revenants from their fallen. We really don't need them anymore, living that is."

IN THE MIDST OF THE chaos that consumed Flameshaven, Kade moved with an almost ethereal grace, his determination propelling him forward. His mission was clear: find the group of Kadus Knights and inform them of the Lich Lords' betrayal. He darted through the outskirts of the battle, hoping to reach his destination before the revenants could catch wind of his presence.

As he neared the city walls, Kade's heart raced. He knew he had to act swiftly, for the undead would stop at nothing to prevent him from delivering his crucial message. Before he could make it to safety, a swarm of revenants closed in around him, their hollow eyes fixed on their quarry.

With a flick of his wrists, Kade drew his distinctive boomerang-shaped daggers. His blades danced in his hands, a symphony of deadly arcs and spins as he deftly cut through the first wave of revenants that reached him. One dagger soared through the air, slicing through the undead with unerring accuracy as Kade seamlessly drew a fresh blade from his arsenal.

In the midst of the battle, Kade's movements took on an almost hypnotic rhythm. He threw one dagger, caught another, and seamlessly transitioned between attacks and defenses. The chaos of the battlefield faded into the background as Kade's focus narrowed to the dance of destruction he orchestrated.

Undeterred, Kade continued his mesmerizing display, his daggers a blur of motion as he fought off his relentless foes. With each throw and each catch, his confidence grew, and a grin tugged at the corner of his lips. "Well, this is a fine mess I've gotten myself into," he muttered to himself, a hint of humor in his voice.

Blows rained down on his Chaos Breastplate, but Kade paid them no mind, his concentration unbreakable. His daggers spun and whirled, becoming an extension of his will as he weaved through the revenants with uncanny agility.

The situation grew dire as the mass of undead closed in around him, a relentless tide that seemed almost impossible to stem. But Kade's determination burned brighter, and he gathered the remnants of his magic, channeling it into a final gambit.

With a swift, coordinated movement, Kade threw the daggers in his hands into the ground, and the spinning blades encircling him changed course in mid-air, embedding themselves in the earth. A surge of magical energy erupted from the ground, a devastating explosion that obliterated the revenants surrounding Kade.

Dust and debris filled the air, and as it settled, Kade looked around triumphantly. A chorus of cheers and laughter echoed in his mind as he pumped his arm in celebration. "Ha! Now that's how you put on a show!" he exclaimed, a mix of exhilaration and exhaustion coursing through his veins.

Yet, his victory was short-lived. Kade stumbled, his jubilant posture faltering. Pain seared through his body as he glanced down, his eyes widening in realization. Two bone spikes protruded from his torso, the cruel aftermath of the battle he had waged. Poison coursed through his veins, a sinister reminder that the battle had taken its toll.

"This isn't good," Kade muttered, his bravado giving way to a grim acceptance as darkness crept at the edges of his vision. His body grew heavy, his strength waning as he fought to stay conscious.

With a final effort, Kade's vision blurred, and he collapsed to his knees, his world fading into blackness. The battle he had so ardently sought had come at a cost, and as he succumbed to unconsciousness, the fate of Flameshaven hung in the balance.

LORD GIDON AGUERIUS awoke amidst the rubble of the city wall, the aftermath of the devastating attack leaving him with only minor scratches and bruises despite being almost completely buried. Dusting himself off, he quickly assessed his surroundings, realizing that the battle had moved deeper into the city. Prepared to rejoin the fray, he was halted by a resounding explosion from outside the former city wall.

Intrigued and concerned, Gidon hastened toward the source of the explosion. There, he found a child of the Kadus Knights, writhing on the ground in pain, poisoned by bone spikes that a revenant or lich had struck him with. Gidon's healer instincts kicked in, his compassion overriding any differences in allegiance. He knelt beside the boy, channeling healing magic into his small form.

Just as Gidon's efforts began to take effect, a shadow fell over him. With swift reflexes, he drew his sword to parry an incoming strike. His eyes locked with those of his attacker-Deleta, his nephew, and leader of the Kadus Knights.

"Murderer!" Deleta spat, "Now your attacking children?"

"Deleta, wait! We need to talk, but there isn't time! Things aren't what you think!"

"I know what I saw!" Deleta said slashing at Gidon again.

Suddenly another voice cut through the noise of battle. "Deleta, wait! Look"

Deleta glanced over to where another Kadus Knight was kneeling by the injured boy. The knight pointed out the bone spikes.

"The undead did this, not a human."

"I was trying to heal him. I'm the only one that can stop the poison from doing any more damage, but each second that we fight lets the poison do more damage.

Deleta's voice wavered as he spoke, seeking affirmation. "Can you really save him from the poison?"

Gidon's gaze held steady as he repeated, "I can accelerate his body's natural healing and protect him from further damage. But the extent of his recovery depends on how much the poison has already harmed him."

Deleta glanced at the other Kadus Knight and said, "He's your son."

The Kadus Knight looked at Gidon and nodded his permission.

Gidon worked tirelessly, his hands glowing with healing magic, as he explained the process to the boy's father and Deleta.

"He will need water as I speed up his kidneys to cleanse the poison from his body. His body will expel the poison once he empties his bladder in a few moments. You'll have to try to ignore the smell."

In the midst of his healing efforts, Gidon took the opportunity to share the truth of their past, recounting how he and Deleta's father had tried to go to his rescue when they heard the town he was at had been attacked. They could find no survivors and had left believing him to be dead.

Deleta's eyes bore into Gidon's as he accused, "I saw you kill my father!"

Gidon's voice was filled with sadness as he corrected the misconception. "You must have seen me kill the revenant he had become. We were attacked by revenants. He was killed in the fight and turned. I had no choice but to put his body to rest."

The boy stirred and started to open his eyes. Seeing his father and Deleta standing over him he whispered with great difficulty, "Tornal...betrayed. Trying to sacrifice...all of us. Almas...needs help."

Gidon's eyes opened wide in surprise at the mention of Almas while Kade's voice faded as he lost consciousness once more. Gidon looked at the boy's father with a mix of relief and concern. "He's stable for now, but there may be lasting damage that could affect him in the future. All he needs now is rest. Did he say Almas was there?"

"Deleta nodded as he said, "He did say Almas, although last I heard Almas was still at Beaver Dam. I heard his brother and friends had managed to free him from Tornal's control. If Tornal has completely betrayed us we are all in danger now." Looking at Gidon he continued, "I've judged you harshly, uncle."

Gidon placed a hand on Deleta's shoulder. "We all make judgments in times of conflict. The important thing is to learn from them. Now we need to act quickly before more lives are lost."

Deleta pulled out a signal horn and blew a series of signals, conveying orders to his fellow Kadus Knights. He explained that they would withdraw from the battle to rescue their children. Gidon mirrored his action, blowing his own signal to his men, commanding them to not pursue retreating enemies.

Looking at Deleta, Gidon's expression was resolute. "I need to go help you rescue the children."

Deleta nodded, the tension between them finally easing. "Let's go, uncle. Let's go save the children."

AMIDST THE CHAOTIC battlefield, Almas fought side by side with Ulec, and Uncle Marpel, their individual skills merging into a symphony of defense. The children of the Kadus Knights, fortified and trained, fought valiantly alongside them. Revenants pressed relentlessly against the makeshift defenses; their unyielding assault met by the combined might of the defenders.

Ulec, armed with Changing Hand, flowed through the chaos with a grace that belied the deadly precision of his strikes. His weapon seamlessly shifted forms, each change designed to counter the threats he faced. He sliced through the undead horde, his movements a dance of calculated speed. He made swift work of any revenants that dared breach their defenses, leaving behind nothing but dissolving dust.

Uncle Marpel, wielding his battle staff, infused each swing with his bardic magic. Bolts of energy and arcs of chain lightning lanced through the air, finding their mark amidst the undead ranks. The powerful vibrations of his staff cast a harmonic pulse that disrupted the revenants' advance, buying precious moments for the defenders to regroup and counter.

Hovering just behind the front line, Almas played his ocarina, channeling his bardic magic through his music. Each note he played served as a catalyst, empowering his comrades with heightened reflexes and focus. He did his best to direct the defense of their small, fortified position, his strategic mind working in perfect harmony with the flowing battlefield. He directed his creeps, summoned from the remnants of dead plants and small animals, to attack relentlessly, seeking out weak points and providing crucial support.

"Don't forget about me," Almas heard Fireweaver say. *"Now that you are free from Tornal's control. Let me help!"*

"I'm not sure how," Almas replied.

"Whenever there is fire, imagine what you want it to do and channel magic into me. And remember, we can only control fire, not make it." Fireweaver taught.

"So, in other words, after the battle, you'll need to teach me Teanas' recipe for his fire cloak." Almas said as he tried using the fieles to control some fire on a burning log and turned it into a fireball and flung it at a group of revenants.

"This is going to be fun," Almas thought to himself.

From then on, Almas was able to control and manipulate the fire around him with his newfound magical ability. He used it to incinerate hordes of rampaging revenants, his flames engulfing them in a sea of searing heat. The sheer power of the blaze forced them back, giving Ulec and Uncle Marpel some much needed breathing room. With Fireweaver's guidance, Almas quickly learned how to craft walls of flame that could protect their position from further attack. On top of this, he used his magic to create illusions and distractions that caused confusion among the enemy ranks.

Feeling better about their odds, Almas quipped, "Ulec, could you show the undead your 'shape-shifting weapon' trick again? I think they missed it the first time."

Ulec's focused expression didn't waver as he slashed through another revenant. "No time for jokes, Almas. And be careful with those flames, Metal is oozing around out there. I don't want him fried."

"Don't worry, I have a creep keeping track of Metal...wait, no, Metal just ate it. Tell your slime the creeps are on our side!"

"Will do. Now let me fight!"

While Almas added a touch of humor to the battle, Ulec's silence was his own form of communication-a focused determination that spoke louder than words. His small frame darted through the fray, a blur of motion as he engaged the enemy. He relied on agility and speed, slipping through the undead's grasp like a shadow.

As the battle raged on, Almas noticed a few of the older children stepping up, defending their younger counterparts with fervor. It was a testament to their training and determination that they were able to hold their own amidst the chaos. They worked in concert with the seasoned warriors, a united front against the encroaching darkness.

Just when it seemed the defenders might be overwhelmed, a resounding horn call cut through the din of battle. Deleta, flanked by the Kadus Knights, had arrived to turn the tide. The surge of reinforcements bolstered the defenders' spirits, and they pushed back against the relentless tide of revenants.

Almas' ocarina continued to weave its musical magic, lending strength to their efforts. "Deleta, fashionably late as always!"

Deleta's lips curved into a fleeting smile as he struck down a revenant. "Fashionably victorious, more like."

Almas smiled, happy to be willingly fighting alongside his cousin finally. Then he noticed his father among the Kadus Knights.

Lord Gidon Aguerius, his presence radiating authority and determination, fought alongside Deleta. His sword cut through the undead, towards his son.

"Father! How has Deleta not killed you yet."

Gidon smiled at his son, "Trust me he tried. We came to an understanding." Gidon embraced his son quickly and returned to the battle, his movements a reflection of his years of combat expertise. The combined forces of the Kadus Knights and the defenders formed a solid front, a united resistance against the malevolent forces that sought to destroy them.

As the battle raged on, the collective efforts of the defenders held back the tide of revenants. The children of the Kadus Knights, under the guidance of their elders, fought with fierce resolve. Almas, Ulec, and Uncle Marpel continued to weave their unique skills into the defense, each contributing to the symphony of protection. Soon the remaining revenants retreated and the defenders found the fighting over.

Amidst the aftermath of battle, as the Kadus Knights prepared to withdraw with their children, Almas hesitated before approaching his father, Lord Gidon Aguerius. Uncertainty gnawed at him- his father had been happy to see him but how would his father react to having seen him in his undead form? But all doubt was erased as his father turned to him, his arms outstretched in a warm embrace.

"Almas," Lord Aguerius said, his voice full of pride and love. "You've shown courage and strength beyond measure. I couldn't be more proud of the man you're becoming."

Tears stung Almas' eyes as he embraced his father back, the weight of his fears lifting in that single moment. "Thank you, Father," he managed to whisper, his voice choked with emotion.

As the father and son shared a heartfelt moment, Almas couldn't help but ask about Kade, who Almas had seen brought in unconscious and taken to the healer's hut. Deleta, who had joined their conversation, stepped forward with a somber expression.

"Kade is still unconscious, but the healers assure me he will recover," Deleta explained. "He's tough, that one."

Almas nodded, a mixture of relief and concern flooding his thoughts. "Thank you for saving him, Deleta."

Deleta nodded, his gaze softening. "Thank your father, he found and saved him. Thanks to him he should recover. We'll keep an eye on him regardless."

With the Kadus Knights preparing to withdraw, the group of defenders gathered to discuss their next steps. Ulec spoke up, his determination evident in his voice. "I need to go to my father. He needs help."

Almas understood Ulec's urgency. "Go, Ulec. We'll hold the city."

Handing Almas his shoulder back Ulec asked, "Will you take Metal? I can move faster without him."

"Sure, I'm always safer with Metal around," Almas answered taking the bag.

Ulec nodded and sprinted off, his figure disappearing into the aftermath of the battle. Almas turned to his father and Uncle Marpel, a sense of purpose returning to him. "We should head back to the city. Our work here isn't done. With the Kadus Knights gone they will raise those who have fallen and commit all their revenants now."

Uncle Marpel offered a wry smile. "Well, I do believe then that there are some undead that need a stern talking to."

Lord Aguerius nodded in agreement. "Let's make our way back to the city. Flameshaven still needs us."

Chapter 6

"WITH LICH-EL HIDING in the rear and the Kadus Knight fleeing the battle, it looks like it will be up to me to end this battle."

"What is your plan Tornal?"

"Simple, Lich-El isn't the only one with a fieles. I will use my wind staff to break through their defenses where they are weakest, the south. We can then quickly take the keep. Be ready to attack."

BENEATH A SKY CHOKED with ash and the stench of fear, Lord Teanas stood at the edge of the Undead rear lines, his fiery resolve evident in the embers that flickered around his clenched fists. The once lush landscape of Aguerius was now a charnel house, an insult to the memories of past generations. As he looked upon the legions of shambling revenants guarding Lich-El, the Elvish Prince's thoughts burned like the fires he commanded: How could anyone betray their own like this?

"Look what you've wrought, Thodien!" Teanas roared addressing the Lich by his human name, his voice like thunder in the gloom. Sparks danced between his fingers as he summoned two blazing whips of flame. With a flourish, he lashed out, incinerating the nearest undead abominations. The revenants not even see what hit them as they were reduced to ashes.

"Ah, the esteemed Lord Teanas graces us with his presence," Lich-El drawled, his voice dripping with sarcasm. He stepped forward, his pale visage twisted into a mocking grin. "And to think I was beginning to worry you'd never show. How are you doing old friend?"

"Your betrayal of your friends, family, and the Aguerius line is unforgivable," Teanas spat, the air around him crackling with heat. "It sickens me."

"Does it now?" Lich-El replied, feigning surprise. "That's rich, coming from someone who hasn't seen what I have, who doesn't understand the necessity of my actions." He paused for dramatic effect, reveling in Teanas's barely contained fury. "Besides," he continued, "it was Tornal who cursed dear Almas, not I. And by doing so, he inadvertently made that boy the key to our world's salvation."

"Salvation?" Teanas scoffed, his eyes blazing like twin suns. "You call this carnage salvation? This perversion of life?" He gestured to the devastated landscape around them, the fallen warriors who would never return home, and the grieving families left behind.

"Your self-righteous indignation is almost endearing," Lich-El taunted, his laughter as cold as the grave. "But it matters not. Soon, you'll understand that my actions are for the greater good."

"Twisted words from a twisted soul," Teanas muttered under his breath. His heart ached for the friend he had once known, now lost to the darkness. "If this is your vision of the future, I will stop at nothing to change it.

"Nothing can justify what you've done," Teanas said, his voice dripping with disdain. "It's not too late to end this madness. Command your forces to withdraw."

Lich-El shook his head, a wicked grin ghosting across his skeletal face. "I'm afraid I cannot do that, my dear Teanas. And while I bear you no ill will, I must warn you: if you continue on this path, I won't hesitate to defend myself."

"Is that so?" Teanas asked, sarcasm lacing his words as he summoned forth the heat inside him. A torrent of flames erupted around his body, outlining him in a deadly aura, daring Lich-El to challenge him.

"Very well," Lich-El sighed, raising his enormous war hammer. Its intricate carvings seemed to come alive, writhing and pulsating with power. As Lich-El slammed it into the ground, massive cracks snaked through the earth like the jagged scars left by an ancient battle.

"Always were one for theatrics," Teanas muttered to himself, leaping nimbly out of the way as the fissures shot towards him.

"Can't let you have all the fun, now, can I?" Lich-El sneered, using his hammer to raise giant, sharp boulders from the ground. With powerful swings, he sent them hurtling towards Teanas, who weaved between them with the grace of a leaf caught in the wind.

"Your aim hasn't improved," Teanas taunted, sending a barrage of fireballs towards his former friend. The searing heat met the cold, dark air surrounding Lich-El, creating a maelstrom of steam and ash.

"Nor has your sense of humor," Lich-El retorted, gritting his teeth as he deflected the fiery assault. His hammer moved in a blur, cutting through the air like a scythe through wheat.

"Your foolishness will be your undoing," Lich-El growled, his eyes blazing with rage as he brought his war hammer down again. The ground shook beneath them, sending clouds of dust billowing into the air.

"Better to die laughing than to live as a monster," Teanas whispered to himself, dodging another boulder. He knew that only one of them would leave this battlefield alive, and he prayed that the legends would remember him as the hero who stood against darkness.

"Let's see if you still find humor when you're buried beneath the earth!" Lich-El roared, raising his hammer for a final, devastating blow.

THUNDER RUMBLED IN the distance as Lady Alixia, standing on a crumbling parapet, surveyed the western side of the city. Her eyes narrowed, accentuating the fierceness of her elven features. The wind whipped her hair into a frenzy, mirroring the storm brewing within her.

"By the stars," she muttered, her voice dripping with sarcasm, "it's as if the very gods themselves have sent this army of rotting flesh just to spoil my day."

Below her, a nauseating sea of revenants and Lich Lords clawed their way through the defenses like a swarm of ravenous insects.

Their groans and screams filled the air, creating an eerie symphony of death.

"Enough!" Lady Alixia shouted, transforming again into an elder dragon with a deafening roar that shook the very foundations of the city. With scales as black as midnight and eyes that burned with the fury of a thousand suns, she descended upon the undead horde once more, her wings casting dark shadows across the battlefield.

Her massive claws slashed through rows of revenants, sending bodies flying in all directions. She swung her tail with such force that it created shockwaves, toppling entire formations of the undead. And then there was her fire breath, a torrent of flames so intense it consumed everything in its path, leaving nothing but ash and despair in its wake.

"Is that all you've got?" she thought as she roared, a booming and guttural sound as she continued her onslaught against the seemingly endless tide of undead creatures.

But as the battle raged on, she sensed that her husband was using a huge amount of magic. As they both shared the same source of magic created by life, she knew with them both tapping the that source they could run out very quickly. She knew that Teanas only had that one source of magic. She on the other hand had another. Being half desert elf, she could tap her own life force for magic; a far riskier source but was the only way both she and Teanas could continue fighting as they were.

Soon however she began to feel that she was pushing her limits and quite quickly even the mighty Lady Alixia began to feel the weight of her enemies' relentless attacks. Her once-graceful movements grew labored, her breath coming in ragged gasps.

"Can't... give..." she panted, heaving herself forward for another swing of her claws. "Up..."

As Lady Alixia continued her desperate fight against the horde, she could feel the Lich Lords drawing nearer, like vultures circling a dying beast. Their presence only fueled her determination, each breath filled with bitter defiance.

"Let them come," she thought, her mind swirling with dark humor. "I'll take as many of these wretched creatures with me as I can."

She roared again, the sound a mixture of pain, rage, and an unyielding will to survive. The battle for the western side of the city was far from over, and Lady Alixia would not go down without leaving a legacy of destruction in her wake.

SEACRA, IN THE FORM of a tiny fly, buzzed silently through the chaotic battlefield. Her compound eyes darted back and forth, taking in the devastation wrought by her mother, Lady Alixia. The dragon's fire had scorched earth, leaving blackened scars amidst the ruins of the city's western defenses.

"Is this really how my mother wins all of her battles?" Seacra mused as she flitted past the broken remains of revenants, their shattered bones still smoldering. "To reduce everything around her to ash and ruin?"

Her attention shifted to the Lich Lords, who stood at a distance, their skeletal forms practically vibrating with eager anticipation as they watched Lady Alixia's struggle. Their yellow eyes gleamed like arrogant stars in the dusk, mocking and cruel.

"Time for some poetic justice," Seacra whispered, her voice barely audible above the din of battle. With a sudden shift, her small fly body transformed into that of an Elder Demon, her dark wings unfurling and casting ominous shadows across the battlefield. The very air seemed to shiver at her presence, the ground beneath her trembling ever so slightly.

"Surprise!" Seacra wished she could yell, but settled for a terrifying roar with a thunderous echo that shook the heavens. She lunged at the Lich Lords, her massive claws tearing through bone and tattered robes as if they were nothing more than parchment. The Lich Lords staggered back, caught completely off guard by the demon's sudden appearance and ferocity. Then before they could even comprehend what was happening, a hail of magic energy bolts started raining down from Tricker, the mischievous imp.

"Knew I had a flair for the dramatic," Seacra thought, grinning wickedly as she crushed yet another Lich Lord beneath her monstrous foot.

But the surprise could only last so long, and soon the Lich Lords regrouped, their undead minions swarming towards Seacra like a tidal wave of rot and decay. She fought valiantly, her laughter tinged with bitterness and fury as she tore through the endless ranks of revenants.

"Mother always did say I had a talent for making an entrance," Seacra mused, her energy waning as the relentless assault continued. "But it seems my grand exit might need some work."

Finally, overwhelmed and exhausted, Seacra collapsed to the ground. Her Elder Demon form flickered and faded, replaced by the lithe figure of a fire salamander. Tricker continued to rain down energy bolts but was forced back by arrows and bone spikes. The Lich Lords stared at the fire salamander Seacra had become, momentarily confused by the transformation.

"Isn't this just the perfect metaphor for my life?" Seacra thought. "From grand demon to harmless lizard in the blink of an eye."

As the Lich Lords hesitated, a vast shadow fell across them. Their decaying faces turned upwards just in time to see Lady Alixia's dragon form swooping down from above. Before they could even scream, the world was consumed by a cataclysmic inferno.

The blaze raged on, a storm of fire and fury that obliterated everything in its path. When the flames finally cleared, only two figures remained: the mighty dragon and the small fire salamander.

As the flames dwindled, Lady Alixia and Seacra reverted to their elvish forms. They both collapsed in exhaustion on the scorched battlefield, their clothes singed and faces streaked with soot. Their chests heaved from the effort of battle, and exhaustion weighed down their limbs like leaden anchors.

"Ah, the sweet taste of victory," Seacra muttered sarcastically as she swayed on her feet, a bitter smile playing on her lips.

Lady Alixia, not one for sentiment, fixed her steely gaze on her daughter and said simply, "Well done." And with that, they both succumbed to their fatigue.

ALMAS, LORD AGUERIUS, and Uncle Marpel raced toward the embattled city. The wind whipped at their faces as they ran towards the city. Upon reaching a hilltop, they stopped and stared at the scene below them.

"Nothing like a good ol' apocalypse to remind you of just how insignificant you are," Almas quipped, his expression dark despite the humor in his words.

"Almas," Lord Aguerius admonished, surveying the battlefield with a furrowed brow. "This is no time for jests."

"Sorry, Father. It's just... hard to take all this in," Almas replied, his tone subdued.

"Indeed," murmured Uncle Marpel, his eyes squinting as he observed the chaos below.

The wind whipped around them, carrying the acrid scent of burning wood and the distant cries of terror as they surveyed the city from their hilltop perch. Almas shuddered involuntarily, his finger tightening on his ocarina. Below them, the eastern defenses of the city held strong, a testament to the bravery of those who fought for their lives and homes. But it was the southern side that drew their horrified gazes.

"Snipies," breathed Lord Aguerius, his face paling as he took in the sight before him. The once-proud southern wall lay crumbled and undefended, leaving nothing but a gaping maw through which the undead poured like a river of death. Their unliving forms swarmed toward the keep at the heart of the city, where the innocent cowered in fear.

Lord Aguerius urgently beckoned, "Hurry, to the city! The undead breached the southern wall and threaten the keep! We must protect our kin and people."

Almas halted him, asserting, "Wait, Father! I must aid Ulec and Lord Teanas. They're locked in combat with Lich-El on the southern hill, and I have to go help them."

"Almas, hold on!" Lord Aguerius cautioned, deeply concerned. "You can't face Lich-El alone; he wields immense power. You can't fathom the extent of his abilities."

Desperation in his voice, Almas implored, "Please, Father, I must try. He's too powerful for Lord Teanas and Ulec."

Lord Aguerius, torn, urged, "Listen, Almas, we just got you back, I can't lose you again."

"Father, trust me," Almas implored. "I have a plan, but I can't reveal it now. It will work, it has to."

Lord Aguerius, exasperated, protested, "Almas, this is madness! You're risking your life for nothing!"

Almas responded firmly, "Father, this is something I must do."

Lord Aguerius gazed at his son, torn between love and frustration, knowing he couldn't stop Almas. He understood his noble heart and unyielding determination. He reluctantly agreed, releasing his son and embracing him.

With a sigh, he relented, "Fine, Almas. Go, but be cautious, and return safely."

Almas expressed gratitude, "Thank you, Father. I'll be careful and return."

They exchanged "I love you's" and parted ways. Lord Aguerius turned to Uncle Marpel, asking him to accompany Almas.

"Lord Vatan, go with Almas. Protect him," Lord Aguerius instructed.

Uncle Marpel readily agreed, "Of course, Lord Aguerius. I'll watch over Almas and keep him safe."

Lord Aguerius expressed his gratitude, "Thank you, Uncle Marpel, a true friend and loyal brother-in-law."

Uncle Marpel reciprocated, "You're welcome, Lord Aguerius, a courageous leader and valiant warrior."

As Lord Aguerius faced again the besieged city he pledged, "I'll head to the city to aid the keep's defense."

Almas wished his father luck, "Be careful, Father."

Lord Aguerius reciprocated, "You too, son."

They exchanged a final, heartfelt glance before parting ways.

Chapter 7

"WE CANNOT WIN THIS battle, we should withdraw!"

"Their southern line of defense has collapsed; Alixia is out of the fight! Now is the time to take their keep, kill all inside and watch the remainder of the city crumble!"

"We are losing too much; we need to withdrawal and build back our forces!"

"Do as you're ordered, take the keep and then we will destroy all of our enemies here today."

TEANAS GRITTED HIS teeth, the heat of battle and the weight of responsibility bearing down upon him. His heart thundered in his chest like a thousand hooves pounding the earth, and he knew that if he didn't act soon, all would be lost.

"Enough of this charade," Teanas muttered, glancing at the fieles on his finger: the ring that could transform into any weapon he desired. With a flick of his wrist, the fieles morphed into a gleaming sword, its edges kissed by flames. "Time to show you what I'm really capable of."

"And just when I thought you were running out of tricks," Lich-El sneered, his voice dripping with sarcasm. "Do proceed, my old friend. Regale me with your legendary prowess."

"Your wish is my command," Teanas shot back, launching himself forward, sword ablaze. As they clashed, the world around them seemed to warp and change. The once lush, green fields now resembled a scorched wasteland, the air thick with smoke and ash. Each swing of their weapons left a trail of destruction in its wake, as though the gods themselves were warring upon the mortal plane.

"Is this all you've got?" Lich-El taunted, narrowly evading a fiery slash. "I expected more from the great prince of the elves."

"Careful what you wish for," Teanas growled through clenched teeth. He changed tactics, allowing the fieles to shift into a bow, each arrow tipped with searing flame. Yet, despite his best efforts, Teanas felt his strength waning, drawn away by the very forces that fueled his enemy.

The sounds of battle from Flameshaven echoed in the distance, a cacophony of death and despair that only served to strengthen Lich-El's dark power. With each fallen soldier, his might grew, while Teanas' own connection to life dwindled.

In that moment, Teanas felt the crushing weight of inevitability bearing down upon him. He had given everything, and yet it seemed it would not be enough. As Lich-El's hammer came crashing down, Teanas managed to dodge, but only just - a glancing blow was still enough to send him sprawling to the ground.

"Any last words?" Lich-El asked, looming over the fallen Teanas, his tone dripping with venomous amusement.

"Only this," Teanas gasped, his vision blurred by pain and exhaustion. "No matter what happens here today, you will be stopped."

"Bold words," Lich-El sneered, raising his hammer once more. "But ultimately, meaningless."

The hammer's descent halted mid-air, a shadow of doom arrested by the sudden intrusion. Lich-El whirled around, displaying agility that belied his undead form, just in time to block a swift attack from Ulec, who had leaped down from a nearby tree. The young elf's blade met the haft of the war hammer with a ringing clash, his blue eyes blazing with fierce determination.

"Ah, Ulec," Lich-El crooned, his voice as smooth and poisonous as black ichor. "I didn't hear you slithering up behind me. Quite an impressive feat, I must say."

With a flick of his wrist, Lich-El sent Ulec flying through the air, but the agile youth managed to land on his feet, skidding to a stop amidst the scorched earth and shattered rocks left in the wake of the titanic struggle. He gritted his teeth, anger mingling with frustration at his failure to land a decisive blow.

"Your praise means nothing to me, monster," Ulec spat, his heart pounding like a drumbeat in his chest.

"Such bitterness," Lich-El mused, an amused grin etched upon his face. "How very fitting for one so young."

Ulec's grip tightened on his sword hilt, the cold metal biting into his palm. He could feel the life force ebbing away from Teanas, every shallow breath a fading ember in the darkness. It was up to him now.

"Leave my father alone," Ulec demanded, his voice shaking despite his best efforts to sound strong. "You've done enough damage here."

"Damage?" Lich-El echoed, feigning shock. "Why, my dear boy, I'm simply doing what's necessary. History often remembers such actions as necessary evils."

"History can choke on it," Ulec retorted, his anger fueling his resolve. "You'll not write another word of it today!"

"Such spirit," Lich-El mused, as he readied his war hammer once more. "But spirit alone won't save you or your father."

"Then let's see what steel and fire can do!" Ulec shouted, launching himself at the lich lord with renewed fervor.

As Lich-El grinned wickedly, their weapons clashed again, the sounds of battle echoing through the ravaged battlefield. Teanas' eyes fluttered open, watching the fierce duel from the ground, his thoughts a mix of pride and desperation for the boy who had come to mean so much to him.

"Fight well, my son," he whispered, the words barely audible amidst the cacophony of destruction.

RAIN PELTED DOWN, A merciless beat upon the worn cobblestones as Creetan slashed his way through the ranks of the undead. His breath came in ragged gasps, each one mingling with the cold air and the scent of death. Jarad fought by his side, their blades singing in unison as they held the eastern line of defense.

"Can this day get any worse?" Creetan grumbled over the din of battle, his voice a mix of sarcasm and exhaustion.

"Ask me again in five minutes," Jarad replied, parrying an attack from a particularly stubborn revenant. "I'm sure I'll have a better answer then."

As if on cue, a messenger sprinted towards them, slipping on the wet stones in his haste. "The southern line has collapsed!" he shouted, breathless.

Creetan's heart sank like a stone tossed into the castle moat. He exchanged a quick glance with Jarad before beckoning to a handful of nearby soldiers. "We need to reach the keep! Follow me!"

They fought their way through the twisted maze of alleyways, the rain never relenting as it drenched their armor and souls alike. The only path left to them was up; Creetan led his ragtag group to the roof of a nearby building, scrambling for purchase on the slick tiles. From there, they had a clear view of the entrance to the keep.

"Snipies," Creetan muttered, surveying the scene. The door to the keep lay shattered on the ground, splinters of wood strewn about like the broken dreams of the people within. The last defenders stood their ground, forming a thin line between the living and the dead.

"Look!" Jarad pointed, his voice tinged with awe and disbelief. "It's Lemuem - the one-legged ranger!"

There, amidst the chaos, stood Lemuem. He balanced on his peg leg with the grace of a dancer, dodging and weaving as he cut down revenants left and right. Beside him, Creetan's mother, Lady Izybel, fought with a slender war axe in one hand and a delicate war hammer in the other. She moved like a storm - swift, fierce, and beautiful.

"Your mother's truly a force to be reckoned with," Jarad said, admiration evident in his voice.

"Indeed," Creetan agreed, watching her with a mixture of pride and fear. "I just hope it'll be enough."

As they looked on, a massive metal golem tore through the ranks of the undead, its arm a deadly mace and the other spewing forth torrents of flame. The revenants fell before it, their dark forms reduced to ash.

"Thanks to that golem, I'd say our chances just improved," Jarad remarked, clapping Creetan on the shoulder.

"Let's not count our blessings just yet," Creetan replied, gritting his teeth. "We still have a long way to go."

"True, but every little bit helps," Jarad said, trying to remain optimistic.

Despite the golem's impressive display of power, the horde of revenants seemed endless. The few defenders still standing fought valiantly, but it was clear they were being overwhelmed. Lemuem, now cut off from the others, battled a group of undead on his own, while Lady Izybel continued her fierce dance with several more revenants.

"Mother!" Creetan cried out, his voice strained with worry as he watched her struggle.

In the heat of battle, one revenant managed to land a lucky blow against Lady Izybel, knocking her out cold. Seeing her fall, Creetan acted on instinct. He quickly notched an arrow, imbuing it with holy light, and released it. The arrow flew true, striking the revenant and reducing it to a pile of ash before it could land a killing blow on his mother.

"Nice shot," Jarad commented, but Creetan barely heard him; his focus remained on his fallen mother.

With Lady Izybel unconscious, the golem she had been controlling came to a sudden stop, leaving the remaining defenders without their greatest weapon. Desperation began to take hold, and Creetan could see the fear in the eyes of those who still fought.

"Jarad, we need to get down there," Creetan said urgently. "If we don't act now, it'll be too late."

"Right behind you," Jarad replied, determination settling over his features.

The undead horde surged forward; their ghastly forms illuminated by the dying light of day. They rushed past the motionless golem, eyes set on the prone figure of Lady Izybel and the door to the keep.

"Jarad, hurry!" Creetan shouted, desperation creeping into his voice as he watched the scene below. The two young warriors scrambled down from their perch; their descent hindered by the chaos erupting all around them.

Just as the revenants closed in on Lady Izybel, something miraculous happened. The once-still golem began to move again, its limbs creaking and groaning with each clumsy swing. It tore through the undead ranks, scattering bones and rotting flesh in a haphazard dance of destruction.

"Snipies," Jarad whispered, his eyes wide with disbelief. "How is that possible?"

"Never mind that now," Creetan snapped. "We need to get down there."

At the same time, a golden wall of magic erupted before Lady Izybel, halting the revenants' advance. Creetan's relief was palpable, but it quickly turned to confusion as he noticed two small figures just outside the keep's entrance.

"Is that...?" Jarad trailed off, squinting at the scene below.

"By the heavens, it's Cady and Giddy," Creetan breathed, his heart swelling with pride and terror in equal measure.

His little sister, Cady, stood strong despite her trembling hands, a determined look on her face as she cast the protective barrier. Beside her, Giddy stared intensely at the golem, his brow furrowed in concentration.

"Seems your siblings have more tricks up their sleeves than we thought," Jarad remarked, a hint of amusement in his tense voice.

"Indeed," Creetan agreed, his thoughts racing. "Giddy must have helped Mother build the golem and formed a connection with it. And Cady...I never knew she had such power."

"Neither did I," Jarad admitted, a grin breaking through his worry. "But now's not the time for family revelations. We need to reach them before it's too late."

"Right," Creetan nodded, his mind focused on the task at hand.

Together, they forged ahead, determined to join the siblings in defending their home.

Chapter 8

"COME NOW BOY, YOU CAN do better than that! I almost killed you there!"

"I thought that was the point. Isn't that your goal? To kill everyone?"

"My goals are my own. But if you wish to ever achieve your goals you must do better. If you die now this world will soon follow. You don't want that on your conscience, do you?"

"Can't you stop speaking in riddles and just tell us what you're trying to do. We can find another way!"

"I... can't. "

CADY KNELT BESIDE HER unconscious mother, her hands trembling as she struggled to maintain the golden barrier protecting them from the ravenous revenants. Sweat dripped down her brow, stinging her eyes as she glanced over at Giddy, who was staring intently at the golem.

"Can't you do anything to help me hold this up?" she asked, desperation seeping into her voice.

Giddy frowned in concentration, his small fingers twitching as he tried to command the battered golem. "I'm trying, Cady. But it's like asking a three-legged cat to juggle – the golem's just too damaged."

"Great, so we're stuck with a clumsy circus act," Cady muttered under her breath, her frustration mounting.

As she focused on the barrier, she couldn't help but feel a pang of fear for her brother and herself. They were children, facing an army of undead monsters – it was like some twisted bedtime story come to life.

Her eyes darted to where Creetan and the other soldiers were engaged in battle, still too far away to reach them in time. As much as she wanted to rely on their help, Cady knew that she and Giddy had to stand strong on their own.

"Dig deep, Giddy," she urged, trying to sound more confident than she felt. "We can do this."

Suddenly, the revenants began to retreat, leaving Cady momentarily confused. Her heart sank as she realized the reason: two dozen undead archers had lined up, their arrows aimed directly at her, Giddy, and their fallen mother.

"Of course, because things weren't bad enough already," Cady said bitterly, her sarcasm masking her terror.

Just as the revenants released their arrows, a large form stepped in front of Cady. She looked up, her heart lurching with fear and hope as she recognized her father, Lord Gidon Aguerius. He stood tall and resolute; his arms spread wide in an attempt to shield his family from the deadly rain. The corner of his face that was visible to Cady bore a resigned expression; he knew the odds were against him, but he was prepared to give everything for their protection.

"Father!" Cady's voice cracked under the weight of her emotions. Her hands shook, but she maintained the weakening golden barrier as best as she could.

"Keep your focus on the shield, Cady," Gidon said firmly, his voice barely carrying over the sounds of battle. His eyes met hers for a fleeting moment, filled with love, pride, and something else – an acceptance of the sacrifice he was about to make.

"Please..." she whispered, tears streaming down her face. But she knew better than to beg her father to reconsider – this was who he was, the noble and brave High Lord they all loved and respected.

"Go on, Dad! You can do it!" Giddy shouted from behind, his small voice wavering with the weight of the situation.

With a nod, Gidon turned his attention back to the incoming arrows. As they drew closer, it seemed impossible that he could block them all with the little magic he had left. Yet, Cady felt a strange sense of calm wash over her. This was her father, the man who had faced countless trials and always emerged victorious. If anyone could save them, it was him.

Just as the first arrow was about to pierce Gidon's body, he burst into bright light, blinding Cady and everyone around them. The searing brilliance disintegrated the arrows mid-flight and incinerated nearby revenants. At the same time, the light washed over the city's defenders, healing their wounds and revitalizing their spirits.

"Whoa!" Giddy gasped in awe, clutching at Cady's arm for support as they both squinted against the glare.

Gidon strode forward, the light surrounding him like a vengeful angel, annihilating revenants with each step. The lich lords, sensing the tide of battle turning against them, began to kneel in pain from the sheer intensity of the light. With one swift swipe of his sword, Gidon unleashed a single blade of light that arced towards the lich lords, severing the evil that held them together.

As the final cries of the undead faded away, Cady blinked back tears of relief and pride. Her father had done it; he had saved their family and their people from certain doom. Somehow, despite everything, Lord Gidon Aguerius had once again risen above the impossible and secured victory for the living.

"Father... you're amazing," she whispered, her voice filled with wonder and gratitude. She knew that this moment would be forever etched into her memory – the day her father became not just a legend, but a true hero.

ULEC'S HEART HAMMERED in his chest, a rapid drumbeat echoing the tremors shaking the ground beneath him. Lich-El towered over the battlefield, eyes burning with unholy fury as he raised his hammer and slammed it into the earth once more. The ground cracked, fissures snaking outwards from the point of impact, threatening to swallow Ulec whole.

"Watch your step, boy!" Lich-El taunted, the words slithering through the air like venomous serpents. "Wouldn't want you to trip and break that pretty little neck of yours."

Ulec gritted his teeth, refusing to let the lich lord's words distract him. He clutched Changing Hand tightly, feeling its familiar weight shift and transform in his grip. It wasn't his father's fire magic, but it was enough – for now, at least. The fieles had taken on the form of Lich-El's own hammer, imbued with the same earth-shattering power.

"Your sarcasm is almost as heavy as your hammer," Ulec shot back, swinging his newly formed hammer in a wide arc. The ground before him roared to life, boulders ripping free of their earthen moorings and soaring towards Lich-El with deadly force.

"Careful, Ulec," whispered the voice of Changing Hand in his mind. *"He's stronger than he looks."*

"Isn't he always?" Ulec thought bitterly, narrowly dodging a massive slab of rock hurled his way by the lich lord.

The two adversaries danced across the battlefield, a twisted ballet of destruction and near-misses. Ulec used his agility to weave between the obstacles Lich-El hurled at him, while the lich lord relied on brute strength and raw power to shake the very foundations of the earth beneath them. It was a dance as old as time, the struggle between life and death played out on a stage of dust and shattered stone.

"Is that all you've got?" Lich-El spat, a wicked grin stretching across his skeletal face. "I expected more from the son of Alixia and Mundial."

"Trust me," Ulec panted, sweat dripping from his brow, "you haven't seen anything yet."

"Bold words for such a small creature," Changing Hand murmured in his mind. *"But I believe in you, Ulec."*

"Thanks," he thought back, trying to ignore the ache in his muscles and the weariness threatening to drag him down. *"I just hope it's enough."*

Ulec leaped into action once more, hammer swinging through the air with a force that belied his slender frame. The earth trembled beneath him, answering his call like a loyal steed charging into battle. He could see the surprise flicker in Lich-El's eyes, but only for a moment – a brief crack in the lich lord's otherwise unbreakable facade.

"Let's see how you like a taste of your own medicine," Ulec snarled, slamming his hammer into the ground with all the strength he could muster.

As the ground shook and split under the force of their blows, the bitter dance continued, each step bringing Ulec closer to victory or defeat – whichever fate the fickle gods had chosen for him. And as the dust swirled around them, obscuring their vision and choking their breaths, Ulec couldn't help but feel that the world was watching, holding its breath.

In the midst of their relentless battle, Ulec and Lich-El were suddenly bathed in a brilliant light. The fierce combatants paused as if time itself had stopped, each squinting against the blinding brightness that seemed to emanate from the city itself.

Lich-El smirked, his eyes narrowing with amusement. "Well, well," he drawled sarcastically, "Lord Aguerius finally found his inner power. It's about time."

Ulec panted, sweat trickling down his face, mixing with the dust and grime of battle. His voice was hoarse as he retorted, "Do you even care that you're the last lich lord left?"

"Ha!" Lich-El laughed bitterly, the sound echoing like the rumble of distant thunder. "All is as it should be." And with that, he lunged back into the fray, the ground trembling beneath him.

As the earth roared and cracked under their hammers, Ulec's thoughts raced, mingling with Changing Hand's whispered advice. *"I just don't have the power to beat him!"* Ulec thought to the magical creation.

"Yes, you do," the fieles answered.

Ulec wiped the sweat from his hands and noticed a smear of red, blood from one of many scratches he had received during the fight. Suddenly he had an idea.

Chapter 9

"WHAT IS IT, WHAT ARE you trying to do!"

"Many things, just a little longer and you will see."

ALMAS AND UNCLE MARPEL sprinted, their breaths ragged and hearts pounding, desperately trying to reach Ulec in time. The air around them crackled with tension, the very atmosphere charged with magic and danger.

"Almas, look out!" Uncle Marpel cried, shoving the boy aside just as an energy blast tore through the air where he had been standing mere moments before. The blast struck Uncle Marpel instead, sending him crashing to the ground with a pained grunt.

"Ruined everything," Tornal snarled, his voice like poison dripping from his skeletal lips. Almas scrambled to his feet, fury and fear igniting within him as he took on his undead form.

"Alright, you bony buffoon," Almas thought bitterly, feeling the darkness swirling inside of him, "let's dance."

As Almas faced down Tornal, the bitter taste of vengeance filled his mouth, and his thoughts burned with a singular purpose – to protect those he loved from the nightmare that stood before him. In that moment, he knew that there was no turning back, no other path but the one that led straight through the heart of darkness. And as his eyes met Tornal's cold, yellow gaze, he knew that this was the battle that would define them both – for better or worse.

Gritting his teeth, Almas snapped off one of his bone spikes and hurled it into the grass. The ground shuddered as a grotesque, insect-like undead creep burst forth, its chitinous legs skittering in anticipation.

"Really, Almas?" Tornal sneered, his voice like shattered glass scraping over stone. "You'll need more than a few undead insects to save you."

As if to prove his point, Tornal thrust his arm forward, launching another energy blast straight at Almas. Without missing a beat, Almas flung another bone spike into the grass before him. A wall of writhing, undead tentacles erupted from the earth, blocking the blast and sending sparks flying in all directions.

"See, that's where you're wrong," Almas replied, his voice dripping with sarcasm as he stared Tornal down. "The lich lords never realized the power they had. You always thought bigger was better. Bigger, stronger revenants. More and more death to fuel your magic."

In the background, despite his injuries, Uncle Marpel began playing a haunting melody on his flute. The notes seemed to weave themselves around Almas, bolstering his resolve.

"Your kind never saw the power in small things," Almas continued, a smile tugging at the corner of his mouth as he listened to his uncle's song.

"Small things?" Tornal scoffed, his pale eyes narrowing with disdain. "What good will that do you when I crush you beneath my heel?"

"Ah, but there's beauty in the details," Almas retorted, his mind racing with strategies born from the wisdom of his father's training. "Take this wall of tentacles, for example. It's not just about brute force – it's about timing, precision, and finesse."

"Enough!" Tornal roared, the air around him crackling with dark energy. "I'll show you the true extent of my power!"

"Go ahead," Almas taunted, his heart pounding with a mixture of fear and exhilaration. "Show me how wrong I am."

As the battle raged on, Almas knew that his words had struck a nerve. Tornal's arrogance and obsession with raw power had blinded him to the subtler aspects of magic.

The wind whistled around Almas like a living thing, tendrils of air swirling and snapping at his face as Tornal's staff glowed with power. It was as though the very atmosphere was crying out for vengeance – but Almas knew that the true force behind this storm was the seething wrath of Tornal.

"Did I say something you don't like?" Almas called out; his voice barely audible above the howling gale. "You know, they say the truth hurts!"

"Silence!" Tornal bellowed, unleashing a torrent of wind that threatened to rip the grass from its roots. Almas braced himself, raising a hand adorned with the fieles Flameweaver. A shimmering wave of fire sprang up around him, drawn from a nearby burning tree, deflecting the worst of the assault.

"Almas," Flameweaver whispered in his mind, the voice urgent yet reassuring. *"Watch for the gusts between his attacks. That's when he's most vulnerable."*

"Got it," he replied silently, his eyes fixed on the lich lord even as he continued to weave protective flames around himself. Every muscle in his body tensed, ready for action.

With a flick of his wrist, Almas sent another bone spike into the earth, summoning more undead creeps and tentacles to bolster his defenses. He could feel their power coursing through him, like dark threads connecting him to these creatures born of death and decay.

"Face it, Tornal," Almas shouted over the roaring wind, his heart pounding with equal parts fear and determination. "Your time is over! The world has moved on, and you're nothing but a relic of the past!"

"Over?" Tornal sneered, eyes blazing with hatred. "I'll show you over, boy!"

The lich lord's staff hummed with energy, the wind around him growing even more ferocious as he hurled himself at Almas. The young bard met his charge head-on, a symphony of fire and undead magic surging forth to meet the oncoming storm.

"Almas, now!" Flameweaver urged, sensing the lull in Tornal's onslaught. *"Strike while he's weak!"*

"Thanks for the pep talk," Almas thought wryly, then lunged forward, his fingers dancing across the strings of his lute. A stream of acid from Ulec's shoulder bad distracted Tornal as a discordant melody rang out, weaving its way through the cacophony of battle and wrapping itself around Tornal like a noose.

"Wh-what is this?" Tornal stammered, his skeletal form shuddering as he struggled to break free from the ensnaring tune.

More undead tentacles burst from the ground around him, their slimy coils winding around his limbs and torso.

"Sorry, old man," Almas said, a bitter smile playing on his lips. "But you're not going anywhere. Uncle Marpel's song is blocking you from simply teleporting away. No easy escape this time."

As Tornal's face twisted with fear, Almas knew that he'd won – not just the battle, but the war for the future of their world. The age of the lich lords was over, and a new era was dawning.

The sky above the city pulsed with a brilliant light, casting eerie shadows as small undead creeps emerged from the ground. They hopped and scuttled like demented locusts, swarming over Tornal's struggling form. The Lich Lord's once-proud visage was now tainted with terror as he fought desperately against his impending doom.

"Almas," Flameweaver whispered into his mind, *"the time is now."*

"Right," Almas muttered under his breath, his expression hardened by determination. With one last strum of his lute, he sent a final surge of power rippling through the air, bolstering the onslaught of undead creeps. The sound echoed like the tolling of a funeral bell, marking the end of Tornal's reign.

As if sensing their victory, the creeps writhed and gnashed at Tornal with renewed vigor, tearing away at his undead frame until, with a final, pitiful cry, the Lich Lord disintegrated into a cloud of dust that scattered on the wind.

"Good riddance," Almas muttered darkly, feeling a bitter satisfaction at the sight of Tornal's demise.

But there was no time for celebration or reflection. Turning his attention to Uncle Marpel, Almas rushed to his side, concern etched across his face. "Uncle, are you okay?"

"Never better, my boy," Uncle Marpel replied, a wry grin tugging at the corners of his mouth despite the pain that flickered in his eyes. "Now go help Ulec. He needs you."

Almas nodded, relief flooding through him at his uncle's assurance. But before he could race off towards the sounds of battle, he took a moment to mark the spot where Tornal had met his end.

"Kade will want to know about this place," he murmured, a sly smile playing on his lips. "He has plans for this spot. I hope I can let him know."

"Knowing Kade," Uncle Marpel chuckled, "he'll probably want to build an inn here and name it 'The Lich Lord's Last Stand.'"

"Ha," Almas snorted, shaking his head at the absurdity of the idea. But as he sprinted towards the cacophony of Ulec's ongoing battle, he couldn't help but imagine what that might look like – a place where heroes and legends would gather to share their tales, bards immortalizing their deeds in song, and ordinary folk reveling in the knowledge that they'd been part of something greater.

But first, he had to make sure that there would be stories worth telling. And so, with Flameweaver's voice whispering encouragement in his mind, Almas charged headlong into the fray, determined to prove that even the smallest among them could make the greatest difference.

Chapter 10

"NOW YOU ARE TRULY THE last Lich Lord, you have lost! End this!"

"I can't. Not just yet. Now give me all you have."

"If you insist."

THE SUN DIPPED LOW in the sky, casting long shadows across the battlefield as Lich-El and Ulec clashed once more. Their weapons danced through the air, the sound of steel-on-steel echoing like a symphony of peril. Despite Ulec's valiant efforts, his youthful strength paled in comparison to the ancient power of Lich-El. Beads of sweat rolled down Ulec's brow as he struggled to keep up with the relentless onslaught.

"Is that all you've got, boy?" Lich-El sneered, his voice dripping with disdain. "I'd hoped for more of a challenge."

Ulec gritted his teeth, his grip tightening around the hilt of his weapon. "You won't defeat me so easily," he spat back, determination burning in his eyes.

Ulec decided that since Lich-El already knew his true parentage that he could show him his true power. The blood from Ulec's cuts and scratches began to glow as his Kaynarian blood turned to magic. Ulec launched an offensive that left Lich-El truly tested for the first time since his last battle with Ulec's mother. The elvish demigod used Changing Hand to again mimic the powers of Lich-El's Warhammer, sending boulders, rock spikes, at the lich lord as chasms opened in the ground to swallow. Yet Lich-El matched him every step. Ulec attacked relentlessly moving around his enemy in a blur of attacks.

For a moment, it seemed that Ulec might have been right. It appeared that Lich-El might have found his match. But alas, luck was not on his side. A misstep left him vulnerable, and Lich-El seized the opportunity, striking him with a vicious blow that sent him sprawling to the ground near his father. The earth ceased its constant quaking as Changing Hand turned back into a rusica on Ulec's hand.

Lich-El raised his hammer high above his head as he prepared to deliver the finishing blow. Time seemed to slow as the hammer began its deadly descent, and just as it was about to crush Ulec beneath its weight, a voice rang out across the battlefield.

"Stop!"

AT ALMAS' COMMAND, Lich-El froze in place, his hammer hovering mere inches above Ulec's battered body. Slowly, the lich lord turned to face the young bard, a twisted smile spreading across his decayed visage.

"As you command," he said, his voice dripping with a bitter sarcasm that made Almas' skin crawl.

Almas took a few cautious steps forward, his heart pounding in his chest. "So, it is true," he said, trying to keep the tremor from his voice. "You have to obey me, don't you?"

"Congratulations on your astute observation," Lich-El drawled, his eyes burning with an unsettling intensity.

"I thought so, I can see magic now, and when we were in Beaver Dam, I saw a magical connection between you and members of the Aguerius family, just like the one between me and Tornal that he used to control me."

Lich-El's smile broadened, revealing rows of jagged teeth. "Well, well," he taunted, "very good my boy. Keep figuring it out."

Almas felt his anger rising, but he forced himself to remain calm. He knew that letting his emotions get the better of him would only make things worse. Instead, he focused on the strange bond that connected him to this powerful and terrifying enemy, determined to unlock the secret that might save them all.

Almas stood firm, his eyes locked on Lich-El, his mind racing as he pieced together the puzzle. The air was thick with tension and the smell of battle, but Almas barely noticed. He swallowed hard, feeling the weight of responsibility resting on his shoulders.

"From what I can see," Almas began, his voice steady despite the fear gripping his heart, "you were once the Retainer to the Aguerius Family, which means you were honor-bound to them." He glanced at Lich-El's undead form, noting the undrawn sword that hung at his side, never used but ever present. "Even now, you're still bound by that oath, aren't you?"

Lich-El tilted his head ever so slightly, the hollow sockets of his eyes seeming to bore into Almas' very soul. "Clever boy," he replied, a hint of grudging respect in his raspy voice. "I did indeed make that vow on this Sword of Honor." He tapped the hilt of the weapon with a bony finger, the sound echoing through the battlefield like a death knell. "This sword ensures that I am magically bound to keep all my vows."

Almas' gaze narrowed as he studied the lich lord, keenly aware that there was more to this twisted creature than met the eye. "But you're not just bound to my family, are you?" he pressed, his heart pounding with anticipation. "There's another connection - one that ties you to something... darker."

The lich lord remained silent, the shadows around him seeming to grow darker and more oppressive. Almas clenched his fists, knowing he had to push for answers. "Explain it to me," he commanded, his voice ringing out with a newfound authority.

"Your sight is keener than I thought," Lich-El conceded, his voice tinged with bitterness. "The ancient gods, imprisoned deep within this world, granted me the powers of a lich lord, but in return... they bound me to their will."

Almas' eyes widened as he grasped the terrible truth. "And so, you've been trapped," he said softly, his voice barely more than a whisper, "caught between honoring your old oaths to my family and obeying the evil orders of those ancient gods."

"Indeed," Lich-El hissed, his eyes glowing with a hatred that seemed to burn through the very air. "A torment I have endured for far too long. But, I needed the power. I did not see the cost and I was tricked and forced to find a way to serve both of you."

"That's why sometimes you seemed to help one side and sometimes the other. You literally had to serve both sides. Let me guess, you couldn't tell anyone either?"

"No, only if you specifically commanded me to."

Almas chuckled, "And who would think to try giving a super powered leader of the Lich Lords a command? One last question.

You commanded me to save Ulec, but you were about to kill him. Why?"

" I had to follow my orders, I had to destroy him if I had the chance. But you will need him in the future. Just as your father found his true power today, by letting go of his own life and will for others, you and Ulec must find yours."

As the revelation settled on Almas like a heavy cloak, he knew that the fate of his family - and perhaps even the entire realm - hung in the balance. With courage he never knew he possessed, he stared into the face of darkness itself, determined to save them all from the clutches of the cruel gods and the twisted creature before him.

Almas stared into the cold, dead eyes of Lich-El, feeling the weight of the situation pressing down on him. He thought back to his own enslavement by Tornal, the humiliating submission and utter lack of control. A grim smile spread across his face as he prepared to issue his next command.

"Believe me, Lich-El," Almas began, a bitter laugh in his voice, "I know what it's like to be forced to obey someone else's orders. So, I order you to be free from the control of all others, and make your own choices from now on. As Seacra did for me, I do for you."

Lich-El's eyes widened, and for a moment, the darkness surrounding him seemed to shudder as if in protest. "You would do this?" he asked in disbelief. "Freeing me was unwise, young Aguerius. Your family now lacks my protection."

"Ah, but I don't think that'll be a problem," Almas replied, a hint of sarcasm creeping into his tone. "We're quite resourceful, you see. Besides, when you made that oath to the Aguerius family, you chose to do so."

The lich lord hesitated, then gave a thin, chilling smile. "Very well, Almas Aguerius. I shall return to the eastern wastes, but know this: if you ever have need of me, I will return."

With that, Lich-El withdrew, his dark presence fading like the last embers of a dying fire. Almas checked on Ulec and Lord Teanas and realizing they weren't seriously hurt, released a breath he hadn't realized he'd been holding, the tension in his body gradually dissipating. The battle was over; they had succeeded.

Almas stepped away from the battlefield, feeling the familiar warmth of his human form envelop him once more. His heart pounded with a mixture of relief and pride as he approached his uncle, Marpel, who stood waiting with an expression of awe etched onto his face.

"Almas," Marpel whispered, his voice thick with emotion. "I am so proud of you."

"Thank you, Uncle," Almas replied, humbled by the compliment.

"Come closer," Marpel beckoned, tears glistening in his eyes. As Almas obeyed, he watched his uncle remove the crest from around his own neck, a symbol of authority and lineage. With trembling hands, Marpel placed it around Almas' neck, the weight suddenly feeling heavier than any armor.

"By giving you this crest," Marpel said solemnly, "I name you my heir, sharing with you all my titles and authority as High Lord. There is no one I would rather have by my side as we rebuild the Vatan Province."

Almas blinked back his own tears, stunned by the honor bestowed upon him. The journey had been long and treacherous, but in that moment, he knew that it was over.

Epilogue

AS THE FIRST RAYS OF sunlight peeked through the heavy curtains, Lady Izybel stirred from her slumber. The warmth of life had returned to her cheeks, a stark contrast to the cold grip of the injuries that had nearly claimed her.

"Ah, you're awake," Lord Gidon said, his voice as soothing as a lullaby.

Izybel turned her head towards the comforting sound of her husband's voice. She found his blue eyes gazing down at her, filled with relief and love. The sight of him brought a spark of happiness amidst the fog of memories that still haunted her.

"Is it... Is it over?" she asked hesitantly, fearing the answer.

Gidon smiled gently, a hint of weariness in his eyes. "Yes, my love. We've won."

A sigh of relief and gratitude escaped Izybel's lips, but her thoughts quickly turned to their children. Her heart ached with worry, and she couldn't help but let the question tumble out. "The children... are they safe?"

"See for yourself," Gidon replied, the corners of his mouth lifting into a smile. He gestured toward the bed across the room.

Izybel followed the direction of his arm, and her heart swelled like a golem brought to life by her expert hands. There, in peaceful slumber, lay Creetan, with Cady and Giddy nestled on either side. At the foot of the bed, the Elvish children Ulec and Seacra dozed, both Teanas and Alixia stood nearby watching with her father, brother, and King Yucaipa.

And there, sitting on the edge of the bed, was Almas. His once-lost smile beamed like a beacon as he met his mother's gaze. Izybel felt tears prick her eyes, and the weight of worry that had burdened her for so long evaporated like morning mist.

"Mother!" Almas exclaimed, leaping from the bed and bounding to Izybel's side. He threw his arms around her, and she held him tight, savoring the warmth of his embrace.

"Almas," she whispered through tearful laughter, "my sweet boy."

In that moment, with all four of her children safe and sound, along with the two Elvish children she had come to love as her own, Izybel knew that her family was whole again. The darkness that had threatened to consume them had been vanquished, and in its place shone the light of hope and a love that refused to be extinguished.

As they stood there, entwined in each other's arms, the room seemed to glow with a warmth that defied even the darkest of shadows. For now, at least, the bitter taste of fear and loss was replaced by the sweetness of victory and the joy of being reunited.

Don't miss out!

Visit the website below and you can sign up to receive emails whenever Marc Van Pelt publishes a new book. There's no charge and no obligation.

https://books2read.com/r/B-A-HGIT-HGIVC

BOOKS 2 READ

Connecting independent readers to independent writers.

Did you love *Lich Lord Wars Collection*? Then you should read *Mathen's Flight*[1] by Marc Van Pelt!

[2]

Mathen is a successful businessman thanks in no small part to a magical crest he wears around his neck that gives him glimpses into the future. His life is turned upside down when one of these glimpses shows him someone destined to become the worst and most evil tyrant the world will ever know, and shows him this person in the form of a small 8-year-old boy who just attempted to pick his pocket.Now Mathen must face the most difficult decisions of his life. Decisions that hold the life of millions of people and the very world itself in the balance. As he makes his choices he must deal with slave traders, magical beings and a living forest that all seem to have their own interest in the boy.

1. https://books2read.com/u/3RLq8B

2. https://books2read.com/u/3RLq8B

Read more at Facebook.com/catseye1979.

Also by Marc Van Pelt

Devil's Peak Chronicles
Dream Walker

Fate's Foe
Mathen's Flight

The Lich Lord Wars
Lich-El
Escape Through the Sacred Forest
The Necromancer
Paladin's Rise
Lich Lord Wars Collection

Standalone
Stories From the World of Mundial
The Doctor's Apprentice
Forest Spirit and the Dragon Queen

Watch for more at Facebook.com/catseye1979.

About the Author

Growing up in Bay Point, California Marc spent much of his time creating and exploring worlds and stories. He finally realized that once he got the stories written down they stopped haunting his sleeping and waking dreams. So he started writing them down.

He writes the kind of stories that he enjoys which are stories about families written for families.

Marc currently lives in northern Utah with his wife, and kids. He can be contacted through his Author's Facebook page at facebook.com/catseye1979

Read more at Facebook.com/catseye1979.

Milton Keynes UK
Ingram Content Group UK Ltd.
UKHW020645040324
438885UK00017B/920

About halfway up Almas asked, "How come you don't have any shoes on?"

"You never take a break from the questions, do you?"

"Sorry, I was just wondering."

"I don't like shoes; I like the feel of the forest on my feet."

They soon arrived at the top of the tree, which was much taller than any of the other trees in the forest. Almas looked wide-eyed across the carpet of treetops. "You can see the whole forest from here."

"This is the oldest and tallest tree in this part of the forest; I like to spend a lot of time here."

"Don't you get lonely?"

"Not really," Ulec lied. "I have the whole forest to keep me company. Plus, I spend a lot of time with my father. He's been training me in weapon mastery."

"Why," Almas asked.

"My father says having skills to protect yourself and others is important."

Almas nodded. Almas was also the son of a weapons master and Ulec was sure his own father taught similar things. So, he knew he didn't have to explain much more than that.

"What about your sister? Doesn't she play with you in the forest?" Almas asked after a moment.

Ulec shrugged his shoulders. "My mother and sister spend a lot of time up north on the other side of the Dividing Mountains. The magic most elves use is stronger up there."

"Why is it stronger there?"

"Elves use magic created by life. The forests up there are much denser and produce more magic than the ones here," Ulec explained.

Almas seemed to think of that for a few moments. The mention of Ulec's mother being gone much of the time must have reminded Almas of the situation with his own parents. Almas commented next, "My dad is away a lot too. He's the royal strategist, and there is a war against the Lich Lords right now. He's been gone longer than normal this time. Normally they just do small raids. But I've heard some of my father's men say this was the biggest attack in 40 years."

Almas nervously fingered the crest he wore around his neck. Ulec's parents had both fought in a war before he was born but never in his life had he gone to war. Ulec responded, "Don't worry. I'm sure he's fine," then thought it best to change the subject. "So why did you come into the forest alone yesterday?"

Almas hesitated then answered, "I was playing with my younger brother and sister a few days ago and Creetan snuck up behind me and scared me. He said I screamed like a girl and was the biggest coward he had ever seen. So, I wanted to prove to him that I could be brave."

"Being scared doesn't mean you're not brave," Ulec said, "Being scared is what helps keep us alive when there is danger. Being brave is what helps us do things that need to be done. You can be scared and brave at the same time. It isn't one or the other."

Almas thought about that for a moment before responding, "I wish someone had told me that sooner. Trying to be brave almost got me eaten by a dragon."

"I'm glad you weren't. I haven't had anyone new to talk to in years."

"So, you do get lonely," Almas exclaimed triumphantly.

"I guess I do," Ulec admitted.

A few moments of silence passed before Ulec spoke again and asked, "Can I see your crest?"

Almas took the crest from around his neck and handed it to Ulec. "How come you don't have one?"